I0187667

Victoria

Of
DALLAS

*How One Woman Learned to Give Men
Exactly What They Wanted Before Discovering
How to Give Herself What She Needed*

by Victoria McCormick

2017

ISBN # 978-1-7323076-0-5

Library of Congress Control # TXu 2-078-739, #TXu 2-072-032

© 2016,2017 Jennifer MG, LLC. All rights reserved.

Written permissions must be secured from the publisher to use or reproduce
any part of this book, except brief quotations in critical reviews and articles.

Badass Cat Press TM United States of America

This is my story. I lived it, and I remember well the parts I remember at all. To protect the privacy of loved ones, clients, and even a few people that probably don't deserve it, I've changed names and a few details throughout this memoir.

This is dedicated to J.M.T. who first told me that I am "Pretty Good," when I thought my whole life was falling apart. He gave me the hope and strength to never give up.

To my sons, N and J who kept me from the road of self-destruction and gave me a reason to keep fighting no matter what. I thank God for you two every day of my life. You have given me light when I thought it was only dark. You have given me hope when I thought there was only despair. I love you more than you will ever know.

I want to thank my wonderful editor Luke G. You gave me the strength to persevere and get this done. Without you I could have never made my dreams come true. Thank you for all your support and always believing in me.

TABLE OF CONTENTS

WHAT DO YOU WANT?

I'm on top of Howard, and he pulls his tongue from my mouth to ask, "Whadya like darlin'? Whadya want?"

What I want is to take a break from the taste of his sour coffee breath, but I don't say anything right away. Instead, I slide my lips slowly down his neck, and I think of what to do next to keep him hard.

What do you want? My clients often ask me this question. Of course, they'd be shocked if I gave an honest answer. I think, *Well, baby, what I want is a stack of crisp hundred-dollar bills and some alone time with a bottle or two of Chardonnay.* But I learned early that when clients ask this question, they mean something specific. They're asking me to figure out what *they* want. They need me to decide what'll get them off without them having to say it out loud. In a split second, I have to guess a client's secret desire, and then I have to pretend that I want it (whatever it is) even more than he does.

"Listen, sugar," I say. "Would you like to slide your dick between these titties?" That answer hardly ever fails.

I can feel his excitement grow. "Yeah, Victoria," he mutters. "You're my little whore, and after I fuck your titties, I'm gonna pull your head back by your hair, and I'm gonna shove my cock down your throat. And if you're a really good girl, I'm gonna spank that hot ass of yours and put my big hard dick in it." I know from his sudden spasm of creative planning that I've said the right thing.

I lower my chest to his cock, and he pushes his dick over my ribcage for a minute or two. Then he pulls hard on my hair, as promised. I moan, as if nothing feels better than having my follicles nearly ripped from my scalp. He smirks and slaps my face before pushing my head toward his cock.

I've only known Howard for a few minutes.

We first met online from an ad that I ran on an upscale escort website. As with all my clients, the first thing I did was check his references, including details about his likes, dislikes, and possible red flags from past escorts he'd been with. Howard checked out, and from his profile, I knew I'd have a repeat client. We booked a date, and since he was a prominent client with sterling references, I gave him my private home address for the meeting.

I live in a condo in Plano, Texas, just north of Dallas. It's in a gated community with every possible amenity. I've furnished the apartment with antiques and a massive, four-poster bed that you can just melt into. I also have a security camera on the intercom—if I don't have a good feeling about a new client when he shows up at my door, I'm not afraid to call the whole thing off. The clients I work with generally understand. Many of them are as experienced in the game as I am. These are the clients known as "hobbyists"—men that spend enormous amounts of time and money booking escorts as part of their weekly—or even daily—routine. Generally, with a hobbyist, you can count on a professional encounter.

Howard introduced himself at the door with courtesy. He was clearly a man with refined manners. But I'd been around long enough to know the man I met in at the doorway was never the same as the guy who'd be fucking me a few minutes later. Howard is a prominent Dallas attorney and used to getting his way, and I figure any frustration he suffers in the courtroom he'll bring with him to the bedroom. Plus, I've read what the other escorts have to say about him: *Dominant / likes to take charge / dirty talk.* I know he wants absolute submission from me. I'm his little whore for the hour. If I want his business again, I know I must make it seem like I want nothing more than to be poked and prodded like a thirty-two-ounce ribeye at a Dallas power lunch.

I can make any client believe. I've had prominent doctors that believed I wanted nothing more than to tie them up and take away their burden of responsibility for just a few precious minutes. I've had professional ball players—sometimes one right after another—that believed I just wanted to be a good team player. I've had politicians that believed I wanted to explore kinks that would make a Kennedy blush. There's even times I can make myself believe that this is the life I was born for. That this is what I always wanted for myself, and what I was always meant to be. Victoria McCormick of Dallas—the woman just a phone call away.

But sometimes doubt creeps in.

Howard is getting closer to the end, pushing faster and faster. I clench my teeth, pretending to be nearly overwhelmed by his passion. Suddenly the track on the stereo changes over. It's Bruce Springsteen and "Thunder Road." I hear poetry about flying from Midwest farmhouses in some rusted-out Chevy and making a big new life somewhere important with a boy who makes big promises. It's the story of my life, my real life.

For a moment, Victoria McCormick vanishes. I'm me, the real me, Jenny Lynn, the girl who grew up in Canal Bottom, Ohio, who danced in a sundress surrounded by chickens and cows while the sun's rays made my red hair glow. The girl who dreamed of being an artist, a model, an actress, a poet, a sophisticated business woman. The girl who wanted to be anywhere else, to get out of the home with the abusive father and neglectful mother, to find real love, real intimacy. Suddenly I'm that person again, and I'm scared and alone—except of course for the man I hardly know pounding away on top of me.

"Oh Howard, that's the spot. Oh God, that feels so good! A lil' more and I'm gonna come—oh my God!" I practically squeal with a practiced imitation of pleasure. I need this to be over as soon as possible—for the moment I'm not confident my act will hold up. Howard hovers over me with an intense look on his face, a look I recognize in an instant. "Come on Howard baby, harder, harder, harder!" He lurches into me one last time and I feel his body clench while I stare deep into his eyes. Then he collapses. I assure him that he's the best I ever had.

Funny how having sex with a stranger can change that person into someone new, someone you'd never expect when first meeting them. And then when it's over, they're someone new all over again. Lying together sprawled out on my bed Howard turns back in to the gentleman that I'd initially met only an hour ago, only now he's full of boyish enthusiasm. He tells me how amazing he feels, and that no other woman has ever made him feel that way. The moment is almost tender. In this moment after sex, so many clients reveal themselves. Sometimes I think it's this moment that they're really paying for. They feel romance, they feel they've found someone who accepts them, who understands them. It's a beautiful illusion, and for a few moments I do sincerely care as they tell me about their problems at home.

I smile and look right into Howard's eyes. I ask, "Baby, when am I going to see you again?" He tells me that he'll call again next week. My heart races. I've done my job well. We chat until the hour is up, and then Howard finishes dressing and leaves my money by the bed. With his jacket back on, he's once again the polite stranger I met in my foyer, and again he reassures me that he'll call again soon. Now I can't wait to count my money and open a bottle of wine. For me, that's the climax. Counting money with a drink in one hand is an intoxicating feeling better than any other I know.

While I relax in the bedroom with my drink and my cash, I'm Victoria McCormick, the culmination of my own long fantasy life— a woman who has money, big expensive car, pricey condo, and beautiful clothes, including glittering diamonds and designer Louis Vuitton bags.

This Victoria McCormick is just one mask, though.

During the day, I'm also a real estate broker, buying and selling dreams of big city Texans. I have two hustles going at the same time and trying to balance the two on any given day only *sometimes* leads to awkward moments.

I've got a third gig as well. The one that's most important to me. I'm a thirty-five-year-old mother of two amazing young children. My oldest son, Jeremy, lives with his shithead father in Ohio much of the year, but he's with me during summers and holidays. My seven-year-old, Noah, is with me almost every day. I split custody with my ex, a man who knows one or two of my secrets. Being Victoria McCormick affords me the opportunity for my oldest son Jeremy to attend a prestigious all boys school. One that his dad nor I could ever afford if it weren't for this double life I lead. Jeremy is brilliant, a nationally ranked athlete, and a young man with unlimited potential. I'll do whatever I can to support his dreams, even if I know I'll never have him in my life as much as I want. Noah, my baby, gets everything he wants as well, and is my truest sweetheart. He sees my best self, and I'll make sure he'll never have any needs that can't be met.

Who I am on any given day may change, but one thing does not: the desire to prove that I can have a big life, one of adventure and success for me and for my family. One far away from that little Ohio town that my family and neighbors seemed to accept without much of a fight. One that my parents said I would never escape from and find success. Sex was always a way out for me, starting as a Go Go dancer at age seventeen. For all my adult life, I've been paid to make men happy. Now I happen to get paid *well* to make men happy.

I'm down to the bottom of the bottle of Chardonnay. I make some quick calculations and realize I have about two hours left before I must look fresh for my sons who'll be coming home from summer camp. I must sober up before then… *Dear God*, I think. *How much more of this can I take?* I watch the Chardonnay swirl for a minute in the glass, and then suddenly I can't raise it fast enough to my lips.

Chapter 1

HARD TO SAY I'M SORRY

I wasn't always a Texas bad girl.

In fact, I'm not even from Texas. I grew up a good country girl in northeast Ohio. I spent my childhood wanting to be good—*needing* to be good—thinking that was the only way I could stop my dad's angry, violent outbursts. I also thought if I was good enough, one day I'd be discovered, find fame and fortune, and escape what seemed like a life with little to hope for. But being good didn't help. Not really.

I was born in 1970 in Rust Bucket, Ohio, one of a string of dying towns scattered around bigger factory cities like Akron, Canton, and Youngstown. These cities and towns had sprung up around World War I and II and supplied the steel, tires, and machinery that helped win those wars and build the country up afterward. When my parents were growing up in the 50s, working class folks in the area might have believed they were chasing the American dream. People came from all over the country and resettled around those factories and made good livings. Then on weekends, factory workers might take their families to catch a picture with Clark Gable, the local Ohio boy made good—the biggest movie star in the world.

But by 1970, when I was born, all that was gone. Recessions, worker strikes, race riots, and shuttered factories were changing the area forever. And the men and women in Rust Bucket and those other Rustbelt towns were mad about it. Bitter, in fact. Bitter and mean.

My father was like that. My first memory is of me standing up in my crib, listening to my father hit my mom. I'm not sure how old I was. Maybe two? I just remember my father closing my bedroom door so I couldn't hear or see. I still knew exactly what was happening, and all I did was scream and scream until he stopped.

In 1974 when I was about four, my family moved from gritty Rust Bucket to a place in the country not far away. Our new house in Canal Bottom, Ohio, was a converted old barn that still had dirt floors when we moved in.

Most of my early memories are from that home in Canal Bottom. So many of those memories are of escape of one kind or another. I had a brother, Tom, who was one year younger, and we spent most of our time trying to get out of the house and away from our dad.

In the mornings, my brother and I would creep downstairs as quietly as possible. Our mother would have breakfast waiting for us. My father worked second or third shift at a nuclear power plant, and our hope was always to move in absolute silence before we could slip out the door and be free. If my brother or I got into a fight and woke our dad up early, there'd be hell to pay. First came the cussing, and then a backhand, or his belt. He might hit us, and he might hit my mom if she asked him to stop. Sometimes he'd lock us in our rooms all day upstairs. He told us if he heard footsteps, things would be even worse for us. I can remember spending whole weekends planted in bed, afraid to even walk across the room.

By most afternoons, my father had shaved and dressed and put on his uniform—a plain white T-shirt and black pants, with a black satchel that held a meal my mom made for him. In fact, he'd wear a white T-shirt and black pants whether he was off to work or not. He liked to keep things simple. When he was finally out the door and on his way to work, my brother and I would breathe a sigh of relief—though we were so well conditioned, we'd make sure that sigh wasn't loud enough for anyone to hear.

My father's mantra was "children should be seen and not heard," but truth be told, he didn't like seeing us much either. The easiest way for us to stay safe was to make ourselves scarce. Any chance we had, we'd be outside.

Behind our house we had an acre of land that sloped down to the edge of the Ohio–Erie Canal. The canal hadn't been used for much of anything since the invention of the railroad, but parts of it still flowed through northeast Ohio, a convenient dumping ground for factory runoff and a trap for tourists that might think old, man-made creeks are "picturesque." My brother and I used to sit out on the lawn and watch a mule team pull the "St. Helena," an old canal barge, while the boat's loudspeaker blared up the hill, explaining to onlookers the workings of the lock system and other fascinating details of 19th century hydraulic technology.

When we weren't out back watching the canal, we were across the neighbors' yard and into the woods, exploring nature. I loved animals. They were my first friends, and the only relationships I had that didn't involve fighting. We had cats, a dog, chickens, and a pet duck named Donald, whom my brother and I kept well fed. My first dreams were of becoming a veterinarian, and I can remember nursing birds, kittens, chickens, and bunnies to health. On days when I feared my father's temper, I'd run to the woods. I remember once falling asleep in a deer bed. I woke up with the deer nearby staring at me, and I imagined they were my new family, a family I could trust to keep me safe. They would love me, accept me, and understand me, no matter what. They stared at me unmoving for a few, beautiful moments. Then they ran off to find something better to do than eye a human child mussing up their favorite pile of leaves.

My mother was a sweet woman, and everyone that met her liked her. She had no enemies. But she was lost inside herself. My father would cuss her out for her weight, and he would demand she be firm with us. I remember one day when she tried to defend us, he turned to her and yelled, "Dammit, Betty, if you don't teach these bastards who's boss, they'll do this to you one day!" I guess my father couldn't imagine a house where the members of a family simply sat down to dinner and discussed their days without someone—mother, father, brother, sister, family dog—hitting someone else.

I must have been not much older than four or five when, after a big blow-up, my parents came to my brother and me with a bottle of pills. "These are hush-me-up pills," my dad explained. From that point on, my brother and I would be given "hush-me-up pills" whenever the rule of quiet needed to be imposed. It was many years later that I learned we were being given Valium. Give him credit, though—he was always the first to pop a Valium when things got tense. He never drank much. But a bottle of pills was always close by, whether he wanted help hushing-up or otherwise changing the course of his rapid-fire mood swings.

As I got older, I tried to make things better by being as good a girl as possible. By age eight or nine, I was doing much of the housework. Both of my parents were poor housekeepers, and given over to collecting—my mother would hold onto any old thing she found (magazines, papers, and other scraps built up in drifts all over the house). My father collected old Corvettes, which he'd leave rusting on cinderblocks around the yard. In fact, it was collecting Corvettes that had brought my parents together. My mom went one day to visit her boyfriend who was in county jail. It was there that she met my dad, who was being held one cell over for grand theft auto. (I grew up knowing there was probably a story I didn't want to hear behind every Corvette rusting on the lawn.) My dad gave my mom the eye, and the rest was history.

My folks must have had a grand old time together finding things to fill up every corner of the house, but it was left to me to keep things in order. I did what I could in most of the house, and I kept my own room immaculate. Every morning I'd clean my room, line up all my stuffed animals, and give them a pep talk before I went downstairs.

I also took up the strategy of apologizing for everything. Too much noise? That's my fault, sorry. The dog pooped in the house? My fault, I'll take care of it. Dishes not done? My fault! One day my grandma visited and lit into my mom for relying on me to keep house. "She's just a girl! She should be playing," my grandma pointed out. My mom looked at me, stricken, and all I could say was, "Sorry!" My grandmother was like me, and she insisted on keeping things neat. We'd work together to get things picked up sometimes. Though I was a bit afraid of her as a child, she came to be one of my most trusted friends.

When I couldn't escape outside, I'd escape in other ways—into homework, into drawing and painting, into my fantasy life. I was a good student, but dreamy, and all my time spent locked in my room was taken up with dreaming of getting away one day and making it big. I wanted to be a veterinarian first, then a business woman, then a Hollywood star. Maybe I wanted to be all three at once—an entrepreneur-veterinarian-movie star. I just wanted a future where I might be loved and respected and show love to others without fear. What a fantasy!

I grew up in the age of Farrah Fawcett, but while all my friends at school were teasing out their hair to look like Farrah's big dirty blonde waterfall, I was obsessed with the classic era stars. Especially Marilyn Monroe. How to explain it? Maybe it was seeing her starring with local hero Clark Gable and knowing that if I wanted to make it out like he made it out, one way would be to become the kind of woman he'd fall in love with. Or maybe it was just that mysterious Marilyn magnetism and sensuality. I didn't really know what that was all about when I was a kid, but I was fascinated by it, and I knew I wanted it when I grew up.

So on those days when my parents gave me a Valium tablet and sent me to my room to be quiet, I'd think of Marilyn, and I'd imagine my house—just like Marilyn's, but purple, my favorite color. And I'd have my purple car, my purple dress, my puppy with a purple collar… and someone like Clark, a little rough around the edges but a perfect gentleman who would always treat me with respect.

As the years passed in Canal Bottom, things were getting worse around the house. My dad was becoming more erratic with my brother and me, my mother, even the neighbors. When my dad began to fight with the next door neighbors over who-knows-what, they put up a small fence. My dad responded by building a huge wall out of cinderblocks and bricks. The neighbors fought back with a higher fence made of white pickets. Soon the space between our two yards looked like a World War I trench, with thorny blueberry bushes serving as barbed wire.

Soon my dad was more and more out of control with us kids, as well. One day he was outside swinging a sledgehammer, trying to knock the engine out of a Corvette. My brother went out to help, or just to see what he was up to, and must have got underfoot in a way my dad didn't like. Dad cracked my brother in the head with a short swing of the sledge, knocking him out. I don't know what excuse my parents gave the doctors, but that blow has affected my brother to this day.

The older we got, the more paranoid my parents were about us going out. My brother and I were more and more confined to the house, especially when both parents were out. The only thing to do those days, other than dream or draw, was to snoop, and this is how I found a suicide note my mom had written back when I was five. In it, she blamed me for her unhappiness and volatile marriage. If I hadn't come along, she reasoned, everything would have been just fine between her and my dad.

It was after finding my mom's note that I began cutting myself. It's hard to explain, other than to say the physical pain relieved the pain I felt inside. One day my mom noticed the cuts and gave me a long look. Instead of a hug, or tears, or apologies, or simply the sympathy of someone that had gone through the same feelings I was going through, she told me that I was crazy, and if I wasn't a better girl, I'd end up in a mental institution one day.

I remember thinking, *How good a girl, exactly, do I have to be? Do I have to take as much as you take, mom?* For once, I didn't say I was sorry.

And while I was still a good girl, I started taking little breaks from being perfect. My brother and I would race around the neighborhood on an old Honda 50, fearless and free. I don't know how I didn't break my neck, but we were daredevils. And when my friends came over to get me, we'd head out as far from home as we could manage.

My dad had an old three-wheeler, fixed up with a ski on the front like a snowmobile. You had to start the thing with a ripcord, like a lawnmower. We'd take it out of the garage when dad wasn't home. My mom would get in on it too, sometimes. One day when I was around nine, I stood with my mom in the backyard with my brother mounted on the three-wheeler, ready for a joyride. It was my mom that pulled the ripcord, but it was me that whispered into my brother's ear, "*Full throttle!*" Once the thing started, my brother took an unfortunate turn downhill and zoomed 100 yards downslope in the direction of the neighbors' blueberry bushes, and beyond that, the canal.

"Jump off!!!"

He hit the blueberry bushes just as the St. Helena rounded the corner. As we watched in horror, shouting, we heard the familiar speech on the Helena's loudspeaker: "AND HERE IS WHERE THE WATERS OF WAYNE CREEK WERE PULLED INTO THE CANAL BY A SERIES OF—HOLY SHIT! *WHAT'S THAT!!!!*" My brother bailed just in time as our father's three-wheeler sailed across the bank ten feet in front of the clattering mules. We could hear the startled screams of the tourists just before the big splash. My brother was okay. Hell, he probably felt better than he'd ever felt before, despite the blueberry branches that peppered his ass.

You wanna talk about getting in trouble. My father was livid. His three-wheeler was trashed and had to be dredged up by some of his buddies who owned a canoe rental. Still, I couldn't help be a little jealous of my brother, despite the trouble he was in. He'd destroyed something important to our dad and lived to tell the story. In a way, he'd gotten even just a little bit. And he'd had a lot of fun doing it. *Oh, to feel that free.*

Steve M.

Salt Lake City

Adventurous / role play / dress up / travel / overnight / would definitely see again

He picks me up at the Salt Lake City airport in the morning. He's tall, has curly silver hair, a boyish smile. I know right away this is a client that I'm going to enjoy spending the day with.

"I see you packed light," he says. "That's not always easy, I know."

His request via email was specific. I like that. Tell me what you want, and I'll tell you if I can deliver. I was to pack light, but wear a leather jacket if I had one, since we'd be going on a bike trip. Oh, and a pretty evening dress.

It wasn't an unusual request. You might be surprised how many grown, straight men like playing with living Barbies. Being Barbie was one of my specialties, and I was happy to play along with the costume changes.

Steve offers his arm and escorts me out to his waiting Harley Fat Boy. He sticks my carry-on in the bike's saddlebag, and I tell him I need to get something out of it first. I fish out a purple bandana and tie it around my neck.

"You're gorgeous," he says.

I know how to work accessories. "What's first?" I ask.

"Let's grab lunch."

He starts up the Harley, and I feel it through my entire body. I lean in close, hold him tight. Soon we're off, past the city, and up into the mountains to the east.

What's better than sex? This. Freedom. Peace. The air is clean and *the sky is blue. This is what I want as much as anything, but I know it's only a fleeting moment. I know to not let myself fall for the open road, for a man who seems perfect, but whom I'm paid to only see the most joyful side of.*

We ride and ride. If I was newer at this, I'd be wondering what the hell Steve was getting out of it. But I've been around long enough to know. He wants the same thing I do. Freedom. Freedom and the company of a good looking person. And he wants to not have to know what the hell my real name is, or what makes me sad or afraid or unsure of myself.

We ride to Park City, where he buys me lunch, and then off to Wyoming and back again to Salt Lake City. It's a day I know will stick around my mind for a while. I know I'm gonna try and make this day linger in his mind for a while, too.

He's rented a room at the Grand Hotel. Our room has a damn crystal chandelier in the foyer, and the bathroom is bigger than my entire apartment. I shower, and then we jump in to bed. Later I change into my dress and he takes me to dinner. "This," he says, "This is what I've wanted. A beautiful woman that can ride through the mountains and then come to a place like this and look like a million bucks."

It's also what I've wanted. It's a dream. But I know it's just a dream. Tomorrow I'll be back in Dallas, selling new dreams to some new client.

Chapter 2

BALLAD OF A TEENAGE QUEEN

Sometimes, good girls do make it. But it ain't easy being good in a world that's no good.

When I was still a kid dreaming of fame and fortune, I'd sometimes think of the Johnny Cash song that they'd play on the oldies station, "Ballad of a Teenage Queen." It's a song about a nice girl who gets discovered, but who never turns her back on where she came from.

"There's a story in our town," the song begins, of a girl with blonde hair and blue eyes, the prettiest girl anyone knew. Sometimes, she'd meet the looks of boys she passed by in that small town, and her eyes seemed to "flash" at them (according to the boys, anyway). She was smart and talented, too, but she didn't let it go to her head. Her heart still belonged to the "boy next door/who worked at the candy store."

Of course, that's not all she wanted. The teenage queen had ambitions, too, and wanted to be recognized. Lucky for her, one day a talent scout happens through her podunk town, flips his wig when he sees her, and drives her off to Hollywood, where she becomes instantly rich and famous. Why did she get in a car with a man she'd never met? That's never addressed. He probably had a real nice car and smelled like money. But she goes off with him, and everything

18

works out. Once she's been rich and famous for a while, she returns home to the candy store, loved by everyone, a hero, and she married her candy-selling boyfriend.

Aw, how sweet!

At ten years old, I pretty much thought that was how my life was going to go. I even had the hair. Some of the popular boys had crushes on me, and teachers liked me too. I got good grades, was a Peewee cheerleader, a talented artist, and a real social butterfly.

The way I thought that you got attention from other people was if you were skinny and beautiful. Never do I remember my mom or dad telling me I was beautiful. I remember flipping through magazines and seeing the long blonde haired models in advertisements that always had a huge perfect smile on their face and they always seemed to have the attention I wanted. They were happy in my eyes.

I think by nature I'm an introvert, but I always knew how to turn it on when I was in public. Whether it was auditioning for the lead in the school play or pushing myself to the front of the cheerleader formations, I was determined to be noticed. My home life was rough. My town was depressed. And the only way my life was gonna make any sense was if I got the chance to start a new one, in a better place. The kind of place I saw in the movies, or that I heard about in songs.

But when you're a pretty ten-year-old girl, it's not just cute boys and talent scouts that take notice. Like most young girls, I was naïve about the ways some grown men might be noticing me. What could I do but wonder at the stares? What did they mean? I didn't know.

One day in sixth grade after cheerleading at a basketball game, a man with a heavy mustache dressed in denim approached me while

I was chatting with my friends. "Hey girl, what's your name?" he asked. He told me he was a talent agent, and that he thought I would make a great hand model. I couldn't believe it! I mean, I literally couldn't. This wasn't the talent scout from the song, the man I'd imagined sweeping me off to Hollywood. Instead of a nice suit and a big cigar, he wore jeans, smelled like stale menthols and beer, and had dark circles under his eyes. And the way he looked me up and down, I could tell he wasn't interested in the expressive qualities of my hands. In fact, the way he looked at me made me suddenly think of my parents as the safe option, and I slunk away to go find my mom.

So there was no scout, and there was no boy at the candy store, either. For me at that age, my life was my friends. There was Becky, blonde like me. A good girl who I could draw out and have fun with. Then there was Ashley. She was the crazy one. We'd been in class together for years, and why she picked me to hang out with, I don't know. She was beautiful, with porcelain skin and raven hair. And she loved getting into trouble. I even had my boy next door. Well, maybe that wasn't exactly the same as the situation in the song. I didn't want Tony to be my husband someday. Just my best friend. Tony was a friend from way back. Our families were friendly—Tony's dad was Canal Bottom's police chief, and my dad became friends with him so he could get away with shit.

We'd see each other a lot, and Tony and I became very close. I'd go over to his house, and it was the opposite of my own. His mother, Darla, was like the mom I wished my own could be—warm and affectionate, funny and full of life. And their house was also the opposite of my own. Not only were we allowed to speak above a whisper, we could pretty much do whatever we wanted. When I was ten, that meant going over to visit Tony and Darla and just going crazy—having pillow fights, belly laughs, chases around the furniture. For me, what freedom felt like.

All in all, when I thought of making it big and coming back home someday, it wasn't to a husband—it was to my best friends, the people who seemed to truly love and support me. The people I could be myself around.

There were other friends, too, like Krista, a quiet, dark haired girl that I went to school with and would play with in the park. In the summer of 1982, we got word at home one day that Krista had disappeared. Everyone in town was worried, since another girl named Tina, only twelve, had disappeared just a year before. Tina's body had been found not long after, and a man had been sent to prison for her rape and murder. Later, he was acquitted.

It was six days before my friend Krista's body was found. Word got around fast that she'd been raped, tortured and murdered. I was devastated, and confused. I couldn't understand why someone would want something like that from a sweet, small girl like Krista, and I couldn't understand how such a sleepy town could harbor so much evil.

As much as I was stunned by Krista's death, my parents were affected as much. Suddenly, I wasn't allowed to leave the house. They were jealous and suspicious of any attention my brother and I received outside the house, and were always finding excuses to keep us home. Even from school—they were hypochondriacs, and they were always trying to convince us we were sick. I swear they had Munchausen syndrome. It was strange. For as much as my dad

21

couldn't stand us being around, they sure didn't want us out in the world, either.

So my parents were paranoid. But just because you're paranoid doesn't mean the world isn't out to get you. One day after the start of seventh grade, I woke up with a fever. I didn't feel very sick, but my parents kept me home. That night, my whole stomach turned red as a beet. I had no idea what was going on, but when I told my mom, she told my dad and my parents freaked out. I soon found myself in the emergency room. The doctor took one look at me and said, "Scarlet fever."

What! This is what it was like living in Canal Bottom? Not only did we have mules pulling barges in our backyards, we also got diseases nobody had heard of since the Prohibition era. How I picked up scarlet fever, I'll never know, but suddenly all my parents worry over me seemed justified in their eyes.

"Oh, Jenny," my mom sighed. "You're gonna be in the hospital a long time." And I was. But as much as my parents moaned and gnashed their teeth about my strange, antique disease, they didn't really seem all that concerned with how I was doing. Locked away in the hospital seemed like the place they wanted me to be all along—I wasn't bugging them at home, and I wasn't in danger out in the big bad world either. During the few weeks I was in the hospital, my parents didn't visit. Instead, I was cared for by nurses, professionals who were more attentive to my needs in three weeks than my parents had been in twelve years. Though I risked long term effects like hearing loss, I wasn't really feeling that bad, so I spent time with other children in the ward as well, like a girl a little younger than me named Dawn, whose hair I braided day after day.

After my release from the hospital, my parents seemed angry at having me back. Not long after my return, I was home alone one day with my father. I was sitting on the couch in shorts, with a row of bandaids down my thigh where I'd received antibiotic shots. I'd collected them on my legs, and I kept them there because the puncture marks were still tender and sore. My dad slid up next to me, making me a little uneasy. Still, he spoke in a calm, sympathetic voice. "Listen, honey, those look bad. Which one hurts the worst?" I was a little confused—my dad had never worried over me before, but I thought maybe he finally felt bad about what I'd been through. "This one," I said, pointing to the bandage covering my most recent shot. "This one?" he repeated, pointing at my leg. And when I nodded, his eyes flashed bright and he dug his thumb deep into my thigh and laughed—it was an angry, hateful joke.

I'd had it. I leapt up and told him off. He had no right treating me that way and he hadn't even bothered to visit me in the hospital. If he wanted me to leave him alone, I expected him to leave me alone too.

It was the first time I'd ever stood up to my dad. And the last. He stood up slowly off the couch, his eyes wide. I started to tremble. Without speaking, he walked into the garage and came back in a moment later, holding something.

When I saw that it was a hammer, I started to run. He chased me all the way up the stairs, and at the top of the landing he swung at my face, shattering my jaw.

"I will not be disrespected in my own house!" he said.

I can't remember the excuse my parents made up when I was taken back to the hospital. Cheerleading accident? Tripped and fell?

It didn't matter. Nobody asked questions back then.

I wasn't really in school much of the rest of the year. And still, danger seemed everywhere. Not long after I'd been braiding her hair in the hospital, the little girl Dawn went missing one day. Her body was found a few days later. Again, I was scared, and my parents were terrified. They didn't want me leaving the house without their supervision.

I began to put on weight and then fought it off by starving myself. It was my wild friend Ashley who offered the helpful hint that if I was hungry, I could eat as much as I wanted and then just stick my finger down my throat. I'd like to say Ashley was a bad influence, but it truth, I was probably as bad for her as she was for me. The more I was kept locked in at home, the more I wanted to escape.

That summer Ashley and I had our first sips of watery beer while on vacation together on a boardwalk in Ocean City, Maryland. We were with my parents, but they were out for the night. We were supposed to stay in the hotel room keeping an eye on my younger brother, entertained only by reruns of *The Flintstone's* on the tube. Fat chance we'd stick around for that while adventure waited just outside. We snuck out, met some boys, and soon were at a party where we were handed a can of Bud, which we split. We snuck back in to the hotel room, thinking we'd got away with the crime of the century, only to find my younger brother (who we'd ditched) violently puking all over the room. Turns out he was as bored as we were, and he'd discovered a couple liters of Bartles and Jaymes wine coolers my parents had stashed in the room. Uh oh. Earlier that night we'd gone to an all you can eat seafood buffet. So my brother had puked strawberry wine coolers with fried fish, clams, and crab

24

legs all over the curtains, the beds, the ceiling and the drapes. The place smelled like something had died in there. It was so disgusting that Ashley and I decided to sleep on the beach rather than see my parents when they got back.

Eighth grade is awkward for most children. For me it was horrific. I'd already been through a lot as a child, and puberty wasn't adding any real clarity. I was growing up, but also growing out, and despite early battles with eating disorders, I was getting a little chubby. My family teased me mercilessly, and so did kids at school, where my nickname quickly became "Jabba." At home, my dad called me "The Lead Sled." I didn't make the cheerleading team that year, and I was devastated.

But, by far, the worst of all was what came next. In the fall of 1983, police finally arrested a man in connection to my friend Krista's abduction and murder. The man's name was Robert Buell, and he'd been found after a grown woman that he'd abducted escaped his house and called the police. Evidence then connected him to Krista (Dawn's supposed killer had already been arrested and convicted). When the report came on the news, I was watching with my family, doing homework, and I couldn't believe what I saw. "I know that man," I blurted out. The bushy white mustache, the close cropped gray hair—it was the man who told me I'd make a great hand model. The creepy talent scout. I felt chilled to the bone.

"What did you say?" asked my dad, not believing what he heard. I slowly explained to them that this man had approached me one day at a game, while I was cheerleading. Suddenly, locking me up in the house seemed justified to them. But it wasn't enough. They wanted to make an example out of what happened to Krista. When Robert

Buell's trial began, my parents insisted I go with my mom and grandmother. They thought I'd learn just what I was risking every time I left the house, every time I spoke to a stranger, or to a person I barely knew.

The day we went to the trial will always be burned in my memory. It turns out the killer had audio recorded his time with Krista, and that day they played tapes of Krista being tortured. I remember the judge, eyes down, either penitent or dozing, not sure which. And I remember Robert Buell, chained, hands in his pockets, and staring, I felt, right at me.

I was sick for days. And in some way, I think something in me broke forever after sitting in on that trial. After that, I spent the rest of the year trying not to be discovered. I let the introvert take over. Get good grades, get along, stay home, stay quiet. If it wasn't for my friends, I probably would have taken a vow of silence.

Lucky for me, my friends would never allow that. For whatever reason, my parents trusted my friend Ashley. She knew how to turn on the good girl when she had too, I guess. They weren't too worried about me sleeping over at her house. Maybe they should have been. Ashley and I would never stay put. We were experts at slipping out windows by age thirteen. Her parents were gentle and trusting, and they wouldn't check in on us until morning. We knew how to take advantage.

Usually the best parties were thrown by the boys who went to the Catholic school. For one, they usually had money, and they could throw some good parties. On top of that, they weren't around girls much, and they treated us like we were goddesses. Not that they didn't have dirty mouths and dirty minds, but they were clearly a little in awe of us. We'd usually make arrangements the days before the "sleepover." Once we slipped out, we'd go to the corner and wait for an older boy to pick us up in his car and drive us to the party. We felt safe, and we felt cool.

By age fourteen, I started high school, and slipping out was pretty common for me. I was in a state of constant fear. Fear of violence, fear of failure, fear of everyday cruelties. The only way I could fight through my fears was to challenge them. If I stayed cooped up in the house, my mind would wander, to my friends who had been murdered, to my parents, to my own shortcomings. Slipping out into the night, I was free of all of that. I felt in control.

Of course, I was losing all control. My eating disorder got worse. I'd stuff myself to the gills and then throw it up on a daily basis. *That's okay,* I thought. *I'm back on the cheerleading squad now. And varsity, even though I'm only a Freshman!* Boys started noticing me again. And it wasn't just boys—I was popular with teachers. I was on the student council, the pep squad, the debate team, and in the art club. Even my parents were treating me better for a while. They signed the work permit papers that would let me get a job at a local pizza joint (I was still only fourteen) so I could bring in a little money of my own. And they let me hang around school to study and socialize. I was learning that whatever was going on inside, as long as I could make others think I was doing great, things would go smoothly.

And when nobody was looking, I was free to do what I wanted. Ashley and I kept slipping out. One night, we went to a party, and I had too much to drink. One minute, I was sitting on an old couch in someone's basement, and the next I was waking up cold, with a pounding headache. Dawn sunlight blinded me as I came to. "Where am I?" I thought I was outside somewhere. I rolled over and bumped against something hard and smooth. What the hell? I spun myself around, woozy, only to realize I was waking up in a cemetery. Shit!!! In a flash, I knew what had happened. Ashley had dropped me off as a prank. I knew I was miles from her house, and that I had to get back to her house as soon as I could if I didn't want to get busted. When I climbed in the bedroom in my party clothes, caked in mud, Ashley just cracked up. Seeing her, I burst out laughing too.

I thought playing it cool could get me through anything. But I was wrong. At the end of the year, Ashley and I went out one night to go to the party of a much older boy named Jimmy. It was early, and I don't know what excuse we made up, but my parents knew we were going out to a party. I'd been bucking against their control long enough, they were finally starting to loosen their grip, and I'd occasionally be let loose. This wasn't like other parties we'd been to, though. There weren't a lot of other people there, and pretty soon it was just Jimmy, Ashley, me, and a guy who'd already graduated high school. I was nervous and wanted to go home. But I'd convinced myself that I could get out of any scary situation just by playing it cool, by never showing weakness. I took long, slow drags of my cigarette and tried to act bored, hoping Ashley would take a hint. When the man I didn't know walked over to me, I looked the other way, pretending not to notice. And when he asked me if he could show me something in the other room, I acted like I'd already seen it all, but I'd indulge him this one time.

He led me to a dark, cluttered room where he forced me onto a mattress. I knew something wasn't right and when I tried to call out for Ashley, the man silenced me with a forearm on my throat and a hand over my mouth. I could barely breathe and had no idea what he was trying to do to me until he started to take off my jeans with one hand. He pulled his pants down and I could feel his hard penis trying to enter me. I was a virgin and all I could think is this cannot be happening to me. The more I tried to squirm my way away from him, it seemed the harder his penis got. Then the more I tried to scream for Ashley, the harder he pressed on my throat and mouth. I was being raped and could only wait for it all to end.

Afterward, I left immediately with Ashley. I had her walk me home. All I could think of was that I needed to tell my parents, that this was the sort of thing they could protect me from, that they still wanted to protect me from. When I walked into the kitchen, I was bleeding. My clothes were torn. I told them.

My dad stared right through me. "You whore," he said. "Don't lie to us," my mom said.

I was devastated. They blamed me. From that awful night forward, I began to feel completely separate from my own body, and yet in other ways more conscious of it than ever. I knew others would try to use it for their own purposes. Men and boys might try to take sex from it. My parents might try to lock it away, pacify it with drugs, and heap scorn on it. But I was the one that needed to live with it, and if I was going to survive, I needed to be fully in control of it.

For the rest of the year and the summer beyond, I did whatever I wanted. I didn't fear my parents any longer, because I no longer craved their love and support. Instead, I was loyal only to my friends—Tony, Ashley, Becky. They were my life. They'd come to the pizza shop where I worked, and I'd give them free slices. They'd have older friends pick me up and drive me around town—to parties, to wherever I wanted. As far as I was concerned, I was my own person, nearly an adult, ready to live on my own.

My parents had a surprise in store for me, though. One day I walked in the door after work to find a black woman sitting with my parents in the living room. I had no idea who it was, but knowing my dad, it wasn't likely this was a friend of the family. My parents told me that she was with social services, and that if my behavior didn't improve, she was going to take me away and make me a ward of the state. She then lit into me for about an hour, yelling at me like I'd never been yelled at by a stranger before. She was trying to scare me straight, I suppose.

The intervention didn't have the effect my parents intended. That night, after crying by myself for hours, I snuck downstairs and opened the medicine cabinet. My dad was a pill fiend, and our cabinet looked like a pharmacy. I took everything.

I'm not sure how I survived that night, but I did live. After my stomach was pumped, I spent more days alone in the hospital. When I returned home, my parents made no attempt to disguise their anger. They yelled at me so much, hit me so much in the following weeks, inside the house and out, that a neighbor called Child Protective Services on them. Ironically, their plan to scare me straight had turned against them.

By age fourteen, I was a ward of the state. That year, I went to school in Akron and moved from one foster home to the next. Akron wasn't Hollywood, and I wasn't a movie star. I'd escaped home, but I could hardly say I'd made it. I didn't know anyone at my new school, and I missed my friends. Unlike the girl in the song, I hadn't found fame and fortune. But we did have one thing in common—we both learned young how much we gave up when we left home. I knew there was nothing for me there. No happy ending, anyway, in a town full of darkness and a home filled with anger. But there were my friends, and I was determined to get back to the only people in my life that were worth a damn.

Jack L.

Clinton, New Jersey

GFE / married / safe / wants to talk

I'm on the road, meeting clients all up the northeast coast. I have more gigs booked in more cities this year than U2. Jack is a client I know little about. We meet in a drab motel a little off the highway in the shadow of New York City. I'm feeling dark and lonely, thinking of home. He's made an appointment with me for two hours. After that, I'll hit the road again, determined to not let the blues catch up with me and make me drink more than I can afford. Maybe I'll even head into the city and rent a nice room, go out around happy people, try to have a little fun.

I arrive at the motel first, and soon I'm more than a little irritated. It's embarrassing to arrive at a fucking motel to meet a client at all, let alone arrive first. There's no bar, nowhere to wait except by the half empty vending machines. I think of ditching this client altogether, though I know I'd take a big hit to my Coach bag if I did something like that. There must be some kind of excuse I can make up.

Just before I'm about to get back in my car, Jack shows up. When I see him, I immediately think of Jack Lemon in Glengarry Glen Ross. He looks like a down and out salesman. Well, he's paying me well, at least.

"Miss, I apologize," he says. "Please, I'll compensate you for your lost time." The first thing I notice as we are close is the sadness written into his face. We go to the room, and he moves slowly, taking off his suit jacket and lying down on the bed with a sigh. I lie down next to him and stroke his hair. He seems uncomfortable, like maybe he'll start crying.

"Listen, Victoria. Sorry, this isn't easy for me. You see, I just came from visiting my wife. I hope this doesn't sound strange, but I just want to talk."

Oh, that always puts me in the mood. But I'll try anything once, even if it's just talking.

Soon the words are pouring out. His wife is in hospice. She doesn't have more than a couple of weeks left. Jack has had to be strong for her for so long now. He needs to indulge in a moment of weakness. No, he won't cheat on her. Not physically. But he needs to share some sort of intimacy with a woman. He hasn't known how to just open up to anyone. I'm not a therapist, but in some ways, I'm paid to understand sides of people they'd never share with a mere psychiatrist.

Jack's revelations about his wife lead to other stories, other worries, tales of self-doubt and loss. I tell him he's handsome, he's strong. I tell him the people in his life are lucky to have him. I'm not pretending. I don't share anything about my life. That's a no no. But I open up my feelings for Jack. I remember some of my own stories of loss. He cries. I cry. We fall asleep next to each other on the floral print polyester comforter. We wake after an hour, he pays me, and maybe we even both feel a little better.

Men often ask for the GFE—the girlfriend experience. They want the illusion of real intimacy. As I leave, I realize for one night I've provided the ultimate GFE.

Chapter 3

WHY CAN'T THIS BE LOVE?

Tony was a football player. He was a good looking guy, too—he had a big mop of jet black hair and broad shoulders. He was fun—always up for a concert or a party. He was also one of the most caring, responsible people I've ever known.

I think Tony always had a crush on me. From the time we were in junior high, he'd be dropping sweet little hints that he wanted me to be his girlfriend. I liked the attention, but I didn't want to be his girlfriend, and he knew it. After all, I'd known him since going to his eighth birthday party at Chucky Cheese. He was like a brother. A hunky brother, but a brother.

At age fifteen, I was living in foster care, and I think in many ways it was Tony I missed the most. Since my parents had lost custody of me, I'd bounced around between extended family. I was with my grandparents a little while, and then with my mom's second cousin Chrystal, a no-nonsense lady that I could respect but who wasn't exactly the mom I never had. I was also living way outside Canal Bottom—closer to Rust Bucket, where I was born. I didn't really know anyone. So I'd hang out in my room and wait for Tony's call, which would always cheer me up. He'd tease me about being a big city girl (my new high school was in Akron), and ask me when I was moving back. I really didn't know if I ever would.

It's not like I'd found a great new life, though. I went to a huge high school in the city, where I quickly discovered I was a nobody. I wasn't a country queen here—most of the student body was black, and for the most part they weren't too impressed with my cheerleader routines or my watercolors. I made friends—acquaintances really— but for the most part kept my head down.

The year started with me in the hospital again. This time, to break and reset my jaw. It was a procedure I needed to keep my face somewhat regular as I grew, thanks to my dad's handiwork with his claw hammer. For the recovery period, I stayed with my grandparents, and then went back to Chrystal's to hide away and dream. I just didn't want to let anyone see the real me.

And then in the spring, I took a job where I could literally wear a mask. I was the Easter Bunny at Rolling acres mall. You know, the one all of the screaming kids sit on and get their picture taken with? I was supposed to look like your average nice, white, furry, cuddly rabbit. But my costume had seen plenty of Easters already, and clearly been filled with plenty other souls at the end of their ropes. The fur was yellow and mangy, and the gloves were riddled with cigarette burns and nicotine stains. The whole inside of the costume smelled like a men's locker room in late August. I found it hard to be cute in that thing, and mostly just tried to keep quiet and avoid breathing through my nose. I remember some of the high school kids I'd started with that year coming to sit on my lap with their friends as a joke. One of them looked in to the metal mesh where my face was and recognized me as the new girl that transferred from the all-white school. After that, all the kids at school started calling me "Cotton Tail." I spent so much time on smoke breaks just trying to hide out and take off the foul smelling, creepy rabbit head that I became a chain smoker that spring. I remember when I gave my two weeks notice they begged me to stay the rest of the season for weekends; no one wanted that job!

I was changing again, fast. Who was I turning out to be? I didn't know—my life felt completely mangled—but I knew a little of *what* I wanted to be: a sophisticated woman, someone who was never afraid, never had to feel ashamed. I imagined myself different in small ways—different hair, different body, different voice. I may have been scared, alone, full of anger, but in a way, I was free to make myself from scratch.

That's why every time Tony called, I answered the phone like I was annoyed to hear from him, even though I was beaming inside. He brought me back.

"Hi Tony. What is it this time? You finally kiss a girl?"

"Hey, listen Jenny, you're never gonna believe this! I got tickets for the 5150 tour!"

"What's that, some kind of tractor pull?"

"No," he explained. "Van Halen!" It was a band I couldn't care less about, but Tony loved 'em. He had every album, and if you got close to him at a party, there'd be a good chance he'd corner you to debate pros and cons of kicking David Lee Roth out of the band. It turns out Van Halen was playing just outside Cleveland, and he'd got tickets for me and three of our friends. He'd also somehow convinced his dad to lend him the Winnebago, even though he only had his learner's permit. "Come on," he said. "This is our first chance to see Hagar as the front man!"

So that summer, I cut my hair short, dyed a big white streak into it, pulled what was left in the back into a little rat tail. I tried out a brand new look for a brand new life. And then I got a ride to Tony's place, where he was waiting with a few of my old schoolmates.

I couldn't help myself—I gave Tony a big, long hug. "I've missed you," I told him.

But he was a little too nervous to notice me as he sized up the Winnebago. The thing was big. We knew he could handle it though, so we loaded up, snuck a case of Little Kings into the back, and headed off. We should have known the trip was a bad idea when he backed the big RV off the driveway into a ditch, but we were too excited about finally being off on our own.

Tony sat in the front seat in his Van Halen T-shirt with a map of Ohio freeways in the passenger seat. The rest of us partied in back with some beers, while the wildest of us, Scotty, teased Tony about his driving. "Tony! Tony! You're driving on the wrong side of the road, dude! Tony! I think there's something wrong with the engine!" And with that, Scotty set off a smoke bomb in the back of the Winnebago, right in the middle of the highway. We screamed while Scotty laughed like a maniac. "Shit!" Tony barely made it to the shoulder before the cab was filled to the gills with stank black fumes.

"Scotty! I swear to God, if you make me miss 'Eruption,' I'm gonna kick your ass!" We all laughed, knowing how seriously Tony took all this. We had a blast that night, and it was the first time we'd had the power to go wherever we wanted, to do whatever we wanted.

That freedom was addictive, and I wanted my own license bad. And, ironically, the only way I could get that freedom was to move back in with my parents. Because of a loophole in state law, I couldn't get a driver's license without the permission of my parents, who were still technically my legal guardians. They were taking classes and going through the paperwork necessary to get custody of me back. I'd refused to cooperate until I learned about the deal with the driver's license. So in the end I talked to them on the phone and made my return home conditional—I wanted my driver's license, and I wanted to go to Catholic school. I'd always wanted to go to the nearby Catholic school, Virgin Heart Academy, since the girls there went on to good universities. I knew I had a much better chance of flying straight and getting out for good when I turned eighteen if I had a license and a diploma from a good school. That was the master plan, anyway.

So for my Junior year of high school, I buckled down, made a plan, and worked my ass off. Other than going to Catholic school and taking AP courses for college credit, I also held down three jobs. I worked at the pizza place, where I became a manager. I worked at a shoe store (I gotta admit, I was in it for the discount). And on weekend mornings, I'd clean homes. I was probably making less than five bucks an hour at these jobs, but I was saving. And to my parents' credit, they not only left me alone, they also helped me where they could. My dad fixed up one of his old beaters for me to drive around—a tiny 1980 Fiat Strata that he spray-painted purple at my request. Once I passed my driving test and had the keys to that scruffy little purple Fiat, I was on the road more than I was home. And for about a year, I lived a life with a real future in mind. Life was pretty good.

I wish I could say "pretty good" was enough for me back then. Unfortunately, it wasn't. By the end of the school year, I was getting restless. Just making it out wasn't enough. I wanted more—a big adventure, a big life, a new self. And I got one. In 1987, sixteen years after my mama had me, "Victoria McCormick" was finally born.

It happened one night on a whim. Near the end of the year, some buddies from the neighborhood were talking about a place up in Cleveland where we could get some real looking fake IDs. My eyes lit up at the thought. Not only could I get a little card that would tell the world I was already an adult, I could also make up any new version of me I wanted. It was a kind of starting over I'd always dreamed about. Complete self-invention.

A handful of us loaded into our ringleader's van, something that looked like the Mystery Machine from Scooby Doo. And we headed out for the east side of Cleveland, a part of the city that back then was full of freaks and zombies. Not exactly the "good" side. We ended up in an old, abandoned parking lot with a dark, rusted out trailer. All I could think of was hightailing it out of there like Scooby and Shaggy.

But it turns out this operation was run by a biker gang, folks I'd later come to know as Hells Angels. We waited in that smoky, sour trailer for some fat, hairy guy to press our new IDs. He'd point to us and ask us who we wanted to be. When it was my turn, I thought of the prettiest name I knew—Victoria—the name of the most beautiful girl in town while I was growing up. Why McCormick? Why not? It was an ordinary name from the perfect, ordinary life I never had.

For the next few months, I was pretty much Victoria McCormick as often as I could get away with it. I spent nights early that summer at bars all over the area, careful only to make sure I didn't end up in the kind of dive my dad or his friends might go to. I met new people, made new friends, and settled into my cozy and fun little alter ego.

Then one night in the middle of summer, Tony called me up. "Hey, you wanna go out tonight? I thought maybe we could catch a movie. They're playing *Predator* at the Empire." *Predator? Who is this calling me up*, I thought. *A child? I don't go to monster movies; I go to bars. I'm an adult.*

I made up an excuse—I had to study, I said. And then I went down to an Irish bar a few towns away where the bartender had a crush on me and gave me a free beer or two.

The next morning, I had to get up early to go clean houses. On my way, I stopped at the gas station to fill up and grab a coffee.

The sight of the local newspaper in the doorway froze me in my tracks. The headline said two dead, two injured in Canal Bottom single car accident. My eyes immediately found Tony's name. I grabbed the paper, hoping I was misreading. The night before, he'd gone out with a few guys, cruising around in one of the boy's muscle car. It had rained so much that night. The paper said it looked like they'd hydroplaned into a tree.

I had no feeling anymore. I could only think one thought—*If only I hadn't been such a bitch, he'd still be alive.* If only I'd gone out with him. I went home and cried on the couch until I fell asleep. At one point the phone rang, and I woke up with Tony sitting across from me on a recliner. "Tony," I said. "Get that will you, I'm trying to sleep."

He gave me a big, warm smile. "Come on, Jenny. You know I can't get that." And just like that, he vanished. And then I remembered it all. I don't know if it was a ghost or a dream, but I will never forget that moment as long as I live.

Tony's funeral was crowded with friends and family. He'd

touched so many lives in the few years he had, and he died before he could grow into the great man he was on the path to becoming. He was still so young. He was actually buried in his Van Halen shirt. I always wanted to grow up fast, but I never wanted my childhood ripped away from me. Tony died a child, and my childhood died off right along with him. After Tony, there was no home. There was nothing to hold onto.

I began drinking. Not like I'd drunk before—a few beers at the bar, a few shots at a party. I began drinking at home, alone, when nobody was looking. And I was raiding my dad's medicine cabinet every day. After Tony's death, I had Valium and booze in my system, in one ratio or another, almost all the time. I didn't think I could hide it from my parents, and I didn't want to try. Instead, I got a place on my own.

I found a kid that was like me, a seventeen-year-old who couldn't live at home anymore. He was splitting a cheap place downtown, above a Laundromat. I moved in with him and a strange, thirty-year-old woman that was trying to start her life over. Together, we split an apartment for $300/month rent.

My parents didn't make much of a fuss. But they also didn't want to pay for my Catholic school anymore. So when my senior year started, I was back at the local public school with all the old drama. I couldn't believe the world wanted me to go to high school still. I was ready to be done with all that shit. So I dropped out early in the year. I only had one class to take to graduate, government—and I could do that through adult education night classes at a nearby town. No need to waste my time anymore with cheerleading and the debate team, pep rallies, and cafeteria gossip. Not only that, I got myself legally emancipated from my parents. I was only seventeen, but I didn't want to wait. I was a grown woman, living on my own.

Or, at least, I was trying.

As much as I had free time to work, the money just wasn't enough. I'd always been a good girl, but the pressure was starting to make me crack a little. I got my friend Ashley a job at the same pizza shop, and she quickly came up with the bright idea of pocketing the money from some of the customers instead of ringing them up. We never got caught, though I felt horrible about it afterwards.

Still, I made ends meet until I'd finished my last high school class, and I graduated at seventeen—even got to walk with my class. My grades were near the top, too.

So I was free, except for two things.

One, I was always broke. I didn't want to steal from my boss at the pizza place, who I liked, and I didn't really have any more hours in the day to work more jobs.

Two, I was already making myself a slave to alcohol. It had started after Tony's death, but only got worse through my senior year. There were parties, yes, and there was the kind of craziness many teens get themselves into, but for me it had become more than that.

More and more, I needed a drink to face the day. And why not? I'd seen so much already. I'd been beat up. I'd been raped. I'd had friends murdered by psychos, and I'd had friends taken away in the blink of an eye by a car crash. I'd been locked in my home for years, and then I'd been taken from it.

The world out there was a bad one, and that wasn't even what scared me the most. I still shuddered every time I looked in a mirror. This wasn't the person I wanted to be. This wasn't my dream. The voices of my parents, my classmates would come back to me: *You're fat, Jabba. You're a slut. You're not good enough.* It got to the point where I needed to drink to go outside, and I needed to drink to be home alone with myself.

By age seventeen, I knew I had a problem. But I didn't know what to do about it. At that age, everything came down to money. I grew up so poor, I always thought that was the one thing standing between me and real happiness. If only I could make it, I'd be able to face myself in the mirror, and I won't have to drink anymore, and I won't have to throw up to make myself feel skinny and pretty.

I was impatient. I had gotten into college—Kent State! And couldn't wait to go. In fact, I enrolled early, and started taking classes in June that year. I didn't know exactly what to study. I'd always wanted to study art, but I was afraid, and followed my mom's advice to take up nursing. Hey, I was ready to take good money where I could find it, and as soon as I could get it.

And that's what led me to my other big decision.

It started one afternoon when I was hanging out with Ashley at the pizza place. It was a slow day, and we were looking at a newspaper a customer had left on the counter. The wanted ads were filled with all kinds of grim offers, but we were having fun dreaming of more money, bigger jobs, and a little adventure.

"Oh God, Jenny, take a look at this! Pepe le Peu's is looking for dancers. Wanna sign up? Men are gonna pay to see those titties!"

I laughed. "Can you imagine? What if someone you knew came in?"

"Yeah, I think my uncle goes to that place!"

Pepe le Peu's was a Go Go bar at the edge of town. Not much to look at from the outside, but the parking lot was always full when we'd drive past at night. We didn't know much about what went on inside, but we knew it was basically a place for guys to go stare at half-naked ladies after a day at the tire factory. Not too different than the places I was going at night, but with bouncing boobies to stare at instead of just the bottom of a glass. *Damn*, I thought. *I bet the pay is good.*

"I'm gonna do it," I said. "I'm trying out."

Ashley's ice green eyes got real wide. It wasn't easy to shock her, but I had this time.

"No you won't! Will you? Okay, but I get to help you pick out the outfit."

We drove up to Cleveland, where we found a lingerie store, and I picked out a lacy lingerie number that I thought was the sexiest thing any woman had ever worn: it was basically a black leotard, but with plenty of sparkly glitter swirling from shoulder to crotch. The hems at the arms and legs were edged with black lace. I wish I had a photo of me in that get-up. I probably looked like I was trying to pull off the most fabulous onesie ever, or maybe I looked like a slutty majorette.

Ashley drove me to Pepe's the next afternoon. I couldn't drive myself because I was blitzed—the only way I could work up the courage to put my body on display was with half a fifth of vodka. There was only one other car in the parking lot when we arrived, and we walked in with the hair up on the back of our necks. The place was dark and dusty, with a bar on one side and a wooden stage in the middle. It smelled awful, like desperation. Around the stage were orange vinyl seats that looked like they'd been swiped from a condemned Denny's. Near the bar was a tall man with bloodshot

44

eyes. Pepe. The owner of the place. "Afternoon, ladies. Are you both trying out today?"

"No, just me."

"And what's your name, hon?"

"Victoria. Victoria McCormick."

"Well Victoria McCormick, how old are you?"

"I'm twenty-three," I lied.

"Have you ever danced before?"

"No. Not at a place like this."

"Well what kind of place do you think this is?" Pepe said with a big, cold smile.

I couldn't think of what to say.

"No worries, darlin. Just playing. You wanna get up there and give it a try?"

I huddled by the side of the stage and took off my T-shirt and jeans, strapped on some high heels. I got up there and thought about Marilyn Monroe, my icon of female sensuality since I was young. I didn't dance so much as pose—arms behind my head, awkwardly shifting one way then the next. Pepe watched a while, stone faced. Then he smiled that mean smile again and drank a long slow sip of his beer. "Okay, okay, that's enough. You can't dance, but you make up for it in other ways. Listen, meet me here next Thursday afternoon. You've got the job."

I was thrilled. Afterwards, Ashley and I laughed all the way home. "You're not gonna do it, are you?" I told her I'd think about it.

Four days later, I pulled up to Pepe's. It was hours before the bar was set to open, and this time I went by myself. Pepe was alone, too, and he met me in the parking lot, carrying a big shopping bag.

He knocked on the passenger door, and I let him in. "Tonight I'm going to show you around," he said. "First, we're gonna get something to eat. You drive."

I wasn't sure what was going on, but I was up for an adventure. We got on the highway and soon we were in Rust Bucket, where I was born. We ended up at the Green Fern Bar and Grill. I was impressed. All this for me? The nicest restaurant I'd ever been to before was Long John Silver's (a favorite for birthday dinners). Inside the Green Fern, grown up men and women were wearing jackets, dresses, and even a few had ties. I didn't feel like I belonged, but Pepe made me feel a little better. He ordered for me and got a bottle of wine. I sat there quietly and sipped it while he explained to me how it was gonna work. I was going to start that weekend, and I'd do shifts of three or four hours. During a shift, I'd dance for three songs, work as a waitress for three songs, and then get three songs to dance for men for extra tips or take a break.

"And bring quarters, Victoria." Pepe said. "Girls gotta feed the jukebox themselves. Pick whatever songs you want. Also, remember: this is a Go Go bar, not a nudie bar. You can't show your tits. Not all the way. But listen. You can't wear what you wore last weekend, either. I've got something for you back in the car."

After prime rib (which I only barely touched) and a bottle of red (which I handled mostly by myself), we went back to the car, where he reached into his shopping bag and brought out a pink box with a red ribbon. I felt like I was on a date with prince charming—if prince charming smelled like whiskey and looked like he hadn't slept in days. Inside the box was something that looked like a black string next to two black buttons.

"What's this?" I carefully held the string up—it was so delicate, it looked like it might disintegrate between my fingers.

"That's a T-back and pasties. That's what you'll be wearing. Now lets go back to the place and you can try them out."

I didn't know what to say. I settled on "okay." Then I put the box in the back seat and turned to face out the side window, like I was checking traffic before I pulled out. Really, I was giggling, as silently and as still as I could possibly be. I knew he was dead serious, but I just couldn't help but think of Ashley's reaction. Or my parents! I didn't even know how I was going to get those little strings and buttons to fit on my body, let alone dance with them on. *Oh Jenny, what have you got yourself into*, I thought.

Back at the bar, Pepe poured me a shot of whiskey and opened a beer. It was still two hours before the bar was set to open. "Bottoms up. Then you go in back and change. You'll figure it out. Then come back and dance. Listen, nobody's gonna be taking pictures. You're not striking a pose. You're supposed to keep moving. Just keep moving, and move like a woman. There's no trick to it. You'll be okay."

I went back to the dressing room, where I stalled and looked at all the personal items that other girls had left there. Lipstick cases, phone numbers scrawled on business cards, old cigarette boxes. Who were these girls, and what would they think of me? Would they recognize me as an imposter in a way Pepe had not? After all, I was only seventeen still, too young to be doing this. But hey, these days I was more Victoria McCormick. If I could fool myself, I could fool them, too.

I found a couple of old pasties on the dressing table that were filled with half-dry goo that looked like rubber cement. Next to them was a bottle of clear gel labeled "Gum Arabic." I thought there was a good chance I was about to burn my nipples off, but I thought, what the heck. I gotta look like I know what I'm doing. I spread the goo on the back of the pasties and stuck em right over my nipples. It was a little cold, but it seemed to do the trick—they stayed in place. Then I put on the thong. At the time, the fashion was to wear T-backs—they had a little more cloth than g-strings, but not much more. The waist went straight across the hip at top, and then another strip of cloth plunged right down the middle in a straight line, making the shape of a T across the ass. I put that on too, and couldn't help but think the way it cut into my butt crack was not the sexiest thing I'd ever felt.

There was a black robe on a hanger, and I put that on to feel a little less self-conscious, and then I went out to the stage. I was half hoping Pepe wouldn't be there, that something had called him away on important business, and that I could just call Ashley to come pick me up. We'd go to a bar and laugh about it all night.

But he was there, sitting in the same booth near the pool table. "You ready?" he said. I nodded, and he hauled himself out of his seat to go put a quarter in the jukebox. A deep baseline and drums started up. "Okay, let's start, Victoria." I dropped my robe and moved to the front of the stage. I couldn't think of what to do, and I just imagined Ashley there in the front, cracking up. So I just pretended I was trying to make Ashley laugh. I thrust my hips out. I shook my chest, flung my boobs around in big semi-circles. For the finale, I turned around and shook my ass like a wet dog that just stepped onto dry land. The song ended.

I turned around slowly. I thought Pepe would be furious, thinking I was making fun of him with my over-the-top dance. But instead he was leering at me, with his mouth half open.

"Damn, Victoria. That was sexy as hell." He stood staring for a minute, and then went to get me another drink. "Here, come sit by me," he said. I did, not knowing what else to do with myself. I was still mostly naked, so I grabbed the robe on the way over.

I sat down, and sipped at a whiskey while I felt his eyes on me. He didn't let me finish. In a flash, his tongue was in my mouth, and his hand was on my ass. I didn't say no, even though I was dizzy and disgusted. He stood me up and walked me backward to the pool table, where he pulled off my thong.

I'd been raped before. This time wasn't quite like that other time. He wasn't violent. He just wasn't interested in whether or not I was interested. I didn't feel anything. I didn't feel anything about sex, really. I've met a lot of girls and women in this business, and probably most have a history of abuse, a history of rape. Maybe this isn't true for everyone, but for so many of us, once that's happened at a young age, having someone take your body just feels impersonal. It's not that it isn't horrible, painful, or terrifying. It's just not a surprise. And once you're numb to it, it's easy to think of it as an exchange. *If people are gonna take shit from my body*, I thought, *I'm going to use it to my benefit, and I'm going to get something out of it.*

After it was over (which was quick enough), Pepe told me to clean up and leave before the other girls showed up. I'd start Saturday, and he'd prefer I didn't come by until then.

Looking back, I can't believe how proud of myself I was that week, waiting for my first show. Somehow I thought having sex with my employer just because he hired me and shelled out for a few square inches of lycra underwear was not only okay, it was something that made me a sophisticated woman. There was nothing sexy about Pepe's club. It was practically held together with duct tape, and it smelled so thickly of spilled beer, stale smoke, and tired men that you really had to take shallow breaths just to keep from passing out. But I had to admit, I got a little charge from the prospect of having so many men look at me the way Pepe did. It wasn't exactly Marilyn Monroe getting discovered, but it felt like I was about to be noticed.

The big night came, and I had serious stage fright. As with just about anything else in my life at the time, I had to get nice and buzzed before I had the courage to go on stage. I showed up at eight and met some of the girls (who didn't pay much attention to me). The bartender, Lisa, gave me a big smile, though. The only man working at the bar was Pepe himself, who mostly kept to his chair, with one bloodshot eye on the stage and the other on any customers who might be getting a little rowdy.

The place filled up quick. The crowd looked like it was mostly factory guys just off a weekend shift. A few white collar types came in as the night went on. First, one of the girls showed me how to take drink orders. I was half dressed in my T-back and pasties, but with a little more covering me up while I was working the floor. Men noticed, but for the most part were focused on the stage or on their drinks. I gotta admit, I couldn't keep my eyes off the stage either. These women were just a couple years older than me, maybe, but they were grown, and they knew what they were doing. I tried not to be overwhelmed.

I had a secret, though. My ace card. Ashley was there, dressed like a customer in a long coat and baseball cap and sipping a scotch like she'd come here every night for years. She was having the time of her life watching me prance around the floor. Every time I passed, she'd make an indecent proposition.

Finally, Pepe called me over, along with a girl who was just on stage. "Let's get the new girl on stage, yeah?"

"Sure. What song you want, hon?"

I didn't know what to choose, so I picked what was on when I danced for Pepe: The Eagles "Life in the Fast Lane," since I knew I could dance to it.

I got up on stage, and started moving. In the lights, it was hard to see very much, but I could tell the eyes were all on me. It was a rush; I'm not going to lie. I looked at Ashley, who couldn't keep a straight face any more. She was doubled up laughing. I played it for her, swinging my chest and shaking my ass like I'd done the night before. The men started to roar. That made Ashley laugh even harder, and I worked it even harder. A man came to the stage and shoved a five-dollar bill in my thong. It felt like I owned the world.

I had a blast that night. And I got paid. The bills piled up in my purse, I sped back to my apartment where I laid it all out on my bed. I'll never forget the smell of that money. It was the most joyful fragrance I could imagine. There was all my ambition, bravery, craving for attention, need for freedom and independence—all the dreams I ever had for myself wrapped up in that smell.

I was giddy counting it up. Ninety-two dollars. It was a week's worth of working my three other jobs. I scattered the bills across my bed and rolled in them, laughing. I may have had happier moments in my life, but I've never felt so sure of the future as I did that night.

Randy

Plano, Texas

Married / wife has the money / shy / GFE / heartbreaker

"Victoria, we've got to talk."

I run my fingers through the hair on Randy's chest. With my other hand, I reach down low and cup his balls. "Yeah, Randall? You wanna talk?" I say it real low, teasing him. My face is inches from his. "Whyddya wanna talk about, Randall? We've only got half an hour left, and we haven't even got to your favorite things yet." I lick the stubble on his chin. "Or maybe you wanna talk about trying something, new?"

"Okay, take a break, Jenn, please?" He calls me by my real name. He's my only client that knows it. But he knows he's not supposed to use it. I give his balls a twist as punishment, I give him a wink, and then I flip around to ride him. But he pulls up and away.

I'm just messing around, since I feel so comfortable with Randy. We're together in my four-poster bed. Just as we are every Thursday. Randy's my first regular client. And he's perfect. Not only is he good looking, he's also paying my rent and half my other bills with his regular visits. I also like to think we have more than a professional relationship. We know each other. I know about his wife, the corporate VP whose money is paying for our liaisons. He even knows something of my exes. We talk. We laugh. We fuck each other's brains out.

I've fallen a little for Randy. "Listen, hon. Wipe that serious look off your face. I know you've got more to give me today, and I'm over here aching for it. What's so important to talk about anyway?"

"Shit. Sorry, it's just... It's just, I'm not sure I can visit you anymore."

I go cold. I feel goosebumps. I sit up and look him in the eyes. He's not lying.

"Dammit, baby, I don't know how to say this. You know how we first met, and I said I was looking for the girlfriend experience?"

"Of course, and it's not just an 'experience,' hon. You're more than a client to me. I like to think I'm more than just another friend to you."

"That's exactly the problem. I don't want to feel these feelings. I've got a wife, Jenn. I can't put that at risk."

He had a wife alright. I tried not to think about it. And along with the wife, he had the Audi, the house, and the retirement at a young age. In a flash I saw the problem. I'd been paid to give him the girlfriend experience. He was getting paid much more to give his wife the "husband" experience. His feelings—and my feelings—were putting his setup in danger. What had it been? Maybe the week before, when I'd opened up about myself, made some remarks about my exes, about the divorce. I'd been lazy. I'd revealed myself. I'd become too real.

Randy leaves, and I don't see him again for months. He eventually comes back—occasionally—but I've learned my lesson. Never drop the mask, even for a guy you like and start to fall for.

Chapter 4

LIFE IN THE FAST LANE

I was barely eighteen and I was living with a man named Jake Majors. He owned a tow truck company. It was his house, and he had a young daughter that lived there as well. We both slept in the same big water bed, and he didn't charge me rent, but we weren't fucking. It wasn't a romantic thing. We just really got along, and he let me stay there for free in return for helping out with his young daughter while he was at work.

At the time, this was the sweetest part of my life. I had fun living there, and I loved taking care of that little girl. I was starting classes at Kent State, and this one little sliver of my life was happy and safe, and it almost resembled a future, as oddball an arrangement as it was.

Of course, to my eighteen-year-old self, my homemaking with Jake was just a temporary convenience while I moved toward my real destiny—a life of excitement and adventure.

I'd become a regular at Pepe's by June. I loved it. It started as a joke, or a way to make money, but it quickly became something I craved like a drug. I'd lived for years with the fear of older men's eyes on me, their want for my body. But every night I could have a few drinks, slip off my robe, and put it all on display and be in total control. It was like a dare. *You want it, well, here it is.* I wasn't just in control of my own body. I felt in control of their bodies as well.

For the most part, all I got was long looks and catcalls. I did have some special admirers, though. Mixed in with all the tire factory guys were a handful of men in nice shirts and ties. I learned quickly that I could have a nice night if I made guys that looked like that feel special.

After a few weeks at Pepe's I started noticing a regular who would always move up to the front when I was dancing. He had dark, brylcreemed hair with white at the temples, a deep tan, and nice clothes. He'd tip, too. While the factory guys would sometimes put a dollar in my T-back, this guy would stick fives in there, every time I danced. Pretty soon, I started joining him for drinks. He asked me my name, and I told him I was Victoria. "Well Victoria, do you like shoes?" He told me his name was Frank Portini, and he said he was an importer of Italian footwear. He asked me my shoe size and told me he'd start bringing in some shoes he wanted to see me dancing in.

So he liked feet, so what? Frank was a nice guy, something I wasn't completely used to. He treated me like a lady. He'd take me out every other week or so, shower me with pumps, stilettos, and other heels in assorted candy colors. And then we'd fool around in his car, or at a motel off the highway.

To this day, I'm not sure if he was really a shoe "importer" or just a manager at Payless, but all that attention worked on me. I think at that age I'd do just about anything for a man that treated me like a grown woman and showed me a little respect. Respect meant more to me than love. I still didn't know what that was, and I don't know if I believed in it.

That's why I trusted Frank when he invited me with him on a trip to Columbus to visit a secret "club for adults." I didn't know what he was talking about, exactly, but he made it sound incredibly sophisticated and sexy. "There's a secret door, and you have to give a secret password." To my ear, it sounded like he was about to give me the secret password to my dreams.

So one weekend he picked me up from Jake's place and we drove down to the state capital. Frank and I spent the night together at a motel off the highway, and spent the next day in the city where he bought me little presents. That night after the sun set, we approached a non-descript warehouse outside downtown. Frank knocked on a thick steel door painted a dull salmon color. It was quiet. I thought we must have the wrong place. Then Frank punched a code into a keypad, and waited a moment until a voice asked over a small speaker, "What is it?" Frank then mumbled something into the speaker and waited another moment before the door opened. As soon as it did I felt like the portal to another world had been blasted open. We were quickly dragged inside where a rail thin man in leather pants and a flowing, linen shirt welcomed us. Frank discreetly handed him a wad of bills, and we were allowed in. The space was divided up the middle by a long hallway of poured concrete with raw, unfinished drywall, and lots of track lighting in primary colors beamed at odd angles. Off the long hallways were doorways out of which all sorts of sounds and tinted lights seemed to pulse.

There was a small bar near the front of the entrance, and Frank got me a drink. Women passed through the halls wearing lingerie, silky robes, and wild slashes of makeup. Some of the hair I saw was so big, it looked like cake that had just come out of the oven. There were a few men like I'd never seen before, too. Men wearing black leather and some wearing mascara. Probably most of the guys were like Frank, though—middle age guys in half unbuttoned button-ups, slacks, and slicked hair.

A gorgeous red head passed me and gave me a big smile while staring me up and down. I was suddenly feeling like a little girl again, trapped in some kind of vampire movie, but I was determined to prove I belonged. I swallowed a clear, spicy drink Frank had given me and let him lead me down the hall to a room halfway down. On the way, I couldn't help but peek to see what other people were doing. It was hard to tell. I saw skin, and lots of it, but there was too much smoke, too many flashing lights to figure out where one body ended and another began. In one room, I saw a woman hanging from the ceiling in a swing like a hammock, and on a clear glass table some burly, naked men were hunched over a little pile of powder. I quickly looked away. I couldn't help but think of my sixth grade teacher and his wagging finger—"drugs will ruin your life!" I'd smoked a joint before, and of course I'd fallen hard for booze, but this was a whole new world.

Frank led me into an empty room and sat me down on a vinyl sofa. He casually undid a button on his shirt and asked me to make myself comfortable. The space we were in must have been occupied just a few minutes before—there were still drink glasses with ice in them in the corner of the room. Frank put his arm around me and we necked a little while Duran Duran played from a speaker above our heads. I was having trouble relaxing, and I kept one eye on the open door as people passed by. Occasionally a single person or a couple would stop for a moment and watch us. I have to admit, when I could tell my audience was turned on, that turned me on a little too.

After a few more minutes, a group came to the door. "Hi," said a slightly paunchy middle aged man. "Mind if we join you?" I could barely see past the strobe lights, but four silhouettes made their way into the room. There were two men and two women. The men looked like they were probably divorce attorneys who had a few too many steak and martini lunches. One of the women looked like your average chubby Midwest housewife. But the other woman caught my eye immediately. It was the beautiful red head that I saw when I first came in moments before.

I think I caught hers, too.

"Hey," she said. "I'm Sue. Can I sit by you?" I made space, and I told her my name (or, my pretend name, anyway). Our eyes were locked on each other. Sue was older than me, but not old. Maybe twenty-seven. And she was a grown woman. With her soft, shoulder length brunette hair and her full, gorgeous mouth and perfect makeup, she was practically the woman I saw as my future self when I closed my eyes and dreamed. She was like a living dream.

We were the two youngest in the room, so nobody seemed to mind that we ignored everyone else. They were chatting and laughing, trying to get comfortable with each other while loosening shirt cuffs here, blouse buttons there. Of course, the three others kept their eyes on me and Sue as well. We were young, and we were the spark. It was our desire that was at center stage.

After a short moment of silence, Sue leaned in and asked, "Can I kiss you?" I'd never been kissed by a girl before, and definitely not a grown woman. I let her, and when her lips hovered over mine, I felt a jolt like I'd never felt before. Pretty soon, she was unzipping the back of her rose-colored sheath dress, and I found I was doing the same. The others in the room were starting to get a little frisky with each other too, but I had tunnel vision.

Sue's body was perfect. It was like something out of a Greek myth, and the sight of it set off a wave of touching, feeling, stroking in the room. But everything aside from Sue was a blur to me. Soon I was on top of her, and she guided me down the length of her body. By this time in my life, I was pretty new to blowjobs, and I'd never been with a woman at all, but I figured out pretty quickly what to do. Hearing Sue's groans was thrilling, and I could tell that the rest of the people in the room had stopped what they were doing just to watch us. That was even more thrilling. Then I let Sue tend to me while I closed my eyes and listened to the farthest sounds I could hear in the crowded, thumping club.

Her tongue tickled each of my nipples and I felt them getting harder all while I got wet. I'd never been so turned on. She slowly went down on me with her tongue first over my rib cage and then caressing my belly button. I had a flutter in my stomach that was a feeling that I'd never felt before. Anticipating her next move, my clit was starting to throb. I couldn't wait for her tongue to touch it. She pulled my panties aside and teased me with her tongue on the top of the inside of my thighs while she slowly spread my legs apart. Her tongue fluttered over my clit like a butterfly kiss while her finger delicately touched the outside of my pussy and I moaned over and over. Meanwhile, I could tell the others had stopped what they were doing completely because I was getting much louder. This was a fantasy come true that I didn't even know I had in me—being with a woman and being watched by others. My hips thrust forward, I was on the edge. I didn't want this feeling of building up to end. She knew just what to do, and this time I wasn't acting. I trusted her maybe because she wasn't a man. I felt like I was floating out of my body after I finally came. My body quivered and shook and I even became dizzy.

Soon it was all over. The others had finished way before us. Frank took me out to a bar afterward and was a gentleman, but I think he was a little less interested in me after my session with Sue. He knew he could never do for me what she'd just done.

Frank wasn't the only man exposing me to brand new pleasures. I also met a man named Mark, a lawyer, who started taking me out. I didn't meet Mark at Pepe's. I met him at another club.

After just a few weeks at Pepe's, some of the girls started warming up to me a little bit, and I started hearing about some of the other places they worked. "Oh, you can always pick up shifts here at Pepe's, but the good money is closer to the city." They told me about another club called the Love Shack, closer to Akron, where the patrons tipped five times as much as at Pepe's. "The hour rate's the same, but the tips are way higher. You'll make twice as much a night." I asked if it was all white collar types. "Some, but also plenty of bikers. You know the Hells Angels? You have to know how to take care of yourself if you're working at the Love Shack. But listen, honey, Big Al, who owns the Love Shack, he won't make you pay for your own songs."

I thought I'd give it a try. I was making good money at Pepe's, but the shifts were limited. If I could work both bars, I'd be making good money every night, and if I could do double shifts (something Pepe wouldn't allow, since he didn't want tired ladies), then I could really build up enough to have my own huge apartment and anything else I might want. And I'd never have to worry about the cost of school.

So I drove to just outside Akron and picked up a job with Big Al. Al was a biker himself, a former Hells Angel. He was a big bear of a man with a leather jacket and a past, but he was a good guy.

And it was true what the other ladies said: The Love Shack was bigger, and the guys that went there threw around more money. It had a real DJ, and the walls were lined with floor to ceiling mirrors. Dancing there was a blast. The music was loud, the crowd was louder, and the other girls were crazy. There were always men hanging around angling for attention, and they always had money in their hands. They knew the game.

It wasn't long before Mark showed up, and he took a shine to me right away. He was intense. His eyes just burned a hole right through me when I was on stage. I kinda liked it. But when I was off stage, he'd buy me drinks, and he was a perfect gentleman (at least compared to some of the grizzled bikers that showed up in the place from time to time). After a few nights, he asked me out, and I agreed. Mark talked fast, laughed loud, and he never took his eyes off me, which was all a little unnerving. But he never gave off a creepy vibe, and he knew how to make me feel like a lady, which was definitely the way to my heart.

Mark took me out to dinner, to the same place all the other guys took me at that time. There were just a few "nice" restaurants in the area, the kind of place with dim lighting and decent wine where a man could take a barely eighteen-year-old girl who promised she was twenty-three. I sat between a couple of brass pots with ferns, and

Mark tried to make me laugh all night. I didn't get his jokes, always—he spoke so fast—but I appreciated a man with a sense of humor.

Afterward, we went to his car, he pulled into a nearby parking lot where we were alone. "So," he started. "You want some coke?"

"Sure!" I was thirsty and kind of hoping he meant rum and coke. But that's not what he meant at all. Mark took a little brown vial out of his glove compartment. It had a black twist top, like the top of an eye dropper, but it was rounded like a bullet. He unscrewed it, and attached to the top was a tiny silver spoon. Mark loaded up the spoon and held it carefully up near my chin, then looked at me expectantly.

Whoa. It had only been a couple of weeks since I'd first seen people doing this stuff, and I immediately broke character and started giggling. I wasn't a sophisticated woman for a moment—I was a girl again. I thought of laughing with Ashley and my other friends about our sixth grade teacher, about the classroom visits from D.A.R.E. officers.

"I'm sorry!" I managed. "I didn't understand what you meant."

Mark looked at me, a little perplexed. "Huh? You don't want any? You're the first dancer I met that doesn't like coke."

I was embarrassed, and so was he. A little vein at his temple throbbed. And then he broke into a big smile. "Have you ever tried it before? Is this your first time?"

I was a little scared. But I said it was my first time. And that I wanted to try it.

He showed me what to do. He was so calm, so reassuring, it was like a doctor telling me how to administer medicine. "This'll be fun," he said. "You're gonna feel like you never felt before. I love watching people's first time."

It took a little more convincing, but not too much. I tried just a little—sniffed at just a little of the powder on the little silver spoon. How could such a small amount turn into a problem? I'd just try it.

First I felt the burn in my nostrils and deep in the back of my throat, and I knew that little bit of powder was going to hit me in a big way. And then I felt big. I felt huge. I felt important. I felt like I'd leapt across that divide separating me from adulthood. I was Marilyn. I was Sue, the beautiful red head from the club I visited with Frank. I was a woman, and more important than Canal Bottom, more important than my parents, more important than all my old fears.

Then Mark and I had sex in the back of his car. That was pretty much our relationship for the next month or two. We'd meet up, he'd give me coke, and we'd have sex. I thought he was being so generous. I only realize as an adult, he knew exactly what he was doing. He was getting me hooked, and he was buying sex from me with coke. Of course, I didn't see it that way at the time. In my mind, we were two consenting adults, having a good time together. Life had gone from drab and terrifying to colorful and bold.

By the end of summer, I felt like my childhood was a distant memory. I'd done things other kids from Canal Bottom probably couldn't imagine. Wealthy men craved my attention. And I was making more money than anyone I knew back home, and was fitting in college courses to boot.

I felt like I'd made it, and I was ready to show off. One night I called up Ashley. We still talked every week or so, even if we didn't see each other as much since I started working on the stage. I told her about the cocaine, and about how fun it was. I felt like we were in the race to impress each other; I'd not only caught up to her—I'd lapped her. I could imagine her jaw dropping on the other end of the line.

We met up for a drink a few days later, and I showed her a little brown vial I'd got from Mark and informed her it was called a "bullet." She was impressed. "What's that? It looks like my grandma's throat drops!" She tried a little, and she practically squealed. "Oh man, that kind of hurts!" We laughed. She held out her hands, shaking them like she'd had too much coffee. "I feel like I'm gonna have a heart attack. Do you like this stuff? Maybe it's just not for me." Then she gave me a look and started to ask something. But she stopped herself. We giggled some more, and we went and had a drink, and then she left early. She was getting ready herself to go off to college. She was going to study nursing too, but she'd be halfway across the country.

She told me to take care of myself, that she'd see me soon. But we didn't really see much of each other after that summer. I probably thought she'd fallen behind, slowed down, and wasn't cut out for the kind of life I'd found for myself. She was content just being a small town girl who went off to college for a couple of years. I thought that was a little sad, but not worth crying over. I had new friends. They were smart, they were pretty, and they lived their lives fast. And I was one of them.

After Ashley left that night I had a couple more drinks, then went back to Jake's place, where I was staying. I went to check on his daughter, gave her a little kiss, then started to get ready for bed. But I was still too high. I checked the clock—it wasn't even midnight. I put on another dress—a tight dress I'd worn one night for Frank—and went out again. First, to the Love Shack to see if Mark was there with another little brown vial. Sleep? Nah! What was the point of that, anymore?

Connecticut Jim
Hartford, CT
PSE / Safe / Married / Use discretion

Most of the time, when a man says he wants PSE—the porn star experience—he's talking about anal sex. Sure, there are other elements—a lot of hammy, dramatic gestures, maybe you have to pretend to be overwhelmed by his "enormous" member, but you've gotta go into a first meeting with a PSE enthusiast expecting some anal play.

Jim's a new client, and I met him while I'm in New England. He's booked me for 3 to 4 hours, and in emails there was a big emphasis on PSE. I don't know much more, but I'm guarding myself.

We meet at a hotel—nothing fancy, nothing grimy, either. It's fucking Hartford, not New York, and my expectations are pretty low. Jim's in his forties, balding, tall. I meet him at the door of his hotel room, and he's already made himself comfortable, with a hotel robe and a bottle of wine in one hand. Okay, this I like. He offers me a drink, and I take it. We get started right away. He wants to try a little of everything. More SPE than PSE—a sampler platter experience. We screw all around the room, and it's clear he just wants to have fun. Is this a man that has no particular hang ups, no secret needs that I must discover? If so, he's a rare bird, indeed.

After he finishes, we quickly shower, and he has a mischievous look in his eye. "Come on," he says. "Let's go down to the bar." On the ride down, he mentions there's a woman at the bar every night that he's had his eye on. Now he wants more than anything to see us together. "Trust me, I've got a sixth sense about this sort of thing," he said.

"She'll be into you."

Well, I don't know if it's Jim's enthusiasm, or if she's really that into me, but it doesn't take long before we're all back upstairs together. The woman is beautiful—young, adventurous, badass. Our first kiss is natural. I know exactly what to do with another woman. I've done this many times before now, to entertain men, to please myself. I think back to twenty years before, to the club in Columbus, to the first woman I was ever with. This is just an echo of that moment, which was both startling and natural for me, one of the great thrills of my life. Here in Hartford, this is nostalgia, but it's also pleasure. Hey, if this is Jim's idea of a PSE, I'll be more than happy to come up to fucking Hartford whenever he wants.

Chapter 5

WELCOME TO THE JUNGLE

"Hey, baby, why you even bother with that lil bit of string?"

It was the Love Shack, and my friend Tania was dancing next to me. She'd made a friend.

"Here. Hey, let's have a look…"

Tania tried to move away to the other side of the stage. Most men seemed to know how to put money in a g-string without getting too handsy. Every once in a while, you'd get a customer who suddenly wanted to play gynecologist.

"Where you going? Listen bitch, don't walk away from me after I give you a dollar."

Tania's fan was a very drunk man with a very nice watch. These were the types we usually had problems with, if we had problems. The Love Shack was about half filled with bikers, especially Hells Angels, but it was in the Angels' code or something to treat dancers with respect while they were on stage. It was the alcoholic businessmen, the middle manager types, who seemed to have something to prove by embarrassing the girls on stage after a few drinks.

The man followed Tania to the other side of the stage, sloshing his drink at the feet of some grizzled old guys in leather jackets.

"C'mon, baaaby!" The drunk grabbed at Tania's crotch, ripping her g-string to the side. Maybe he thought she'd be flattered? Maybe he thought everyone in the bar would laugh? Who knows, what he thought, but I doubt he was expecting what happened next. You couldn't work in the Love Shack without being able to stand up for yourself, and Tania was no pushover, despite standing only 5'1". The second he began tugging her g-string aside, she reached down and shouted in his ear. "Get off! Now!" She grabbed him by the hair to tug him away. But the hair came away without the drunk guy underneath it. Tania catapulted backward off the stage, helplessly gripping the man's bushy toupee. She freaked out and flung it across the bar where it landed on another businessman's lap. The whole table of men jumped up and then one screamed, "It's alive!" I thought I was at a comedy show! At the same moment, the two older biker guys in the front jumped up and grabbed the man by the arms (which, luckily, didn't also tear free, despite the death grip they used), and pulled him back away from the stage.

"Hands off, fucker!"

While I jumped off stage to help Tania, the biker guys passed the man off to Arvin, Jr, a Hells Angel who worked at the club. I knew what would happen next. The giant Arvin would speak to the man in a gentle voice, escort him slowly outside, and then—I never knew the specifics, but I knew we'd never see the guy again.

I was getting to know Arvin pretty well. He was more than just a bouncer. He was more of a fixer—taking care of any sort of problem that might pop up around the club. And my problem was my growing need for coke, which was harder to come by the end of summer after Mark moved away for work. Arvin was all too happy to help me out, though.

In northeast Ohio at the time, the Angels ran the show. Anything you wanted, you could get through the Angels. To my young eyes, they were like the Robin Hood and his merry men—kicking the shit out of grabby rich guys and bringing drugs and booze to people in need. Soon, I began buying my coke straight from Arvin, which became a pretty regular arrangement once or twice a week when I worked at the Shack. I wasn't the only one, either. All the girls at the Love Shack seemed to like to get high and have a good time, while back at Pepe's the vibe was more booze and tears.

We'd even get invited to hang outs at the Angels club sometimes, where we had our choice of coke, booze, pills, and grass. The space looked like an all you can eat buffet, but with drugs instead of a salad bar.

Even for me, though, life at the Love Shack could get a little hectic, and I was happy to still have a little bit of a life back in Canal Bottom. As the summer came to an end, I was making plans to move out on my own. Before I did, I invited Jake out to see me at Pepe's. I think he was a little embarrassed about it. "Come on, it'll be fun," I said. "And bring some of your friends from the Guard. I would love to meet a hot man in fatigues!" Jake spent his weekends with the National Guard, and I'd seen him pass through with some of his friends from the weekends. Some of em were pretty cute. After spending too many weekends with loud bikers that looked like extras in a ZZ Top video, I was having fantasies of being swept off my feet by a clean cut man with a soft voice and puppy dog eyes. I'd proven to myself that I could take care of myself, but I still wanted someone to share my life with.

So the weekend before I moved into my own place in Massillon,

Ohio, I had Jake bring his buddies in uniform to Pepe's. There were probably a dozen guys in the group, all in their fatigues, and they all made the crowd at Pepe's easier on the eyes than it had been since I started.

My eyes locked onto one guy, in particular. He was a tall guy with nice, strong arms filling out his uniform, cool green eyes, a smooth jawline, and neat blonde hair, slightly receded. He must have been in his late twenties. I did my best up there, and I probably had a big smile on my face, too, while the guardsmen whooped and hollered. I might've even been blushing a little. In between dances and shifts waiting tables, I'd hang out with the boys. The guy that caught my eye introduced himself. His name was Greg. I could tell right away I'd caught his eye, too.

After my shift was over, the boys took me out to an Irish bar and they all wanted to buy me a drink. On the way over in the car, I sat next to Greg, and he asked me what I did when I wasn't dancing. I told him about school at Kent State, about the new apartment I was about to move into. When we got to the bar, I made sure to sit in between Greg and Jake. They both bought me rum and cokes, and I poured em back, one after another. "How about a straight bourbon for the next round?" I asked with a smile and a wink.

Greg's eyes got real wide. "Damn!" he said. "Brains, beauty, and a hollow leg. Where have you been all my life? I know some marines who aren't as tough as your liver must be."

He was a smart ass. I liked that.

I moved in to my apartment in Massillon the following week, and Greg practically came with the lease. He helped me arrange the furniture and picked the perfect place to settle his own ass on the

71

couch. Still, I was smitten. I couldn't put my finger on it, exactly, but there was something so familiar about Greg, something that helped make my new apartment feel like home.

When I was with him, the need to be Victoria McCormick melted away. I could be myself. Or, almost. It was probably the third or fourth time we met up that Greg knew my real name, but I never told him my real age. He thought I was twenty-three, just a few years younger than himself. Greg was twenty-seven, and he'd been a machinist at a factory for a long while. His life was steady. He had an easy way with me and the people we'd meet together. He could be charming—shy one minute and making everyone laugh with a sharp tongue the next.

Being together felt right that first month or two. We lived in a little bubble, with the only tension coming from our jobs.

"Hey, you don't need to dance anymore, I can pay the rent."

Sure, I'd think. *Only I make in a day what you make in a week.* He was shacking up in my apartment and wanted to pretend like he was taking care of me.

"No, honey," I'd say. "I'm trying to pay my way through college." I told him it was important to me to get a degree and be the first in my family to have one. He acted like he understood, but he kept needling me about it. "It's embarrassing," he'd say. "I don't want other men to see you like that." He refused to come to the clubs, which was fine by me. That way, I could play house and be the sweet girlfriend and then go to spend the nights with my other family. Especially Arvin, who'd sell me what I craved before and after my shifts.

Still, things worked out okay for the first couple of months Greg and I were together. Then I introduced him to my parents. At this point, I wasn't seeing my folks too often, but we'd reached an uneasy truce. We were polite to each other when I visited, and we'd talk about my summer classes, how the car was running. I never stayed much longer than I had to. But when I started dating Greg, I thought it would make them worry less if I introduced them to a nice boyfriend. I had him wear his National Guard uniform to really show off.

And my folks did like Greg. He was polite and quiet, exactly what my dad wanted my brother and me to be when I was growing up. After dinner, my mom gave him the tour of the house, with me following close behind, keeping my mouth shut and just trying to get through the rest of the night without any major blowups.

In the hallway, Greg admired framed pictures of me and my brother. "Aw, she's always been cute." He focused in on my high school graduation portrait, with me in my mortarboard and robe. "Holy moly, is this your high school graduation picture? You look exactly the same! You haven't aged at all."

My mom turned and looked at him, confusion spreading over her face. "Well of course she looks the same! This was only taken last spring! She might think she's a grown woman already, but she's practically still a baby. She just turned eighteen!"

I watched Greg's ears turn bright red, then flush spread down his neck. He didn't say anything. A moment later he pointed to one of my paintings on a big canvas. "Oh man, her painting projects. You should see her apartment. She has paint splatter everywhere, even on the ceiling! I don't know how…"

He covered for me, but he knew that I'd lied to him. I wasn' t twenty-three. I was just out of high school, and he must have been wondering if it was even legal for him to be dating me.

We drove back to my apartment in silence. Once we were in the doorway he lit into me. "Goddamnit, I wish you had told me I was dating a child. I feel like a fucking perv. Shit, how old were you when you started showing your tits on stage? Had you taken your SATs yet?"

I apologized again and again, crying. I told him more of my story, how I'd been on my own more or less for years, how I told people I was older so they'd treat me with more respect. How I had a fake ID for years that always worked when I said I was twenty-three.

He punched the wall, putting a dent in the plaster, then went out back and lit a cigarette. After a moment of hesitation, I went out back and joined him. "You know what the most fucked up thing about this is?" he said quietly, without looking at me. "I think it's too late. I'm already in love with you."

We decided to stay together.

Next up was the visit to his folks. It was clear to me he thought meeting his parents was important for our relationship, but he also seemed nervous about it. When I asked him what was wrong, he tried to explain. "You see; my folks aren't like your folks. They're . . . not as high class." I had no idea what he could possibly mean. My parents met in the county jail. My dad kept broken down cars all over the yard. A big night out for them was a trip to Long John Silvers followed by a six-pack along the banks of the canal. I couldn't wrap my head around anyone calling them "high class." "Don't worry," I said. "How bad could it be? I grew up on Wonderbread and mayo sandwiches, too."

It was worse than I ever could have guessed.

If Rust Bucket felt far removed from the big city where Greg's folks lived felt far removed from the twentieth century. His folks had no running water in their home. They lived in an old shack that looked like something out of *Deliverance*. We spent the visit sitting on the porch, staring at trees, watching Greg's parents bicker. It turns out they worked together as cashiers at a K-Mart, and they spent every waking minute together almost, and they clearly hated each other.

Afterward, driving home, Greg was dejected. I tried to cheer him up. "It wasn't that bad. And besides, look how far you've come!" It wasn't working. He stared out at the highway looking like a puppy with no home. Suddenly, I had an idea. "Listen hon. I have a surprise for you. Something that will make you feel better."

I'd always hidden my drug use from Greg. He knew about the drinking, sure. He could keep up with me on that front any night of the week. But some instinct kept me from ever letting him see my coke. There was something about that night, though, seeing him as exposed and vulnerable as he could be, that made me want to open up and share my secret with him.

I had him pull over into an abandoned gas station parking lot. "Listen, I've had my share of hard days, too. Sometimes it's not as bad as you think it is. I've learned whenever I get really blue, I can turn things around with some help." I took the brown vial from my purse.

He stared at me, stared at the vial, and didn't say anything. Very slowly, gently, I unscrewed the vial and dipped the spoon into the powder. I held it up. "Have you ever tried this before?"

Greg said nothing. He just watched. But as I lifted the spoon up to my nose, he suddenly reached out and grabbed my hand. "What they FUCK are you doing?" he screamed. He squeezed my wrists so hard I dropped the spoon and the vial on his car seat, spilling some of the powder into the upholstery. "Great, now you're getting this shit all over my car? Get out!" Greg opened his door and came around to my side. I was paralyzed. He swung open the door, reached across my lap, and grabbed the vial and spoon. He then walked to the side of the abandoned gas station and chucked the vial as far as he could into a stand of trees.

Then he came back to my side of the car. He was fuming. I was alarmed and instinctively held the door closed, but he ripped it open. "Get out of the car," he said. He was speaking in a low monotone. I got out of the car.

He reached into the glove compartment and grabbed some upholstery wipes. He scrubbed at the powder left behind on the seat, and then chucked the wipe across the asphalt.

"Where did you get that shit?"

I was silent.

"Jenny, where did you get it? I want you to tell me right now."

"There are some girls at the club…"

He stared deep into my eyes. "Yeah, right."

"Greg, listen, if you don't like this stuff, I don't have to have it around you."

His mouth curled and his hand shot toward my neck. He pushed me against the side of his car. "Listen. I don't want you to have this stuff, period. This shit is gonna ruin your life, and mine. I'm not gonna let that happen. If I ever catch you with anything like this again, you'll regret it."

I didn't speak. I couldn't. I was completely caught off guard.

"Get back in the car. Let's go. And I want you to vacuum out my car tomorrow. I don't want any trace of that stuff left on the seat."

After that night, our relationship changed. We could go out together and have a good time. We could talk about our families. And we sometimes even talked about our future together. But Greg no longer trusted me, and I didn't trust him either. I'd seen the violence in his eyes, and it was familiar. I'd seen the same look before so many times from my father.

I was spending more time at the clubs. I was comfortable there, and I figured if I kept my party life separate from my home life, I wouldn't have trouble with Greg. I also started meeting Arvin at his house, where we'd do lines together. Arvin never tried to get physical, but he liked to tease me. I'd go over and he'd have me watch a porno with him, or he'd make comments about my body. He probably thought I'd sleep with him eventually, but he wasn't going to be too aggressive. It wasn't his style.

Of course, Greg wasn't an idiot. He knew my hours were suddenly longer, and he knew I hadn't given up drugs.

The first time he hit me, I wasn't home all that late. But he'd been drinking. He took one look at me and said, "Gee, babe. You go to the YMCA to swim tonight? Your eyes sure are red." I tried to brush it off, but he followed me to the kitchen, where he pushed and threatened me. Then he slapped me, hard, across the face.

It got worse. Every time he suspected I'd been out partying, or really any night I was home late from a shift, he'd hit me.

I can't say why I stayed with him. I was earning enough to be on my own. I didn't need him, and I wasn't having any fun, that's for sure. I think a part of me knew I had a big problem, and that I needed help. Maybe he could have reached me. I wanted to be reached. But not like that. I'd had plenty of that in my life already, and I wasn't about to give in to a man with a closed fist. I just knew there was a hurt boy deep inside Greg that wasn't too different than the hurt girl inside me—someone that grew up in a home that was far from okay and who wanted to find someone that would really love him and care for him. I was young enough to think we could get past the problems we were having. I thought we could help each other.

I did my best to keep our relationship going. I was sweet to him. I came home on time every night. I took care of the house.

But I wasn't taking care of myself. I was drinking more than ever, and I hadn't given up coke. Not by a long shot. I just learned ways to hide it better. Some of my other old demons were coming back as well. I was throwing up to keep myself skinny, to keep the reflection I saw of myself perfect. Meanwhile, school was rapidly falling away from my life as I missed a class here, a class there, always thinking I'd catch up soon.

One night in November, after things had been okay between us for a few days, I got home a little late from the Love Shack. I was a little scared, but I wasn't going to show it. When I walked in though, Greg didn't say anything. He was awake, waiting up for me, watching TV. "Hey," he said. He sounded relaxed. "You ever been to Pittsburgh? I've got some buddies there, and I thought maybe we could make the trip down. We've still never taken a real vacation together. We could just go for the weekend."

"Okay!" I said, maybe a little too enthusiastically. I mean, it was just Pittsburgh, but as much as I'd traveled, it might as well have been Paris. I was legit excited, and relieved. *Maybe we have turned a corner in our relationship*, I thought. *He's accepting me for who I am.*

That Friday, we packed some bags. I was getting geared up for a big night on the town. "Which of these dresses do you think is sexier? Maybe I'll bring both."

He stared at me, a little absentmindedly. "What? Ah, forget all that. It's not gonna be that kind of trip. Just pack comfortable clothes. Jeans. T-shirt. That's all."

What, are we going camping? I thought. I was too giddy to argue, though.

The next day, we set out, heading south. Greg was acting serious, kind of gloomy. I couldn't cheer him up, and I couldn't understand it. But then he told me the truth. We weren't going to Pittsburgh. He was taking me to New Horizons down by Columbus. He was driving me to a rehab.

Rehab! I lost my mind. I cried, I screamed, I argued. "You lied to me! You told me we were going on a trip. I thought I could trust you, Greg!"

My very first stint in rehab is a dark spot in my memory. I remember checking in, having the staff go through my purse and take a bottle of Valium. It struck me at the time as unfair as anything that had ever happened to me. *But I'm not here for Valium, I'm here for coke, right?* I had a lot in my system, and I know those first few days must have been hell. I don't remember the feelings, though, just the tiled hallways, the color of toothpaste. The pale, sweaty faces of other girls a little older or a little younger than me. Nobody having anything to say unless we were forced to speak. I realize we were all probably hell raisers on the outside, but in treatment, we were all as shy as could be. It was startling for all of us to have had our own private dramas discovered by the world and lined up next to each other like specimens in a lab. There were pills, booze, eating disorders, violent fathers, violent boyfriends, and violent husbands, distant mothers, lost friends in all our stories. If we could find the strength to speak honestly about our stories, we probably could have finished each other's sentences.

I was in for a month. I could have walked out any time—I wasn't committed or anything. But I felt found out, that I had no choice. At the end of my thirty days, I took part in a group circle. It was a condition I was supposed to fulfill before I could be released. For this circle session, the rehab patients were allowed to have a friend or family member present. The idea was that each of us would admit to the wrongdoings of our past, talk about the lessons we'd learned in rehab, and then share a dream of the future. Our friend or family member would be there to hold us to our words, to be witnesses to our shiny new plans.

Greg came up for my release. He wore a suit and tie, while I was dressed in the jeans and T-shirt he'd thought I should pack when I still believed he was taking me on a trip to Pittsburgh. He smiled wide when he saw me, and he gave me a big hug and kiss. I was happy to see him, too, but I felt like that month sober had made things clear for me. We weren't meant to be together. I was too independent, too much of a dreamer to end up a wife in some tiny house in the Ohio suburbs. I didn't need to grow up so fast. Being young meant having choices, and I wasn't ready to give those up.

I thought long and hard about what I was going to say when my turn came in the circle. I wanted to be able to say I learned that taking care of myself was the most important thing in my life right now, and I couldn't let anything or anyone take that away from me. I wanted to say I had plans, bigger plans than most of the others in the room. I wasn't just going to survive; I was going to thrive. I was going to go back to school. I was going to develop my best talents. And, yes, I was going to dance if I wanted to.

My turn came and I cleared my throat. But before I could start to speak, Greg got up from his chair and walked over to me. First he put his hand on my shoulder and looked deep into my eyes. He gave me a big smile. Then he got down on one knee.

He grabbed my hand. "This woman has made me the happiest man alive, and now that's she's better, I know we can finally start our real life together." He reached into his pocket and pulled out a jewelry box. "I know we've had our ups and downs, but I also know we were meant to be together. I hope you understand now why I did what I did to bring you here. Are you ready to go home now? Are you ready to be my wife?"

I looked down at Greg. I could barely breathe. I looked around the room, at the toothpaste colored tiles, at the pale faces of the other patients, at the beaming therapist. What would happen if I said no? Would I have to stay, be taught the right answer? Would I break Greg's heart? Would I be despised by all these other patients?

"Of course I'll marry you. Yes. Yes. Yes."

And then before I knew what was happening, we were in his car, driving home to my home, to what was apparently going to be our home.

Mr. M

A State Capital, Somewhere in the USA

overnight / gentleman / absolute discretion a must

When the door of the limousine opened, I half expect the flash and smoke of old-fashioned newspaper photo bulbs. I'm dressed in my purple sequined gown, and the man on my arm is in a black tux. We look amazing, if I do say so myself.

This isn't quite Hollywood. But at this point in my life, I'll take it.

The man who offers his arm as I exit the limo is a client. Mr. M has made dates with me a few times before. The first time, I was staying in Cleveland, and he offered to take me out on the lake in his boat. If there's one thing I've learned from other women in the business, it's that you should never meet a client alone on a boat—especially a new client—so I politely declined. We all know horror stories of women that had disappeared far away from land, where there were no witnesses and no police to investigate. I don't know if the law of international waters applies to Lake Erie, but it can get awful dark and quiet out there. Still, Mr. M persisted and ultimately sailed across Lake Erie to Cleveland to see me. Seems he's got a thing for red heads.

I've always had fun with Mr. M. Tonight, though, is going to be special. Mr. M is paying me thousands to accompany him to the governor's inauguration ball. I'm posing as his "assistant." I know what he wants, though. He wants all his friends, all his enemies, to see me on his arm. He wants their jaws to drop. He wants them to wonder if there's something going on between us. He wants the gossip.

Mr. M is a major donor to the new governor's campaign. He wants to make the governor's jaw drop as well. "I need you to be the one that takes the photos of us together," he whispers. "He'll be seeing a lot of other donors tonight, but if you're with me, I'm the one he'll remember taking a picture with. I want to keep everything I've done with this campaign fresh in his memory, if you know what I mean..." He laughs. The implication might be that he's hired me just to curry political favors, but I'm not offended. I know I'm here for much more than that.

As we enter the reception room, we walk through a crowd of the state's powerbrokers. Most of the faces are new to me. Some aren't. There's Dr. David—likes to be tied up but doesn't tip unless the knots are really tight. So that's what his wife looks like. Always wondered. And there's, oh, what's his name. The guy who wanted a blowjob in the backseat of his car while he called out the name of his high school girlfriend. When I pass the governor's staff chatting by the cocktail bar, half their heads duck low. I hadn't realized how much of the new cabinet I'd worked with before. I bet I could make a killing as a lobbyist with this bunch of guys.

After the party, Mr. M takes me back to our hotel and gets his money's worth. He's in a great mood. So am I, and we have sex on and off for hours. The sex is fun, but the night has been about so much more than that. For me, I think back to where I came from, and where I've been tonight. Mr. M and I lie in bed, and the expression on his face looks just like how I feel. I know he's wealthy now, but I've got the sense from the way he talks sometimes when his guard is down that he didn't start out that way. I think tonight meant something more to him than just sex. "Shoot," he says. "I want to see the photos you took again." He grabs his phone and flips through the shots of him and the governor, him and state senators. It may be fleeting, but the feeling of *taking what you never had growing up can be more powerful than any drug, more pleasurable than sex. It's a feeling Mr. M and I share this night.*

Chapter 6

ANOTHER DAY IN PARADISE

The wedding was scheduled for June 1989. I knew in my heart I didn't want to go through with it, not with this man. But after I got out of rehab, it was almost Christmas, and I was seeing lots of family. It was easier to talk about the engagement than talk about rehab. I think everyone else felt the same way. Nobody really talked to me about my time away, or what was going on with me before I disappeared for a month. It was easier to talk about something happy.

My life was still the same, though. I was still working—I needed to now, more than ever. I wanted to get back on track at school, and I had to pay the bills, and now I had a wedding to save up for.

I remember my first couple of weeks back, thinking I could keep business and pleasure separate. In some ways, my family at the Love Shack understood what I was going through better than the people I spent my days with. I remember New Year's Eve that year, with the whole staff toasting me with sparkling wine. These were some people who knew how to party, and they were drinking bubbly juice just to make sure I didn't fall off the wagon.

I wasn't drinking, I wasn't snorting, I wasn't even smoking as many cigarettes. And I was miserable. I started going to some of my first AA meetings during this time. I remember the cracked linoleum, the hot coffee in old, crusty urns, the faded clothes and faded faces of the people gathered. I didn't feel a real sense of connection in those meetings. It broke my heart to hear stories that were so familiar that led to depths I'd never experienced— homelessness, jail time, loved ones dying from addiction. I hadn't had those experiences yet, anyway.

I always felt clear eyed and committed after those meetings. But there was that other thing. That other person. I couldn't help but look at those lined, care-worn faces and feel the fast beat of my own young heart. I wanted to get better, I wanted to live, I just wasn't ready to fade.

I probably fell off the wagon pretty early at the start of 1989. I remember a little about that time. One night, I showed up for work at the Shack, and all the other girls were standing outside in the parking lot, smoking and agitated.

"Hey, Victoria. No work tonight. Al's gotta close the place down for a while."

"What the hell? Why? I've gotta work."

"Take a look for yourself…"

One of the girls opened the door for me to peek in, and all I could make out was the glimmer of glass all over the floor.

"Someone broke in and shot the place up."

Did I mention that Big Al, the owner, *used* to be a Hells Angel? Up to this point, my experience with biker gangs had all been surprisingly positive. They tipped well, generally, hooked me up with great drugs, and the Angels even organized Christmas toy drives. I thought they were a great bunch of guys. But I'd never seen a turf war before.

To this day, I don't know what Al did or who he pissed off (and if I did knew, I would not say a word). But it was my first glimpse of the darkness that was just below the surface of that sort of place.

The Shack was closed for weeks. Partly for repairs, partly, I guess, so Al could handle his business. I think it was during that time that I fell off the wagon. I didn't tell Greg about what had happened. I picked up extra shifts back at Pepe's, and on other nights, I'd tell Greg I was off to work and just go hang out instead. Of course, sometimes those nights by myself would end at a bar, and some of those nights at the bar ended in a drink. Just a little one. A beer can't hurt, right? A glass of wine? It didn't take long. Then after the Shack was back in business, I'd drink before I started my shifts. Then after I'd been drinking, I started looking for Arvin. Before long, I was buying coke and stashing it in secret hiding spots.

I guess it wasn't much of a secret to the people who knew Victoria McCormick. The bikers, the girls, they'd all seen people go through the cycle. Coke and booze, crash. Rehab, honeymoon, relapse. It wasn't just a pattern folks were familiar with; it was a way of life. We were all somewhere on the ride, going up or going down, it seemed like.

But nobody at home knew what I was up to. I was getting a little better at hiding it. It was getting to the point where I seemed perfectly normal when I was drunk or high. It was when I was off booze or coke that I started to get a little weird. Or that's what I thought, anyway.

I told myself it was because of the stress of the wedding. All I needed to do was get through with it, marry Greg, forget my earlier dreams, and accept the Canal Bottom lifestyle. It wasn't so bad. Sure, I didn't live up to any of my expectations for myself and was going to hitch my star to a guy who beat me up and resented that I could make my own living, but, hey, that's life, right?

As the big day got a little closer, things got worse and worse at home. It had really started not long after the engagement—the verbal abuse. Greg would tell me I was getting too fat for the wedding dress one day. Then the next maybe he'd call me a cokehead or an addict. It seemed like even the smallest disagreements turned into a situation where he'd feel the need to put me down, to remind me that he was the man in the relationship, that I was the crazy one who'd needed to be saved And when he still thought I had a little self-esteem after all that, he'd slap me.

Once I started back into drinking, and then into hiding coke, things went from worse to rock bottom. I thought I could hide what I was doing from him. And I could. For a month or two, he never had any real evidence I was drinking or using again. But he knew. He wasn't stupid. He may have been a mean hearted, back handing, trifling red neck, but Greg wasn't stupid. He started waiting up for me again each night. I'd have to sit on the couch and look him in the eye while he talked to me. He'd make me lie to him, again and again, like I was being interrogated by a police officer.

"Did you go straight to the club tonight?"

"Yes."

"Did you come straight home?"

"Yes, Greg, of course!"

"You didn't drink?"

"No!"

"You didn't get into anything else? What about pills?"

"No!"

"Your shift ended at midnight, and it takes you half an hour to get home. But it's 1:30 in the morning now. So you came straight home after your shift? What happened, did you hit a little traffic again? That midnight rush hour slow you down?"

"Greg, I came right home! I just changed and talked to some of the girls, paid out tips and came home! Look, I've got the money right here. I made almost $200 tonight. We can put some of this toward a house one day. That's all I'm focused on right now, baby."

"Okay, then give it to me."

"What?"

"I'll hold your money, then. That way we know it's going to get spent on the right things."

"Greg, I don't need you to manage my money. I can do it myself." I was willing to go along with so much to have peace between us, but I wasn't going to pretend like I wasn't the one supporting the two of us. That money wasn't his, it was mine.

But he just took this to mean I wasn't serious. I was fooling around—with drugs, with other men, even. That's what he suspected. And so he'd hit me. Slaps and shoves soon became closed fists. I shielded myself the best I could, worried that he'd leave marks that others could see while I was dancing. That's all I cared about then. So what if my life was falling apart—I just didn't want anyone to be able to see the scars.

I learned how to use concealer to hide the marks, how to use makeup just right. It changed my look. When I went out or was on stage, I was wearing a mask. I wasn't even there on stage anymore. It was just Victoria. It was Victoria who could make a bruise look like a beauty mark. It was Victoria who could turn a swollen face into a sultry look. It was Victoria who could turn fear into control, stomping the stage in the bright lights for men who would do anything to keep her looking down on them for just one more minute.

Soon it was late spring, and the wedding was just a couple of weeks away. I was too busy to think about what I was getting myself into, and I was too high to ever think I could make a mistake. But I knew things were about to head straight south when Greg wouldn't even talk to me for three straight days. We were about to get married! He was already treating me like I was dead to him.

Then, one night after work, he was there, waiting up for me.

"You fucking liar," he said.

"Greg…"

"I found some of your shit. I know where you keep it in your car. Tucked under the casing of the stick shift? You're not exactly a criminal mastermind, are you? What if I'd been pulled over with that shit in the car? Huh? If you want to fuck up your life, fine. But now you're trying to fuck up mine, too?" He was screaming. Then he was choking me. He hit me harder and longer than he ever had before. All I could do was try to cover my face.

I sometimes wonder, if he had stopped there, how my life might have turned out different. Maybe we would have married anyway. Maybe I would have gone back to rehab. Maybe I would have ended up just like my mother, and Greg would have been just like my dad, and we'd settle down in northeast Ohio and both regret our life decisions for the rest of our days. But what happened next changed everything for me.

Greg threw me out my front window. Through the glass. It was the window overlooking the front porch, and it was half open, but it shattered and fell with me onto the concrete outside. I must have blacked out, because I heard nothing, felt nothing. But the neighbors must have heard.

I remember blood, the swelling around my face, the sound of sirens getting close.

The next thing I remember was sitting up, trying to focus on the scene in front of me. There was an ambulance, paramedics. There were the flashing lights of police cruisers. *Oh good, a party,* I thought. *Shit.* Greg was already out front, talking to the police.

"Yes, we had a fight, but officer, you don't understand, she's high as a kite right now. She's got drugs in her car. I can prove it to you!"

One of the officers approached as I was checked over by the paramedics. No serious cuts, I wouldn't need stitches. My knee was incredibly swollen after bracing myself from the fall and landing on it.

"Did he do this to you?"

"…yes"

"Okay, that's all we need to know for now. You just sit here and rest."

The officer returned to Greg.

"Officer, check her for drugs. She's calm now, but she was crazy a minute ago. Look, I can show you where she keeps her stash in her car."

"There are drugs in the car now? Can you get them for me?"

I watched Greg nod, and felt like he was getting ready to betray me. If we had a pact, it was that we were keeping things between us. Now everything was confused. He just ran to my car and pulled up the loose gear shift casing where I kept my coke. He came running back up the driveway with it.

The officers opened the vial and poked inside. Then one of them stepped forward toward Greg. "We're going to need you to come with us, sir. You're under arrest for assault and possession of a controlled substance."

I couldn't believe it. They were arresting him for the drugs.

He stood there, confused, as one of the officers handcuffed him. Then he was led to the cruiser. The other officer came back to where I was sitting up on the porch. "Listen. We're taking your boyfriend away for a couple of days. He won't be able to make bail because the courts are closed tomorrow. I'm not going to tell you what to do with your life. All I'm telling you is that you have a day to yourself to make any decisions you need to make. I've seen plenty of nice girls like you look like you do right now at the end of a Saturday night. I'm tired of seeing them the same way ten years later." And after the paramedics finished, they all left me alone.

I had a little more than twenty-four hours to figure things out. I didn't need nearly that long. The first thing I did was call Arvin. Nah. It wasn't to score more coke, though I did lose my stash. Arvin wasn't just my friendly neighborhood drug dealer. He was a guy who was known to solve problems. Before the sun was even up, he had a moving truck at my apartment, a couple of burly dudes with him, and half my stuff packed up.

"Damn Victoria, we're gonna miss you. You don't have to leave town, you know. We can get him to leave instead." I appreciated the sentiment, but I wasn't about to add another heaping spoonful of violence and intimidation to the shit show. I told Arvin thanks, but no thanks. I knew where I could go to be happier.

"Where's that, Victoria? You gonna hide out in Pennsylvania for a while?"

"Nope. I'm getting way the fuck out. I'm going to Texas."

And so that's what I did, after saying goodbye to the wedding dress in the closet and leaving the engagement ring on the kitchen table (and then putting it in my pocket—you never know when something like that might come in handy.)

"Hell no," Arvin said when I asked him to leave. "I'm not going to let you drive this truck by yourself. I'm coming too. I've always wanted to see Texas."

I was touched. That was the Hells Angels spirit I was used to! We hooked my car up to the moving truck and Arvin and I were on the road before the church bells rang. Sixteen hours later, we were in Dallas.

I'd been there once before. The owners of the pizza shop where I'd worked only a couple of years before (though it seemed like a lifetime ago), had taken me with them on a trip. They had family down in Texas, and now they were living in Dallas. As a child, I'd dreamed of Hollywood, where everything was larger than life. But after I'd been to Dallas for just a few days, I couldn't imagine Hollywood being any bigger. It hadn't ever occurred to me that Texas might be in my future. Not until that night in June of 1989. But ever since I'd taken that trip, when I closed my eyes at night, I'd think of the women who were more beautiful than any I'd seen up north. I thought of the prairies I'd seen stretching out forever. And I thought of the cars, the jewelry, the flash. It had seemed all a little funny to me at sixteen, but now, two years later, there was nothing funny about it at all. Dallas was made for me. And I was made for Dallas. Or, at least my alter ego was.

Victoria McCormick and Texas hit it off right away.

Butch

Dallas, Texas

overweight / health problems / treat with care / would not see again

That does it. I've been in Texas too damn long.

The paramedics wheel Butch through the hospital doors, and I slink back to my car. His family has shown up in the lobby of the hospital. At this point, I know it's best if I scram.

There's an expression in Texas, "all hat and no cattle." Well, Butch was the opposite. He was all cattle, with an emphasis on the beef—Butch is over 400 pounds. After living in Dallas for many years, Butch is the first actual cowboy I've met. He's got a ranch west of town with a lot of cows and a fleet of Dodge pickups. Other than the slight whiff of manure and the jeans, you might never know Butch was a cowboy. He kinda looked like a comic book collector.

Butch is by far the fattest man I've ever been with. In fact, I didn't quite know what to do with all that brisket in my way. So I wasn't trying to be ironic or anything when I started riding him reverse cowgirl style. I just couldn't figure out a better way to get on top of him. And I wasn't about to let him get on top of me. I remember thinking, as I faced the wall of my bedroom grinding away, Is that wheezing a sound of pleasure, or should I be worried? *I should have been worried.*

"Dammit, get off. Get off. I can't breathe!" I leapt up. I knew this kind of shit was going to happen. He was grabbing his chest. "I think I'm having a heart attack!" He was. I called 911, and an ambulance was at my condo within minutes. The advantages of a pricey zip code.

Later that night, I sit awake wondering what's happened to Butch. This is definitely the first client I've almost killed, I think. I guess I've made the bigtime now.

Chapter 7

YELLOW ROSE OF TEXAS

Dallas sparkled. I'd spend my first nights there driving past the city skyline and staring at the lights and the skyscrapers like someone might sit on the beach and watch the ocean, or watch a bonfire. For the first week I stayed with John and Jamie, my old bosses from the pizza place. They were so kind to take me in. They put my furniture in their garage, they made me dinners, and they did what they could to get me on my feet. They were like a mom and dad—the good kind. They had two younger daughters who I'd babysat before and who were also like sisters. We'd sit around the kitchen table and talk about our lives, and it was like the family life I never had.

But that's not what I wanted. It was way too late for me to long for a stable family life, or that's how I felt anyway. I chafed at the very idea of family and authority, and I wanted to be on my own. I wanted independence. I wanted fame, adventure, fortune. And I figured I wasn't going to get that by going back to my teenage pizza parlor days.

I had money—a small amount of cash from my work in Ohio—and I was able to find an apartment in Arlington, Texas after my first week. That night after I signed the lease, I drove into Dallas, just admiring the stars above the city lights. I was sober as the day I was born, but so drunk on the beauty and excitement of the city that I ended running my car into a guard-rail while staring slack-jawed at the skyline. I laughed. Pretty soon, I figured, I'd be driving the sort of car that you'd take to a specialist every time you picked up a scratch or ding. I couldn't wait.

I also got a job after that very first week. I walked into Corset, one of the big clubs in Arlington and I was hired on the spot. The owner of the place was a happy drunk named Chris, and he'd had the place for many years. Corset wasn't like any of the places I'd worked for back in Ohio, that's for sure. For one, it had six stages. No poles, no spray-painted floorboards likely to give you tetanus if your shoe slipped off. Corset was professional.

And I enrolled in school again, too. This time, I decided to follow my dreams and started art school at the Art Institute of Dallas. I'd start classes in August, and I'd be studying visual communications. I thought, *Why can't I have it all?* I'll be a dancer, I'll become an actress one day, and I'll also have an art degree. I thought of Marilyn back when she was Norma Jean. She'd moved out on her own from absolutely nowhere, used her amazing beauty, and then she got whatever she wanted. She married or dated artists, athletes, singers, intellectuals. Of course, best not to focus on how things ended—the point was, she used every advantage she had and took as much from life as she could. I could do that too.

Dallas. I was living there, and I longed for even more of the city even when I was out on the streets. The city was like a crush that sat next to me in every class. What was it exactly that I was in love with? Cadillacs and big trucks with gun racks on the back? The giant fountains of hair on all the perfect ladies helped out of the cars by perfectly dressed gentlemen? Big hair, big boobs, big houses, big flags in every parking lot? The money? It was everywhere. I remember that first night I danced, throwing the bills on my mattress and just smelling their scent. The whole city of Dallas smelled like that.

The thing was, back where I lived in Ohio, everyone seemed ashamed of who they were. If they were poor, they were embarrassed, and if they had money (not that many did), they were afraid to show it. They probably thought about sex as much as any adults anywhere else, but they'd act like it was this naughty thing nobody should acknowledge. Here in Dallas, it seemed like sex was part of every conversation, even as everyone you spoke with stuck to their manners. There just was no shame here. People wanted sex, they wanted money, and they wanted to show everyone else that they had a lot of both.

Finally, my people, I thought.

I didn't know then how much of those perfect bodies had cost fortunes, wheelbarrows of cash dumped off at the surgeon's office. I didn't know how many people in those big houses were filling them up with furniture from Goodwill, since they'd spent their last dimes on keeping up with their mortgages. I didn't know how many of those fat snakeskin wallets were full of maxed out credit cards. I didn't understand how much fakery went in to seeming so genuine. Dallas seemed more real to me than anyplace I had ever been— people weren't afraid to talk about what they really wanted. But all that was really on the surface. Sure, people were having fun, but they were all just one misstep away from disaster, from having it all fall apart, from ending up in the trailer park, the shack on the Texas plains, or, more likely than not, the back of a police cruiser.

I sure wasn't interested in other people's problems then, though, and I didn't notice them. I was doing great. I could make twice as much a night in the Dallas clubs. As far as drinking, drugs—that wasn't really part of my life that summer. Being healthy seemed easy—I had nothing stressing me out. I had no fear. I had no shame. I joined a gym (everyone in Dallas worked out), and I met lots of charming men. Men who seemed all too happy to treat me like a lady and introduce me to someone who could get me into movies, or modeling, or something else big enough for my ballooning ego. I started to put on the Dallas costume, too. I went blonde. I got hair extensions at Lord and Taylor, and suddenly had hair as big as anyone in the city. Now about those boobs . . . At that age, I didn't even really know about surgery yet. None of the girls in Ohio did that. But I had some natural assets, and I kept them as pushed up and on display as all the other ladies did in the city. Short dresses, long nails, and makeup that took half the day to put on became my new look. Hard to believe I was only a year removed from trying to perfect my Cindy Lauper look.

And then, after a perfect month, maybe a little more, my phone rang.

It was Greg. He'd found me. He must have got my phone number from my parents. I'd called them a couple of times, but they wanted nothing to do with me. They were still furious, since they'd already dropped thousands of bucks on my wedding, which apparently I wouldn't be attending. Hell, they even bailed Greg out of jail after he assaulted their only daughter. Still, I left my number with them, and they must have passed it along.

"Listen, baby, I just want to say I'm sorry, Jenny. I never should have done what I did to you, and I understand why you may never forgive me. I know how much you were going through too, and I'm glad you've got a fresh start . . . I hope you'll find it in your heart to forgive me. I guess I need a fresh start, too."

I don't know why I didn't just hang up on him. I guess I'd been trained—by him, by my dad—to be afraid of standing up for myself like that. I heard him out, and I started crying. I told him I had to go. That we were through. But as soon as he heard those tears, he knew he was going to keep trying.

Greg called about every other day. He'd check in on me, see if I needed anything. He'd listen to stories about work. Over the phone, he didn't pass any judgments. He didn't talk to me like I was a child that was a minute away from timeout—or worse.

I held out. I was so happy. I was myself. I was living the life I'd chosen without any special drama, without all the baggage from back home. But I couldn't escape it. My life back home knew my number. Back home would always find me. I figured it was just something I'd have to learn to live with.

Eventually, I broke down. I told Greg he could come down and visit me. I knew what I was really saying. I was taking him back. I knew I didn't love him—I just didn't have the will to get rid of him. I was an adult. But he spoke to me as someone that knew. Someone that could see past the surface to my real vulnerabilities. Just speaking with him, all the shame and insecurity came flooding back.

We were together again. And then as soon as we were together, we were made husband and wife by the county clerk in Fort Worth Texas on August 23, 1989.

There weren't any flowers. There was no dress. We did it on a whim, really. Marrying Greg was probably the thing I feared the most, to the point that I thought about it obsessively. I played it out in my mind so much that it came to seem like an inevitable reality. I decided I just wanted to get it over with as soon as possible, and then I'd never have to worry about it happening one day. It would have already happened.

If this all sounds crazy, I'm not going to try to convince anyone that it wasn't. I'd just had my dreams smacked out of my head enough times already in my life that I instinctively cringed when anyone told me I wasn't being realistic. When Greg told me I needed him as much as he needed me, well, I didn't exactly believe it, but I accepted what he was saying.

And it only took a few days before Greg was strutting around my apartment like it was his. I thought, *That's okay. Even Marilyn had her share of rough marriages. Eventually we'll both come to see that we're better off by ourselves, and by then I'll be ready to take the next step and really make it big.* I was planning our divorce before the ink was dry on the marriage certificate.

Greg got a job through my old friends from the pizza place. John had left the pizza business and was working as a corporate manager of a chain of corner stores. He got Greg a job managing one—in the worst part of Dallas. He was an ex-marine, after all, and corporate thought he was perfect for the job. He was glad to have it, since he finally was paid to boss people around. Not that it was easy. His employees would skip shifts all the time, which meant he was driving into Dallas at all hours to keep things going. He was out as late as me most nights, and so he didn't really have the time or energy to worry about what I was up to. And his vision of Dallas was so different from my own. I saw the bright lights, the sparkle. He saw what happened when those lights fell to earth. He saw the misery of all the broken dreams, all the hopes that never got off the ground. To him, the city was a hell that we could survive if we were very careful. To me, it was as close to heaven as I had ever been here on earth.

Meanwhile, I got a job dancing at the Red Room, a beautiful spot in Dallas run by one of the princes of the city's night life. The Red Room looked a little like the set of a bad vampire movie, with black candelabras, red velvet everywhere, and plenty of tall dark men nuzzling into young girls' necks. But it was a well-run operation, and plenty of important people in the city showed up there.

We put on a show for them. On any given night, there'd be 75 to 100 girls working. Stages were scattered all around the floor, with a beautiful bar in the center of the action. The operation was so big that we had a "house mother" in the dressing room—an older woman, maybe someone who used to be a dancer, who made sure our costumes were on straight and squashed any drama as soon as it started. She'd get paid by every girl 5 or 10 bucks a night. With up to 100 girls a night, that meant she did pretty well for herself. The Red Room also had a few fulltime makeup artists, tanning beds, free meals. It was a long way away from Pepe's, where the girls would have to slide their own quarters into the jukebox and buy their own pasty glue direct from Pepe.

Between the Red Room and Corset, I was working six nights a week, typically. Shifts would last from 7 pm to 2 am. Friday and Saturday nights were big and I never missed those shifts, but the rule was we'd have to work a slow shift like Sunday or Monday night to pick up a gig on Friday or Saturday. It was a lot of juggling. Even on those slow nights, though, I could pull in $200, no problem. I'd still have to tip out the house mother and some of the other staff, but by the end of summer I was taking home five to six grand a month. I knew fame was still out of my reach, but fortune seemed close at hand.

After the shows ended, I'd head out with the girls to the gay bars. They were great. We could let loose, have a good time, and we knew nobody would be hitting on us.

Other nights, we had professional obligations. Some of us girls were developing regular customers. For me, one that summer was Joe Avanti, a guy who'd made a fortune selling tomato sauce all around the country. The nights he was in, I could make double the usual tips just by sticking around his table. Afterwards, he'd take me and some of the other girls out to one of the city's best steakhouses, where we'd get an off-hours private room. Joe and his "business associates" (all mobsters) would smoke cigars and drink while we sat around as arm candy, saying little and ignoring everything we heard.

Sometimes during those early hours I'd think of Greg, stuck at his Qwickie Mart, cleaning out the Slushie machine and knocking on the bathroom door to make sure junkies weren't nodding off in there. I was definitely having more fun than him.

We weren't seeing much of each other. Between our complicated work hours and my schooling, we'd be around each other for maybe an hour or two on any given week day. Weekends were worse, since I'd pull longer shifts and he'd signed up with the Texas National Guard.

I think we were both fine with the arrangement. For a little while, we could pretend we had a normal marriage, if a little busy. Sure, we'd just got married and hardly ever had sex, but we were trying to get established. It felt like hard work leading to a better life.

There was something else on the horizon, though. Something coming at the end of the year that I tried to block out of my mind whenever I could. We were going to go home for the holidays. We were going to see our families. And we were going to have a proper wedding, six months after the first one fell through. We still had all the place settings and decorations stored away in my parents' basement. All we'd have to do is dust em off, buy a cake and some booze, and we'd be really, *really* married. Maybe then we'd start seeing a little more of each other.

We flew to Ohio just a few days before the wedding, which was supposed to take place on December 23. I was a little miffed we left when we did—I was gonna miss my biggest night of the week at Corset. Turns out, it was maybe a good thing I wasn't around that night. After the club closed and the girls had gone home, a man who'd been hiding in the air vents snuck into the office. It was a former manager of the club, someone whose life had fallen apart. The house manager, accountant, and the hostess stayed late, as usual, to count the money and close up shop. The former manager robbed them at gun point, and he tried to force the accountant, a young woman, to have sex with him. When she fought him off, he shot her three times, killing her. Then he shot the manager and hostess, took 20 grand, and ran. They caught him, thank god. It was a reminder that in my line of work, evil was always a step away. But from a young age, I'd trained myself to ignore it. It was the only way I could survive.

When I heard it from the girls, just two days before the Ohio wedding, I felt deeply off balance. Of course, it wasn't just the brutal murder. It was being back at home, facing all my old demons. It was a wedding I didn't want to go through with, even though I was already married. It was the fear of suddenly knowing, on some level, exactly how thin the line was I was walking. What seemed in Dallas to be a life opening up to unlimited possibilities now seemed like a life closing in on all sides by infinite dangers.

Two days before the wedding, I slipped out to visit my old friends at the Shack. I said hi to some of the girls, Hey to Al, and then a big thank you to Arvin, who was still working the door. He'd delivered me to my new life, after all. So when he invited me back to his place, I sure didn't think I could say no.

Arvin and I got high together, along with some of his friends. I was AWOL the day before the wedding, flying on coke so high all my problems seemed like tiny specks way below. I missed my rehearsal dinner, telling my mom I was sick. She covered for me, and probably never knew the truth, even if she had her suspicions. Greg didn't even try to find me. He must have known, but he also must have been keeping himself from doing something he'd regret.

I came down in time for the wedding, though. It was in the middle of a deep cold snap, -5 degrees outside. Not many people bothered to show. Maybe it was the cold, maybe they didn't have any faith the wedding would take place. But it did, and there I was, twice married to a man I didn't love.

We left that night for our "honeymoon" in Cleveland, Ohio. On our wedding night we slept in the same bed, facing opposite directions. We didn't touch each other. We spent a couple days in the city pretending to be happy. We did end up making love one night. Probably one of the last times we'd ever do so. And that was probably the night I got pregnant.

Tyler
Lancaster, PA
Into dress up / definitely looking for GFE / won't see again

"No, honey, I can't come."

"What do you mean? I don't want to be alone on New Year's Eve. Come on, I'll wanna drink if I'm alone. I need you to come. You know payment isn't going to be a problem."

"Look, I just have other plans. I'm not trying to give you a hard time."

"What, you're seeing another client? I know that's a lie, since you already told me you were taking a break for the holidays."

"Yes! Exactly. I'm taking a break, and I'll be with family."

"Seriously? You consider me just another client? You want to take a break from me? Okay, great. Glad to know I can count on you when I need you."

Then Tyler hangs up. Shit. Have the lines blurred again? Yes, I think they have.

Tyler has been a client now for a few years. He works in construction, and our first meeting had been an overnight. Expensive, and I gave him his money's worth. I liked Tyler, because I could see myself in him a little. His life wasn't off in the clouds. In fact, it was remarkably like mine. He was a single dad from Pennsylvania, and like me he was trying to stay sober. I loved that. It was always a struggle for me with clients who drank. I'd often join them for a glass, just a glass, but sometimes that glass turned into a whole bottle back at home. It was an occupational hazard. But Tyler understood. We spent our first night together talking about ourselves as much as screwing around.

As we met more and more often, Tyler became more and more adventurous. Soon he was buying me outfits to wear for our meet-ups. One time he'd bought me ten separate sexy outfits and patent leather boots that went up to my thighs. "But Victoria, you can't wear these unless you're seeing me. You understand?" I understood. I'd heard that tone of voice before.

For the last couple of months, Tyler has been pushing me harder and harder to leave my life, to be his girlfriend. The more he pushed, the more I heard my first husband's voice, telling me what I should do, what he needed, never asking me what I needed.

I know after our phone call I'll have to break Tyler's heart. I have to resolve to never see him again. I know he'll just want more and more from me, and that I'll never be able to give enough of myself to make him happy. This is a real profession I'm in, but it can be damn hard to keep it professional sometimes.

Chapter 8

CRADLE OF LOVE

I learned I was pregnant in January 1990, and my life changed, instantly. I didn't drink, and I didn't do coke, and I even stopped smoking cigarettes. Looking back, I think my pregnancy was my first true experience of grace, of a divine presence in my life that protected me when I needed it most. I'd spent plenty of time in AA meetings already by age nineteen, and had heard plenty of older men and women yap about the power of God in their lives, how He was there when they hit rock bottom. How He spoke to them and showed them a way out. How He offered them the greatest love they'd ever known. I'd never experienced anything like it, and, honestly, religion was something I felt I'd left back in Ohio along with the shame and guilt.

But as 1990 started, I felt different. I wasn't visited by a white robed angel with hair like the bass player in Warrant or anything. I just had a sense of calm, a sense of purpose I'd never experienced before. Suddenly I no longer saw myself as the center of the universe—I was just one person in a sea of them, with a set of responsibilities and duty to protect those around me. Hollywood, music videos, hanging out with bigshot gangsters at the clubs—all of that seemed silly. Victoria McCormick seemed like a dream I had long ago. I was happy to be myself for a while.

But that didn't mean all my problems were gone. I was able to stop drinking, but it had an effect. I spent my mornings puking, my days nervously filling out to-do lists in-between classes, and my evenings compulsively scrubbing floors and doing everything in my power not to chew my nails down to stubs. I was determined to make my marriage work, to raise enough money to buy a house, to stick with art school. This was my life now. I had to use every part of myself to survive.

I was still dancing. Not six days a week as I'd been before learning of the pregnancy, but often enough to pay the bills and put some away for our house down payment. Greg didn't like me dancing. He thought I should be waiting tables at most. I knew I'd have to once I started showing, but up on stage I could make three or four times as much money a night. Hell, a single night of dancing could be enough to cover rent for the month. Anything beyond that was building a future.

It hadn't taken me long to get used to big money. I'd been making close to five grand a month before my marriage through working the clubs a few nights a week. Now, pulling in a few grand a month made me feel destitute. This was Dallas, after all. It wasn't okay just to get by. I had to have the best of everything for my baby, and I needed everyone to know it. I was also still watching the Caddies rolling downtown, and the fat stacks of bills in the money clips at the clubs. Between the oil, tech, and agriculture industries, there was a lot of money in Dallas, and it was money being spent. I'd close my eyes at night and just imagine a river of cash flowing through the city, somewhere. I'd just have to be resourceful enough to go find it and I could fill up my bucket whenever I wanted, just like so many happy people in the city seemed to do. I was so determined to buy a house for me and my family but didn't know the right way to go about it.

Lee was a good friend. Okay, he was a little crazy about me and had been a regular tipper at the clubs in the past. But he wasn't an asshole, and he was very respectful, even after he knew I was married. He was a businessman, and after I got pregnant, I called him up and we talked about ways I could make real money. His first suggestion was to get an accountant and to start keeping tabs on my money. It turned out all the older girls were doing exactly that already. He pointed out I was never going to be able to get a home loan if I had all my money hidden under the mattress. So that year I got hooked up with a guy named Sal whose accounting business was pretty much dedicated to helping strippers figure out how to deduct the costs of pasties and leather shorts when April 15 came around.

Lee also told me all that money from oil and computers in Dallas was locked up, owned by a few old families and a few hotshot newcomers. If I wanted to be around money that moved, I had to start learning about real estate. It was Lee that told me I should buy a house as soon as possible, and he told me which neighborhoods to look into. I was grateful. I've spent a lifetime around creepy men that wanted something from me, but I've been lucky enough to have a few relationships like the one I had with Lee that have saved me over the years.

But seeking advice from Lee turned out to have its drawbacks. One day he took me out to lunch. We talked about my hopes for my new child, life in the city, and he teased me about the Dallas accent I was starting to pick up. Then he drove me home. I didn't feel like I was doing anything sneaky. But when we pulled into the lot of my apartment building, I realized we had guests.

Chuck and Ellen.

Chuck and Ellen Biddle were friends of Greg's. Like us, they were Ohio transplants—they'd been close to Greg's parents way out in the woods before coming down to Texas to chase one bad news scheme or another. They were grifters and disability cheats, and half the reason they left Ohio was to escape the law. Of course, they hadn't escaped for long before Chuck got popped for an armed robbery and spent five years in prison. You'd never know it to look at them, though. They looked like a couple of churchgoing hayseeds. It was part of their grift, really. And the worst thing about them was the hypocrisy. They'd straight up stolen from people, and worse, but somehow when I was around them, I was the bad guy.

"Well, hi there," Chuck said after Larry dropped me off.

"Listen, hon, we didn't know you had a guest. We just came to drop off our old car seat. We want to make sure the baby has everything it needs, especially since you've been so busy running around, you don't have time to think of these things. We don't need to stay."

Chuck looked at me like a priest waiting for a confession. Then they left. I knew what they were implying—that I was slutting around and ignoring my responsibilities. Really, that was the opposite of what I was doing, but Chuck and Ellen had the ability to get in my head. Every time they spoke to me, I lost all words to defend myself—I'd choke on my own anger. I wanted things to go smoothly with the marriage, and I knew Chuck and Ellen were important to Greg, so I'd just smile and nod. Damn, I couldn't stand those two.

Of course, the first thing they did after leaving was call Greg at work and tell him that they'd seen me with another man. When he got home that night, he was angry and quiet in the way he'd been back in Ohio. Since moving to Dallas, we had a sort of arrangement. He wouldn't ask about the people at the clubs or what I did afterward. And I wouldn't tell him. But in his mind, I'd now brought that world home with me.

Things hadn't been exactly warm between us since the marriage, even with a baby on the way. But now they were downright chilly. What made it worse was that Chuck and Ellen were coming over all the time now, dropping by with a few old baby blankets from Goodwill or second hand bottles. I didn't need or want any of that stuff, but I took it since I didn't know what else to do. It was pretty clear they were coming by to keep an eye on me.

One night, after hosting Chuck and Ellen for dinner and trying my best to keep the topic of conversation becoming my past and my uncertain future (as it so often did), Greg came into the kitchen where I was washing dishes. When I heard him behind me, I flinched instinctively. But he just spoke.

"I want to see what you do."

I was so surprised my heart skipped a beat. "What do you mean?"

"I want to see you dance. I want to go out with you wherever you go afterward. Listen, I know I've been jealous in the past. But it's not about that. And I know your work isn't always fun, but you're out there having a real fucking adventure while I'm stocking beef jerky and cleaning out soda machines. I'm bored, and you're not."

I'm not sure what kind of adventure he thought I was having at two months pregnant. And I was worried about what this all would lead to. But, honestly, it was the first time he'd showed any interest in my life in months.

I decided I'd find a way to show him a good time. Maybe it would bring us closer together. Maybe I was worried over nothing.

I wasn't sure what it would be, but the answer came not through work but through school. There was a girl in some of my classes named Janette. She was gorgeous. Smooth skin, bright blue eyes, and beautiful dark auburn hair that flowed all the way down her back. She looked like something out of a fairytale. She was like me, too. She'd seen a little more of the world than most nineteen or twenty year olds. She knew I was a dancer, and she'd done something similar. Janette and I talked about sex. We talked about it a lot. In fact, I had a pretty big crush on her, and I think she did on me, too. She knew I was married, and sometimes we joked about having a threesome. And it was Janette that told me about a private club she'd been to. It sounded like the warehouse I'd been to in Columbus, Ohio a couple years before, but maybe a little more dressed up.

My plan started to come together quickly. I'd take Greg to the club, where we'd meet Janette. We'd show him the time of his life—I was sure Janette would be up for it. So first I asked her, and she said yes. And then I talked to Greg about it, and try as he might to act cool, he couldn't hide his keen interest in the plan.

I thought I'd hatched the perfect scheme. I'd show Greg a little of the wild side like he'd wanted, I'd keep him away from the clubs where I worked, and, for the cherry on top, I'd get to play around with Janette.

Of course, things didn't go according to plan. Greg was into the idea and talked about it for days ahead of time. But the day of, he was incredibly uncomfortable. He kept asking me what he should wear, what he should say, what he should do. He'd messed around plenty before, especially back in his Marine days, but he'd never done anything like this, in a place like this. He kept worrying that some dude would come into the room and make a pass at him.

"Greg, you don't have to do anything you don't want to do. Nobody's gonna bother us."

"How do you know? You've done this a bunch of times before, huh?"

"No! I just know. Listen, this is just going to be the three of us. It's just a sexy place to meet up. You'll do great."

"There just better not be any fucking guys coming into the room. If that happens, I'm going to leave, immediately after puking."

"Greg! It's not going to be a problem."

"How the hell do you know?"

And it went on like that, even in the car ride over. We'd coordinated with Janette and met her exactly where we'd planned. She was wearing a dark, loose dress and looked like she could be Stevie Nicks' daughter—nothing like the dolled up, little red dresses all around the rest of Dallas. I could tell Greg was impressed, but he didn't have much to say. I did, and Janette and I whispered in each other's ears and flirted as we found our room. Greg just followed a few steps behind.

When we got to our room, I got right down to business. What the hell, I didn't want to just stand around like a wallflower. I kissed Janette long and slow. At first we were putting on a show for Greg, but to tell the truth, I didn't care if he was watching us or flipping through a copy of *Readers Digest*. I pulled Janette's dress up her thighs and eased her panties off. I could hear her breathing short, sharp breaths, and I knew she was into what I was doing. I moved my tongue up her inner thigh and stroked her legs with my fingertips. I was down there a while.

After a few minutes with Janette gripping my hair tight in her hand, she suddenly sat up.

"Hey, stop for a second."

I wasn't sure what I'd done wrong.

"No, look. Your husband's gone."

Janette and I looked all over the club. Had he met someone else and wandered off? I had no idea where he was. Then we thought to check the parking lot, and our car was gone. Janette had to drive me home.

I walked in the front door, and spotted him in the kitchen, drinking a beer and reading the paper.

"What happened, Greg? You just left without saying anything."

He looked up, but couldn't look me in the eye. "That place gave me the fucking creeps."

"Well, why'd you just leave me there? I would have gone home too."

"Seemed like you were having a pretty good time," he said. "I didn't realize you were so into muff diving."

And that was that. Greg didn't want to have anything to do with me after that. Instead of bringing us closer together, it was like I'd confirmed all his suspicions, that I was out there having a better time without him.

Home was no fun, so I was trying to spend as much time as I

could out. I'd go shopping for the baby, or I'd stick around school and study, or I'd be at the clubs. I wasn't going to stop dancing until they yanked me off the stage. And, hey, I was still a money maker at those clubs—I had guys coming around just for me. The bosses would probably have let me stay up there until my water broke.

One night, when I was about five months pregnant, I was dancing at the Red Room and spotted some money. A little off to the side, by himself, was a guy in a nice shirt and tie, glasses, a kind face, and a shy fixation on my body. I'd been dancing for a few years by this point, and I'd developed an instinct about the guys with money. It wasn't always the guys in the loud suits and alligator boots with the platinum rings who'd tip me all night. It was often guys like this, alone, shy, and ready for someone to talk to them. Of course, it wasn't hard to see his eyes were stuck on me, so I went over to try to start up a lap dance. When he saw me coming, he briefly made eye contact, but seemed intent on my body.

"Hey Sugar, you here all by yourself? How about a private dance?"

He gave me a warm smile and made space on the seat next to him.

"Miss," he said. "This is a personal question, but are you pregnant? I'm a physician and I thought maybe you were." My face was suddenly the reddest thing in the Red Room.

"Um, yes. A few months now."

"Well, I don't mean to embarrass you. You can clearly still get around with no problem. But it looks like you're in your second trimester, yes?"

"I guess it's about five months now."

"Look, people might not be able to notice yet, but you should really think about taking it easy from here on out. It's not just the chance of hurting your back dancing—you've got to stay real skinny for this job, right? Well part of your job as a mom is to do the opposite right now. You need to give up on the stage bod and start putting on a little weight. Just my opinion, but call me if you want to talk. Here's my card."

I was mortified. But I took his advice. I continued to work, but only waiting tables. I made a tiny piece of what I'd been making before. But it was okay. I'd saved enough that we were able to start house shopping. At age nineteen, I bought my first house. It was in Grand Prairie, just outside Dallas. It was a small ranch, but nice—three bedrooms, and a beautiful kitchen. I couldn't be more excited. The only problem was, when I thought about the new house, I thought about it as my house. Not our house. As far as I was concerned, Greg was becoming a dead weight I was better off leaving at the old apartment. After all, I was the one paying for the house. I was the one getting the nest ready for the baby. I think we both knew that I didn't really need him. And that was a problem.

One day I looked into divorce in Texas. I was so ready. The abuse wasn't as bad as it had been in Ohio, but there just wasn't any love anymore—if there'd ever been. I figured he'd agree to it, as long as I was gentle about the whole thing. Turns out, though, it was legally impossible at the time to start a divorce in Texas while pregnant. I was stuck with him until I delivered the baby.

In truth, Greg was eagerly awaiting the baby for his own selfish reasons too. Greg was in the Texas National Guard, and there was war on the horizon. He'd sometimes talk about the possibility of being sent over to the Middle East, which seemed crazy to me at the time. What would be the point of that? But he knew it was a possibility, and he also knew the best way to get out of it was to become a new dad. So Greg was eager to become a dad, but he may have only wanted to stick around so he wouldn't have to go fight in the desert. His actual interest in the family seemed to be about zero.

I remember one morning a little later in the pregnancy, my baby started kicking harder than usual. By this time, I was so big that I could probably not have climbed up on stage, let alone dance on it. The little guy kicked so hard he knocked something loose it felt like, and the pain was excruciating. I called Greg to come home and take me to the hospital, but he wouldn't do it. He told me I was fine, that I should deal with it. I had a neighbor drive me instead, and it turns out I had a broken rib. Whoever this kid was growing inside of me, I was confident he was gonna be a fighter, like his mom.

And then just before the due date, we had even more setbacks. Greg lost his job. He had employees stealing from him at work, and he didn't want to admit how bad it was getting, so he covered up some of the theft. It cost him his job. I was a little embarrassed, because it was my friends from the old pizza shop that had got him that job.

He was embarrassed himself, and spoke to me even less around the new house. I have to give him credit, though. He was going to do what he had to bring in money. He'd go out every morning to wait on the corner with the undocumented immigrants and wait for day work.

In mid-October, my water broke one night while I was waiting tables at the Red Room. I got to the hospital quick, and Greg joined me there. What followed was the most unreal pain of my life, and my only relief was taking it out on Greg. At one point, as he coached me to breathe, I socked him so hard that I knocked him on his ass. That did make me feel a little better.

Finally, my son Jeremy was born on October 23, 1990. I was elated. I can't even put it into words. Here wasn't just someone to love, it was love, my whole heart there in my hands. I wanted Greg to share some of the moment, but by the time I'd been taken to the recovery room, he was already getting packed up. He was due at the National Guard for weekend training.

"But Greg, don't you even want to hold him?"

He gave a long, cool look. "That's not my baby," he said. "It doesn't even look like me."

I couldn't believe it. "Greg, what are you talking about? He looks just like you! It couldn't be anyone but yours."

"Are you sure?" he asked, a little sarcastically. "And are you sure it's even yours? Or is this 'Victoria McCormick''s baby?"

And then he left. I didn't even have anyone to drive us home.

Semper Fi

Cleveland, Ohio

Much Older/ Uses Viagra / Marine / Never see

I'm done with Marines. And I'm really done with fucking Viagra.

When I saw Semper Fi on the screen of my intercom, I thought I might have to help him up the stairs to my condo. He looked that old. He'd paid for a dinner date, which was four hours of my time. Maybe 90 percent of the guys that schedule a dinner date want exactly that. They take me to a nice dinner and then we spend some time alone. It's an arrangement I look forward to.

I knew Semper Fi was in his mid-seventies, and I'd dressed conservatively, maybe a little old fashioned with my hair pulled back, but also with stilettos to add a little allure. For an officer and a gentleman of a certain age, I wanted to make sure I brought a sense of decorum to dinner. Of course I'd known enough freaking Marines in my life to know better.

As soon as he walked in the door, the old soldier handed me his jacket, and then after I'd hung it up, and turned back to greet him, he pushed me up against the door and shoved his tongue down my throat. He was about four inches shorter than me, so he had to stand on tippie toes to do it.

This isn't okay. He hasn't even shown me the envelope with money yet. There's rules that any client should know without being reminded.

"Slow down cowboy," I say as I pull up a little out of range of his wriggling tongue. "We haven't even had a chance to say hello or get acquainted."

He speaks for the first time. "Listen, babe, I just took my pill and

121

I'm going to get as many pops as I can for my money."

Well, off to the bedroom, where he treats me like a blow-up doll. I can be anything—I'm a professional! But I don't especially like playing the role of an inanimate fuck object. I'm not a damn sexbot. After half an hour, I wonder how long that little blue pill is really going to keep him going. Even young, healthy men have their limits.

Nope. Semper Fi was committed to filling up the whole four hours with the old in and out. It can't be done. And this guy is no Sting—I realize he might have a heart attack any minute at his age. After struggling through for an hour and a half of a missionary position marathon, I'm cooked. I can't go on, and I tell him so. He's disappointed at first, then seems proud. "It's a little too much for you, eh? My wife used to say the same thing. Well, I'll pay you for two hours, sound fair sweetie?" Sure, sweetie. Semper Fi walks out with a swagger, and from then on I remember to suggest an actual restaurant whenever a client schedules a dinner date, and to ask ahead of time if they plan to use a little medicinal enhancement.

Chapter 9

EVERYTHING I DO (I DO IT FOR YOU)

Jeremy was close to ten pounds. It took me a couple days to recover, and when I was ready to go home, Greg still wasn't back. I didn't know if he was coming back, ever. I held Jeremy and looked into his eyes, which were Greg's eyes. His mouth was Greg's mouth. I sighed. If only this *hadn't* been Greg's child, the future would have been so much easier. But a difficult future did nothing to diminish the overwhelming love I felt for my new child. Maybe there was a chance we could start fresh together.

I started making calls, and nobody I knew was around to come pick me up from the hospital. Then a nurse arrived to let me know I had visitors. It was Chuck and Ellen. They came bearing more gifts: a jar of instant formula. "We thought we'd come by and Ellen would show you how to feed him. We know it'll take some time for you to get used to being a mother." ("If you ever do…" mumbled Ellen.) "So we thought we'd help."

Well, this wasn't exactly the fresh start I was imagining. Still, they were around, and I didn't have much of a choice unless I wanted to take a cab home. I let Chuck and Ellen drive me home with a stop at the grocery store for diapers, and then it took me hours to get them out of the house. Once they did, I tucked Jeremy into his brand new, top of the line crib under his luxury baby blankets, and I fell asleep on the carpet right next to him. I was exhausted still, but deliriously happy.

I didn't see Greg again until late Monday. He came in carrying a case of diapers, set it down by the front door, and then went and turned on the TV. I didn't know what to say. Was he even going to acknowledge his child? Did he feel any love for him at all? Did he feel even a shred of love for me?

I was angry, and I went to talk to him, but all I could do was cry. Maybe it was partly the hormones, but I just couldn't fathom how he was behaving. No matter what problems festered between the two of us, I could never imagine trying to get back at him through our newborn son. Did he really not believe Jeremy was his, despite the incredible resemblance? I doubted it. He was just too angry at me, too angry with his life, to feel what should have been natural.

After that first night with him back, I made up my mind to end it as soon as possible. Now that our baby was born, it was legal for me to file for divorce. I just had to wait until I was strong enough to do so.

After a few weeks, I was working again. First waiting tables. I made it my mission to get back in shape. A huge part of me wanted to move on from dancing, get a regular day job, maybe in real estate like my friend Lee had suggested. Or better yet, finish school and start working as an illustrator—a dream older than my dreams of going to Hollywood. But I knew I wouldn't be able to support myself and my new child and start a new career at the same time. I was still so young. Only 20 years old. But I had a plan. If I could work just a few more years, I'd have enough to start a career creating greeting cards, or get a realtor's license. I could live a normal life and take care of my son, and Greg didn't have to be involved at all.

During those first few weeks of Jeremy's life, I don't think Greg looked him in the face even once. He was deeply depressed, and he still didn't have a job. He was spending more and more time at Chuck and Ellen's house. He'd given up on us, and it was clear to both of us we were headed for a split.

Six weeks after he walked in the door carrying diapers, he came into the house again with a few bucks for groceries.

"Greg, I got the papers today. You're about to be a free man. You don't have to worry about us anymore."

He didn't say anything. His shoulders just slumped, and he looked pale, worn. He was a defeated man. I almost felt sorry for him. He took the papers and walked back out the door, leaving his twenty dollars under the key chain. If his contribution to his son's life was going to be twenty bucks and a box of diapers, so be it. I was happy to cut my losses.

I didn't hear from him for a couple of days, though I was doing everything I could not to go crazy waiting for him to sign the papers. Finally, he called.

"Listen, if you think I want this, you're crazy. If you think I'm going to give up on our marriage, you're crazy. And if you think I'm going to leave my son with you, you must be even crazier than I thought. You might not be mine anymore, but you're sure as hell not going to be anyone else's either. And either is he."

Once again, he'd left me speechless. I thought he wanted a divorce as much as I did. There wasn't anything between us anymore. But I underestimated the pride of a wounded man.

Maybe I'd underestimated the power of Chuck and Ellen, as well. The next day they showed up at my door. "Hi, hon. We came to borrow Jeremy for a while. His daddy has been missing him and wants to spend some time with him. And besides, you look like you could use some rest. You're not working yet, are you? We're around anytime, you can drop your baby off with us. That way his daddy can spend some time with him, and he'll be well looked after."

I really hadn't figured out how I was going to do it completely on my own. I had my friends from the pizza shop, but they had daughters of their own, and they didn't have time to be watching a newborn while I worked at night, or even while I took classes in the afternoon.

I was confused, and I wasn't sure what was the right decision, but here were Chuck and Ellen, and they were ready and willing to help out. Whether they were truly able to help out or not, that was another question.

I also figured it might give Greg a chance to be a part of his son's life, if that was still a possibility. Then maybe Jeremy would have a father, and I'd have a little support raising him. I was conflicted, though. I still had nightmares about my own father, and my dreams about Greg were not much different. I would never want Jeremy to go through even a small part of what I'd been through, and if there was even a hint that something like that was happening to Jeremy, I didn't think I could survive it.

So I thought about it carefully, and made a decision that would be one of the biggest mistakes of my life. I decided I'd accept Chuck and Ellen's offer to help care for my son, with my still-husband pitching in.

Greg was refusing to agree to the divorce, but he didn't exactly want to move back in either. It was a strange situation, but I decided he was still just hurt and prideful, and that with a chance to spend time with our son, maybe we'd come to an amicable agreement.

During this time, I wasn't working much, and I wasn't making much. Until I was back in shape and could leave my baby for more than a few hours, it was just a few nights of waiting tables for me every week. Slowly I got back into shape, and Jeremy got to the point where I could leave him overnight at Chuck and Ellen's house.

So I started back, and once I started back, I started fast. I was dancing at the Red Room, and soon I got a recommendation to work at a club closer to home. One that happened to be the biggest, swankest club in Dallas, La Royale. La Royale was slick: marble and chrome, gilt mirrors, and top shelf liquor. Girls would wear elaborate costumes and dance on pedestals, like we were Greek goddesses. It was fancy—like Cirque du Soleil, but with boobs and g-strings. I was a hit right away. Motherhood hadn't slowed me down much. After all, my body was still only twenty years old. If anything, having a baby had made me a little curvier.

La Royale was the kind of place that celebrities would come to. There was a steep cover charge, and the drinks weren't cheap either. I loved it. It wasn't exactly Hollywood— those dreams were on ice, anyway. In the meantime, I definitely got a thrill looking out past the spotlights into the crowd and seeing eyes on me that I recognized from MTV or sitcoms or movies.

I was making great money straight off the starting line, but I knew the trick to making the amazing money was to dance in the

VIP room, where the tips flowed like champagne. I was a popular attraction and bringing in my own fans, but there were girls who had been around longer and seemed to get a little more attention.

I spent a few days trying to figure out what they had that I didn't. Maybe they were better dancers? Maybe they had a little more animal magnetism? Flirtier? Prettier? I watched the girls that made the big bucks, and when it finally hit me, it was like a slap in the face. It's the boobs, stupid.

I was naturally well endowed, and in the real world, I'd be considered pretty remarkable in that category. But this wasn't the real world, and the men that came into La Royale weren't looking for mere mortal tits. They had to be something from another planet. They had to *be* planets—to exert their own gravitational force.

Every once in a while, a dancer a couple years older than me named Vickie would come to the Royale. She wasn't based in Dallas— she was from Houston—but she'd tour around, and whenever she showed up, she'd make money that made my jaw drop.

Vickie was the ultimate Texas dream girl. She had the hair, she had the voice, and, as I was learning was most important, she had a chest that seemed to exist in more than three dimensions. Unlike me, she wasn't just pretending to be Texas. She was the real thing. But she was like me in some other ways. She'd dropped out of school young, supported herself, and met her husband way before she turned eighteen. He was a cook she'd met at a fried chicken joint where she'd worked. He didn't come around much, but when he did, he had that dark, hollow look I remember seeing in Greg's eyes when the subject of my dancing came up. I'm sure the attention his wife got drove him out of his damn mind, but that money was hard to ignore.

It wasn't rare to hear about men that would leave Vickie a grand in tips in a night. She could walk out of the club any given night with over 5,000 dollars, plus a handful of marriage proposals. What was her secret? Well, once the obvious slapped me in the face, it wasn't much of a secret.

Vickie wasn't the only one. There was also Mary Sue, whose enormous gifts made her the steadiest earner at the club. One night after I watched her bring in nearly $2,000 in tips, I couldn't help but express admiration.

"Damn. This place treats me well, but I'm never going to see that kind of cash. Mary Sue, you're blessed."

She laughed. "Oh yeah, Victoria. I'm blessed alright. Blessed by Dr. Ira Goodson."

I asked her what she meant, and she told me her secret. Dr. Goodson was the best plastic surgeon in Dallas. This guy was a boob artisan, she told me. He could make your body do things that defied the laws of physics. She handed me his card. "Give him a call sometime if you want to make some real money. He ain't cheap, but accept no substitutes."

I thought about it. Maybe more money per night could mean I could save faster, and I could also work fewer nights a week and spend more time at home with my baby. I mean, making a few grand a night—I could practically retire by the same time some of my friends from back home in Ohio were just getting out of college.

In the meantime, I had less buoyant concerns back at home. To keep up the mortgage and save, I was working many nights a week. That meant counting even more on Chuck and Ellen, who I hated having around my child. It would hit me at the oddest times—up on stage, getting into costume, counting out tips. I'd imagine Ellen holding Jeremy, rocking him and putting him down in his crib. I thought of Chuck sitting at the kitchen table with Jeremy, giving him one of his earnest lectures about the right way to be a man. I'd think of Greg, drinking a beer with his eyes glued on the TV while Jeremy wailed in his play pen. I'd think of those three with my baby, and I'd start crying, right in the middle of the club.

And apart from that, things with Greg weren't getting any better. He refused to cooperate with the divorce, and so I had to hire a lawyer. The whole thing was getting very awkward. I'd drop Jeremy off in the afternoon and remind Greg about our court appointment the next day. Every time I saw him, his whole demeanor seemed to change a little more from sad defeat to bitter hate. I thought time would ease the anger between us, but it only seemed to be growing.

I decided I needed to do what I had to and make more money at the club while I still could. After all, I'd already invested in a house. Getting a boob job was just one more investment. I scheduled an appointment with Dr. Goodson.

Dr. Goodson's office was as well appointed as La Royale—every detail looked like money. Looking at the tasteful art on the walls, it was clear he was no stranger to spending on appearances. When he initially examined me, he raved. "I think you'll be able to support significant augmentation. We'll be able to do something really special here, I think." I admit, I got a little thrill hearing that. I imagined myself like Vickie, with men down on their knees, begging me to let them buy me a new car, or diamonds, or a ranch somewhere in west Texas. I signed my down payment over and went back to work.

Meanwhile, the greatest moments of my days were spent alone with my son. I had friends still from art school, and I had friends from work and the neighborhood. But I felt like I didn't really need to see any of them. Jeremy was so beautiful. For as much trouble as he caused me while he was still in the oven (I was just getting over my broken rib six months later), he made up for it by never fussing at home. I know moms can sometimes have selective memory, but he was an angel, always. We'd sit out on the porch together, and I'd rock him and tell him stories of our future. About the purple house we'd live in someday, with a purple Cadillac. And of course, he'd have his own car too—whatever color he wanted. I'd tell him he was the only man I needed in my life. And I meant it.

Then I'd go to La Royale. I wanted to be good, one of the top dancers. Everyone thought I could be. But, man, I was having trouble concentrating. Back when I was drunk and high most of the time, taking off my top and shaking my body for four or five hours a night seemed like the most natural thing in the world. But cold sober, I kept thinking about hopping off the stage, grabbing a coffee, and relaxing with a good book for a few minutes before heading home to see my son. I just wasn't feeling it. I pushed on, though.

One morning, I picked up Jeremy from Ellen, and she clucked, "Honey, you look so tired. You're wearing yourself out again. Nobody can be a good mom to a baby when she's working all night. Why don't you quit that foul job and let Greg take care of you?" He'd gotten a job as a machinist again. Chuck and Ellen thought we could still get back together, as if the only obstacle to our happiness had been that he'd been out of a job. Didn't they know about the abuse? Didn't they know about the lovelessness?

"Ellen, I appreciate your help, and it won't be like this forever, but I'm trying to build a home for my son. Greg and I aren't getting back together. He doesn't want that either, even if he might say he does. Believe me, I know there's nothing left there."

"Well, you're trying to throw away a good man, and I don't think he deserves that. And I don't think he's gonna stand for that either, and he shouldn't. If you can't focus on what's best for your child, maybe we need to think about a different arrangement."

I left with Jeremy in my arms and my face burning. In her mind, working was some act of pure selfishness. I was able to calm myself down, and after taking a day off, I went back to my usual routine. Ellen didn't mention anything about our conversation, so I didn't either. Then a couple days later, I heard from my lawyer. He said he had news that might be shocking at first, but that was common in divorce proceedings like mine. Greg was suing me. He was suing me for custody of Jeremy. He wanted to take my baby away.

Wild Bill

Dallas

Likes to drink / Hates to talk / Has money / No wife or GF / Home visits / Safe / Would see again

I arrive in the driveway of the Highland Park mansion, and I know the drill. Walk to the service entrance door along the side. Ring only once. Wait as long as it takes for him to answer.

Wild Bill opens the door, slowly, this time making me wait only two or three minutes. If it was a different regular client, someone I could joke with, I might tease him about leaving me out in the cold.

"Come on in," he says, without really looking me in the face. He turns and shuffles down the hall, swirling the Chardonnay in an oversized globe. "Put your coat over there and take off your shoes," he instructs, again without looking. I do as he says without a word, watching him move slowly into the kitchen to grab his bottle. He walks so slowly and so gingerly, I wonder if he's had an operation recently, or if he's sick. All I know for sure is that Wild Bill isn't so wild anymore.

"Get yourself ready and go to the TV room." He orders me around like I'm hired help at a construction site. I've gotten used to it. He's not my only client that's like that. It didn't take me long to realize that some clients wanted to give up all control to me and others wanted to take all control from me. One of the finer points of my job was figuring out which was expected of me, and fast. You don't want to confuse a dominant for a submissive, or vice versa.

I ready myself the way he wants in the bathroom, fixing my lipstick just so and unbuttoning just the right number of buttons on my *blouse. Then I go to the TV room, where the football game is already on, volume up to a level you might expect at grandma and grandpa's house. I'd guess Wild Bill was still only in his late fifties, but he acted much older.*

While he's getting his snacks and wine gathered, I have time to look at the photos on the wall. I use any clues I can to figure out my clients' desires. Most of the photos are of Bill's race horses, which I know he's sunk a lot of money into. Then there's photos of him in his working days, shaking the hands of Texas politicians and other oilmen. One or two frames are empty. But there's that one photo of Bill, the only one that shows him smiling. He's up in the saddle of a big chestnut mare with a wide brimmed hat and a six-shooter in his leather glove. Next to the horse is a red head dressed up like she was Calamity Jane. They're both smiling big, goofy smiles.

"What are you looking at? I told you to get yourself ready." I apologize and get in position on my knees next to the leather recliner. Through my years of working, I've noticed men who want total power over me are those who feel like they've lost it somewhere else in their lives. Men who want to be dominated have more responsibility than they know how to handle.

I often wondered, during those long hours on my knees trying to bring Wild Bill's cock to life, whether it was work or love that had made Wild Bill feel so powerless. He once mentioned in one of his rare, chatty moods that he'd retired early from the oil business, and he'd been living in that big house for twenty years. Ten years alone. I guessed it was Calamity Jane that had left him feeling helpless.

Bill drinks, shouts at the men running around with the football, and chomps mini pretzels. He's trying to relax, but he's also drunk and upset at the course of the game. It's all making my job harder. I work for what seems like nearly an hour trying to coax his limp dick to life with my hands and lips. I know to be patient. Finally, after his team scores and the crowd cheers, he starts to stiffen a little. Two commercial breaks later, he finally comes.

I go to the bathroom to clean up, and when I return, my money is on the snack tray next to the pretzels. I know not to say anything, and don't expect him to acknowledge me in any way. He's left a pretty big tip. I must have done a good job.

I kind of like Wild Bill, I decide. He's had his heart broken. He doesn't trust women. Well, I don't trust men either.

Chapter 10

SHINY, HAPPY PEOPLE

By the start of 1991, I was twenty years old, and I was a grown woman. I wasn't pretending anymore. And the difference was that I knew something of real heartache. My son Jeremy was slipping in and out of my life, and he hadn't yet learned to crawl.

Greg, Chuck, and Ellen pressured me daily—quit my nightlife, stay home. Stay with Jeremy, take Greg back, and all would be well. I'd be with my baby, and Greg would find a 9 to 5, and we'd get by, somehow, provided we had Chuck and Ellen's expert advice close at hand. My parents would call me and tell me the same thing—Greg had enlisted them. Even my friends wanted me to stop struggling and accept my new role as a devout housewife.

Some nights I would lay awake with Jeremy in the next room, and I'd imagine life exactly like that. A life with no fights. No fears. No wants. An apron around my waist, my baby in my arms. Dinner on the stove and my husband home from work soon. It was a dream, and only a dream. And it wasn't mine.

I grew up in a house with adults pretending they were living that exact dream. They weren't. They were full of anger, full of sadness, shame, and regret. I'd seen the same in Greg, and I'd seen the future with him. It would be just like the life my parents had, full of moody silences, paranoia, and sudden bursts of violence. I'd spent all my life fighting against that future. I wasn't going back to it, and I didn't want that life for my son, either.

I had so little. I was alone in the city, without many friends, and nobody who could take care of me. Every day someone would tell me I should take my husband back. People just liked the idea of reconciliation, of families being together. Of course, I didn't tell people about all the blood and bruises, or all the demeaning words. I was too proud to admit all that, and besides, I'd known abuse since I was a child, but it had never been something I'd had words for. Maybe if I had a way to talk about it, I could have made a friend— there were men and women all around me that knew that kind of household. Many who had struggled just to survive and hold onto self-respect. But I didn't reach out, and because of that, I was fighting alone.

But one thing I'd always had, even when I had nothing else, was my pure bull-headed stubbornness. My looks and my brains have helped me here and there, but everything worthwhile I've ever got came from never flinching. And I wasn't going to this time either.

I had the money to hire a divorce lawyer. My first lawyer was named Jimmie Troccio, and he made me feel like things would be simple. I hadn't really spoken to Greg about dividing our stuff. After all, almost none of it was his. I'd put down the down payment on the house, and almost all the furniture was mine. He had an easy chair and a small TV that he liked, his clothes, and that was about it. He was welcome to all of that. As far as the house went, he couldn't even afford a tiny amount of the mortgage payment. We'd hardly put any money down. He didn't have much of a claim, and I could buy out what he did have. I'd take the rest and start a new life.

137

And my new life started with my new body. That spring I had my new boobs installed, and I went big. With Vickie back in Houston, I was a contender as the dancer with the biggest boobs in Dallas. As a business decision, it was one of the smartest investments I'd ever made. My tips doubled overnight. I suddenly ruled the roost at clubs like the Red Room and a Roman-bath themed club called Satyricon. After a couple of nights, I realized I could be making over $12,000 a month while still having plenty of time for my son. I could do it. All I needed was to find someone else to help care for Jeremy while I worked, and I'd get him away from his father, Chuck, and Ellen forever. I could break the cycle and raise him in a happy home.

In the meantime, I still had to rely on Chuck and Ellen to watch my son for me. I didn't trust them, but they were more than willing, and I didn't have anyone else. They'd keep him for a day or more while I was dancing, and then he'd come home with me. Every time I saw them, they'd ask me to reconsider the divorce, for the child's sake, "and for your own, honey. We're worried about you. Just look what you've done to yourself! You can't keep living this life." I knew their concern was only skin deep, and quite frankly what I did with my skin was my own business. I'd smile and nod, and then tell them it wasn't meant to be, and that I was working so I could take care of my child.

Meanwhile, Greg's life was falling apart. He wasn't working, other than a day job here and there. He was still earning in a month what I could make in an hour or two. And what he did make, he was spending—he was developing a gambling problem, trying to make money fast. On top of that, he was spending money on sex. I knew all of this because Chuck and Ellen would tell me. They used it as

138

evidence that I'd broken his heart, as though he'd been a fine, upstanding citizen before I'd left him. He was the same guy I'd dated. He was the same guy I'd married. If only I'd seen it a little earlier, or had had the nerve to stand up for myself and not just try to please everyone around me. I wasn't going to fall for it again.

Finally, the state of Texas's mandated sixty day waiting period for continuing divorce procedures was over. I was so happy. I only needed to go through the paperwork and I'd be free. Greg already had his clothes, TV, and easy chair. I thought it was going to be as simple as getting a new license at the DMV. But nothing was going to be easy.

First, I came home early one morning after work, and I found the front door of my house wide open. I was scared, and I called a friend to come over. We went in, and found everything was gone. Even my two cats! I'd left a window open a crack with the screen behind it shut and locked. Someone had simply come into the house by cutting open the screen and opening the window. I didn't have an alarm system or anything. What was amazing to me was that the burglar hadn't just taken the cash or jewelry—they took my couch, the bassinet, clothes, everything. Other than a few kitchen chairs and a few trinkets, I'd been cleaned out. I sat alone in my empty living room, crying, and I promised myself I wouldn't let this set me back. I called the cops and then spent the morning looking for my cats. I then called Chuck and Ellen and asked if they could watch Jeremy for a couple of days while I sorted things out.

"Honey, we will. But you need to figure out what's best for you and your son. You can't keep living in that dangerous neighborhood, going out all night, with no man at home. It's just not safe for you.

You should take a few days and think about what's really best for your future—and Jeremy's."

I'd heard this before. If they thought losing my stuff was going to change my mind, they were as wrong as always.

A few days later, I was back in Jimmie's office to finalize the divorce. I sat down by his desk, and watched quietly as he shuffled through a thick stack of papers, humming and occasionally sighing. I realized I'd never before paid so much money to be so bored. "My, my, my," he said to himself. He flipped through more documents. What was he even looking at? He gave me a long, searching look. "This is going to be more complicated than I thought."

I shook myself awake. "Whaddya mean? I don't even have anything anymore to split with him, other than a mortgage."

"Well, you said he wasn't interested in the boy, right? That's not what it says here. He's got a lawyer too, and he's petitioned for full custody."

What? I thought. *Is this a joke? Is my lawyer pranking me?* He was looking at me like he was dead serious, but what he was saying made no sense. Greg had no interest in Jeremy. I don't think I'd ever seen him touch his own child. When he was at Chuck and Ellen's, only Ellen really had anything to do with the baby. And Greg didn't have any money to hire a lawyer. Chuck and Ellen paid for everything, though where their money was coming from was a mystery. Then it hit me like a flash. It wasn't Greg. It was his "aunt and uncle" that were behind this. I thought of Jeremy, who was with them right then, probably getting fed a bottle in front of the TV. I signed some papers and told my lawyer I had to go.

"Of course, I understand. But before you leave, I think we should talk soon about bringing in a specialist. This is turning out to be a delicate case." I told him I'd call soon, and I ran to my car.

When I showed up at Chuck and Ellen's house, I could tell lights were on in the back of the house. As soon as I pulled into the driveway, they went off. I wasn't falling for it. I ran to the door and began banging on it, ringing the bell. "I know you're in there!" After a minute or two, I heard Jeremy's cry.

I wouldn't give up. I stood at the door screaming and pounding for what seemed like hours, listening for the sound of my baby's voice. Finally, I heard footsteps stomping toward the front door. It flew open, almost hitting me.

Chuck stood in the door. "You're trespassing on our property," he spat.

"I'm not leaving without him. He's my baby."

"You're never even home. How are you gonna take care of him? Time to leave. Now. Go drink yourself to death, if that's what you want to do. Get AIDS. I don't care. Just leave."

This was the real Chuck. Not the pious, church going reformed ex-con. The bitter sociopath ex-con.

"Chuck, nothing you say is going to make me leave without my baby." Down the hall, past Chuck's shoulder, I could see Ellen watching from around the corner. I tried to slip past Chuck and he caught me, shoving me back. I tried to move past him again, and this time he balled his fist and knocked me clean off the porch with a right hook.

I felt like I left my body. When I came to a few moments later, Chuck and Ellen were both standing over me. I could hear Jeremy softly crying.

Ellen spoke. "Now honey, you know this is for the best. Greg will take care of his son, and we'll pray you get your life together."

My life was just fine. The only thing wrong with it was the swelling that was closing up my left eye and the kidnapping of my first son.

"Just let me hold him, please."

Ellen wasn't sure what to do. It took some convincing.

"I just want to hold him."

"You can say goodbye, then leave. If you stay clean, you can still visit him. But right now you're no mom. You can't do what you're doing and be a mom."

In that moment, I hated her. She was wrong. Wrong about everything. She handed Jeremy over, and I ran for the car.

This time, it was Ellen that came after me.

"You bitch! I knew you'd try this shit."

As I screamed, she grabbed onto Jeremy's arm and tugged. I held tight, but she was pulling so hard, I was terrified she'd pull his arm out of the socket. She didn't seem to care.

I let go. I had no choice. I couldn't be part of hurting my baby.

Chuck moved in and held me back, just as the police came. The neighbors had called them to report a disturbed woman trying to break into Chuck and Ellen's home. The cops took one look at me with my bloody face, streaking mascara, and torn shirt and immediately assumed I was a crack head or something. I was too panicked to explain clearly what was happening, and Chuck was a natural grifter. Within moments he'd told his account to the police, and they were yelling at me to leave before I was arrested.

I did. I was too hurt and confused to make any sense of what was happening.

Back at home, I cried all night in my empty house. My life made no sense anymore. Just as I'd finally found a life I was happy with, everything was falling apart.

The next fight was in court. My lawyer introduced me to a specialized divorce attorney; someone that could handle the kind of messy case that mine had become. Kris Lightner was more than a persuasive courtroom attorney. He was like the director of a movie. He could change the way the judge saw the case—or so he claimed.

My new attorney took as much money as I was bringing in. Hey, you've got to pay for talent. At our first meeting, he went over my life story, and he asked a lot of questions about my history in rehab, my time as a dancer, the hours I kept. At first I went along, but then I got frustrated.

"Why do we need to go over all this? This should be an open and shut case, right? I'm the mom, and I have an income. He's a bum, he hits me, he has a criminal record from hitting me, and he lives in a house with a man who was locked up for armed robbery. I've never even seen him hold Jeremy. He's completely unsuited to care for him. And Chuck and Ellen are psychos. Chuck smashed my face in! I'll just show the judge this!" I pointed to the large welt that had my eye still partially swollen shut.

Kris put his gold-rimmed glasses down and sighed. He looked me up and down, carefully. I felt like he was sizing me up for a table dance or something, but he just shook his head. He called out of the office room: "Maria, could you come in here please?"

A young woman wearing a business suit came in. She couldn't have been much older than me. "Maria, we need to get our client here ready for her court date. The judge hearing the custody case is Rick Bronner. Could you take her out shopping tomorrow and get her ready? We'll need to have her ready by 3 p.m."

Maria agreed and left. I was confused.

"Look, I don't blame you. You're not from Texas, so you're still learning how it is here. There's nothing a Texan loves more than a Texas mama, but, quite frankly, you ain't that right now. At least not to a man like Judge Bronner." He went on to explain more. Being the primary earner wasn't necessarily going to be in my favor. If I'd had no personal income at all and stayed home all day vacuuming and watching soaps, the court would probably award custody in a flash. The fact that I had a job, and that job took place at night, was a big sticking point. In this court's view, a mother's job was to be home with her baby, and if she wasn't, there was a good chance she wasn't a "good woman." What was a good woman in Texas? It was a woman who might have no problem showing off her body, but who only left the house at night when accompanied by her husband. A good woman was a woman who would go to mega-church every Sunday and spend the other six days shopping. A good woman would have a nanny push her baby in a stroller all day while she tried on Cavaricci's at the mall. A good woman would be in bed by 10 every night, thinking of ways to make her husband happier. And if I couldn't be a "good woman," I'd have to be a "good girl," someone who had lost her way but was now meek and dowdy and ready to throw herself at the feet of the court and beg for mercy. He also asked if I had a serious boyfriend yet. When I said no, he sighed again. "If the court thought there was a good chance you'd remarry soon, this would be much easier. It doesn't matter if your new

144

husband was Lee Harvey Oswald reincarnated, the important thing in this town is showing you're striving to be part of a nuclear family again." Unfortunately, romance hadn't really been on my mind lately. I didn't have anyone to introduce to the judge.

Then he moved on to my appearance. "There's not much we can do about your bustline, but we're going to have to change the hair, the nails, and the clothes all by tomorrow. Don't wear much makeup, but cover up the bruise as much as possible, and make sure you're otherwise well groomed. Maria will take care of the rest."

I waited for my court date with a sense of confused panic. I thought, *For what I'm paying this guy, he must know what he's doing, right?* But I just couldn't understand what he was saying. Sure, I was a stripper, but if I could make the judge see why I was doing it, how much I was earning for my baby, all I had fought for my whole life, all I had overcome, surely he'd understand. *But what if my lawyer's right? What if all that doesn't matter?*

The next morning, I went out to the mall with Maria. First, we plucked off my long red acrylic nails and I got a manicure. Then we went to a specialty bra shop, where I was introduced to sports bras for the first time. Maria had me try on a sort of harness that looked like something you'd put on livestock, but with lace. The bra flattened my boobs way back and made me look like a woman who happened to have a large throw pillow strapped under her shirt. We bought a modest brown suit that made me look a little like Dana Carvey's Church Lady. And then we went to work on the hair—first having my extensions removed, and then picking up a brown, bobbed wig to stuff the rest of my long locks under. Finally, we went to a beautician to conceal the bruise Chuck had left on my cheek.

"Tough day, honey?" the beautician asked.

"It's getting there," I said.

The initial court appearance was no more than twenty minutes. Greg showed up with Chuck and Ellen looking like everyone's favorite grandparents. They didn't recognize me at first, and when they did, they snickered. Greg entered into the court along with just his attorney, as did I. Our lawyers presented our stories, and the judge asked us questions. Greg's lawyer claimed I was an addict, that I was drinking and using still, and that I was an immediate danger to Jeremy. They didn't have any evidence but my time in rehab years before. My lawyer painted me as a poor young woman led astray who had attended AA and was seeking help to become the mother she knew she could be.

Nothing seemed right. It was like I was an actor in a bad play. When it was my turn to testify, I had trouble speaking, between my nerves and the shrink wrap binding my chest.

"All I've tried to do these last six months is to be a good mother to my son."

"So miss, explain to me why he hasn't been staying in your home the past few days."

"Well . . ." I started, looking to my attorney. My wig itched, and I scratched near my hairline, accidentally pulling a loose blonde lock from under the brown mop.

"You see . . ."

"Excuse me, miss," the judge interrupted. "Are you wearing a wig?"

I was hyperventilating. I couldn't answer.

"Miss, is there a medical reason why you need to be wearing a wig? Otherwise it's not appropriate in family court."

And the appearance just went downhill from there. After a half hour, the judge ruled that Jeremy would stay in Chuck and Ellen's house until the formal hearing. In the meantime, Jeremy was to be appointed a private attorney—an ad litem—to look after his interests and observe my interactions with him to ensure I could provide for his welfare.

I was still working long hours every night to keep up with the bills. My new lawyer was costing a fortune, and he hadn't won anything for me yet. I spent the next few days in tears, and the nights determined to make the money I needed to win the battle.

I got home early one morning and fell asleep on the couch. I woke near ten, and went to check the answering machine. It was my lawyer, who had called the evening before. It turned out the ad litem would be at Chuck and Ellen's this morning to watch me interact with my son. I was supposed to be there at 10 a.m. Five minutes from when I heard the message. I leapt to the bathroom and brushed my teeth, then threw on a T-shirt and jeans. I pulled into Chuck and Ellen's at 10 past 10, yanking my hair into shape with an old brush I had in my glove compartment.

I rang the bell, and Ellen answered. "Here she is, finally," she said, her eyes down and her voice sounding like a disappointed nun at Catholic school. "Jeremy's sleeping." I was bewildered, but I went into the living room, where Jeremy was asleep at the bottom of a play pen near a stern looking gray-haired woman in a navy blue suit. I wasn't sure what I was supposed to do, but my heart ached to hold my son. I scooped him out of the play pen, and he yawned, curled up in my arms, and went back to sleep. For the next hour, I sat perfectly still with a smile plastered to my face and Jeremy's ad litem watching me intently. She was taking notes. What could the notes possibly be about? Nothing was happening. Was she making a record of my mussed hair, my sleepy eyes? The way my jacket smelled of the club—stale beer and cigarette smoke? Was it a quick note about the little blue and yellow half-moon bruise an inch below my eye?

Nobody spoke. And then it was over. I was told that I was legally required to leave the premises and wait for the formal court hearing. I gave Jeremy a kiss on the forehead. He was starting to wake and cry. Ellen came in the room with a bottle. I told him we'd be together again soon, and fought every instinct I had to grab him tight and run out the front door.

I wouldn't see Jeremy again for almost a year and a half.

We had our court hearing, and our attorneys duked it out over which household was the most dangerous for Jeremy. The judge seemed tempted to take him away entirely and grant custody to the state. Chuck and Ellen testified as witnesses, and they played their role well. They knew how to dress, how to speak, how to drop enough talk of church and redemption and hope for salvation to seem like wise elders, like good Texans. Ultimately, the judge granted custody to Greg, while I was to have visitation rights on weekends and for a few hours' mid-week. I was to pay child support as well based on a formula that averaged my recent income with Greg's non-income. Not only would I only see my son rarely, I'd be responsible for over one grand a month that was basically going directly to Chuck and Ellen's household. I could see the smiles spread across their faces. They were about to become very well compensated babysitters.

And, I soon learned, they used money from child support to pay attorney's fees to keep me in court. They would file petition after petition arguing that I was a threat to Jeremy's welfare. That I was a drunk, an addict. They wouldn't let me have my visitation rights, so I had to file petitions myself. I was losing thousands and thousands of dollars a month, and I couldn't keep up with my mortgage. All I could do was pick up more shifts, work more hours.

One night, weeks after the hearing, the stress got to me. I was despondent, exhausted. The word that comes to mind is "shattered." I was getting ready to start another shift at Satyricon, and I couldn't handle it. I remembered back to my first nights dancing, way back in Pepe's, and the shots of vodka I'd slam back to work up my nerve. They seemed so quaint, so harmless. I went to the bar at Satyricon and knocked back a double shot.

And that was it. Alcohol was a part of my life again.

My focus was on my court battle, and I took my eye off my battle with addiction. Once I was drinking before shifts again, it wasn't long before coke was back in the picture. After all, it was as common in the club dressing rooms as glitter and spandex.

In the period of a week or so, I'd slipped quietly into becoming the caricature Greg and his lawyer had painted of me in court. I hadn't been that person. I hadn't been weak. But now I was.

Alpha Dog

Washington, DC

Shy with clothes on, uninhibited with clothes off / enormous /
married / meet and greet

It's quite simply the biggest dick I've ever seen. I'm no size queen, but I know this one is going to be one to remember. The memorable organ is attached to a nondescript man. Alpha Dog is a software engineer, and he's otherwise slightly built, middle aged, professional and sweet.

We met at what's called a "meet and greet" in Alexandria, Virginia, which is something I don't normally do. Basically, you get invited by the organizer to show up with a bunch of other call girls at a club or restaurant that's been rented out, and a bunch of vetted clients come and mingle. While it's generally safe and some working girls seem to think it's fun, I've always been weirded out at these things. Maybe it's the introvert in me, but I'm much more in control one on one than in a group of interested guys. Plus, they've all seen our profiles ahead of time, while we have no idea who they are. Sometimes it's kind of like being at a party full of stalkers that know way more about you than they should. Alpha Dog introduced himself and could tell I was uncomfortable. He took me back to my hotel and we exchanged info.

Now, the next night after the meet and greet, we're meeting up at the hotel in the flesh. Alpha Dog is wild. It's like he's got this secret super power he's been hiding, and I'm the only one he trusts to show it off to.

After, he wants to talk about his wife. They so often do. It's a kind of justification, I suppose. He says he's unhappy. They're always

150

unhappy. In fact, it's always a little refreshing when I get a married man who basically says, "Marriage is great, I just like to fuck around!"

"I'm going to end the marriage soon," Alpha Dog says. "In fact, most likely it'll only be three or four more years."

That soon? At least he's being honest. I can't count the number of guys who say they're just about to leave their wives, then continue saying the same thing month after month at the end of our sessions.

"Why three years, is she unwell?" I know it's never a good idea to pry, but I'm generally curious.

He gets out his phone and swipes until a picture comes up. It's a pair of German Shepherds. "No, it's our children here. We think of them that way, anyway. I wouldn't want to split up the family while they're still alive. They're getting on in years, though, and when they're gone, there really won't be any reason for us to stay together anymore."

For real? It always astonishes me the reasons unhappy people stay together. For the fucking dogs? I get a little pissed off when people don't seem to know how free they really are.

Chapter 11

TEARS IN HEAVEN

In October 1992, my son turned two years old, and I was going to see him for the first time in over a year.

I'd missed Jeremy's first birthday. I'd missed his first steps, his first words. I didn't know what kind of child he was growing into. I didn't know what kind of life he had with my ex. The year after I lost custody was a slide to the bottom—the first of many—and to this day I'm not sure how I crawled my way back.

During the previous year and a half, I wasn't just worried for my son's safety, I was worried for my own. The first stalking laws in the country were enacted in California in 1990, and they were still a year or so off from coming to Texas. While it was still legal, Greg was perfecting the art. He rarely worked. Instead, his full-time job seemed to be trailing me in his car. It wasn't like he was trying to win me back anymore. He never tried to talk to me. His creepy game was just pure intimidation. He knew where I worked, and he seemed to figure out my schedule. He'd come to the clubs and watch me dance. I would look down from the stage and see him standing there against a wall with a single beer, mouth screwed up tight, with hate in his eyes. I'd never felt as scared, even back when I used to dance for bikers who'd been on the road for weeks. I told the club owners about him, and they'd have the bouncers throw him out. Then he'd just wait in his car until I was done with my shift. I'd stay in the club until closing, nursing a soda water some nights, some stronger stuff on others.

One night I worked up the courage to confront him. I was clear-eyed and sober, and my anger had built up over a night of knowing he was waiting in his car to tail me home. It helped that a couple of the biggest bouncers in the Red Room were heading to their cars at the same time. I stomped up to his rusted out Bronco with my hands shaking. I told myself I needed to control my voice. He rolled down the window and leaned out, calmly waiting for whatever I had to say, and his smug smirk let me know he had a few nasty things on his mind he'd been waiting to tell me.

I asked him what business he had following me. I wasn't his wife anymore. He said if that was the case, I shouldn't worry about what he did. Following me around was his business. He said he was collecting evidence to use against me in court. He was going to catch me drinking and driving and turn me into the cops, or he was going to catch me buying coke. He said if my business was shaking my ass for strangers and getting drunk, his business was making sure I'd never have a hand in raising his son.

"I'm not doing any of that! I'm clean!" I screamed. This was partly true. I was trying to stay clean. So much depended on it. But I would slip now and then. I was at an emotional and psychological low, and there were nights I just had nothing left to fight my addictions. But at that time I was clean, and I'd been clean when we'd had our custody hearing, and I was determined to get and stay clean for my son. We argued. He told me I could end this in a minute if I agreed to come back to him. I told him that was ridiculous. He told me I still had a

153

chance to make things right. He'd be watching me, and if I slipped, I wouldn't get another chance.

"Greg, you've been watching me for a year now, and you haven't seen anything. I'm not doing drugs!"

"That's not what I'm talking about," he said. "I know you're going to drink again, it's just a matter of time. I know you're going to get yourself into trouble, and I'll be there to see it, and I'll be laughing my ass off. We both know that's going to happen. But if I see you with someone else, then it's over. If you go home with another guy, you'll regret it. You won't have another chance." He told me if he saw another man touch me, he would mess the guy up, then walk away forever with my son. He was determined to make sure I'd pay for leaving him, that I'd learn to see he could take everything and anything from me if I defied him. Then he pulled away. I was stunned, and I sat in my car and cried.

More and more, it seemed like he might have the power to do whatever he wanted. By this time, I'd been fighting Greg for custody of Jeremy for months. I sent my now ex-husband a huge chunk of cash every month for child support, but since he paid no rent, most of that money went to his attorney fees. I'd blown most of my money on attorneys already, and I had nothing to show for it. Not only had Greg been awarded primary custody, he was refusing me visitation as well. He was filing petition after petition that I was a threat to my child's welfare. In the meantime, when I'd file to take him back to court over not allowing visitation, it would cost me thousands in attorney fees. Each time, Greg would get a slap on the wrist with no real consequences. I was soon broke, behind in my mortgage payments, and unable to afford my lawyers. Greg was bleeding me dry.

I had a few nights in a row where I slipped—went on a bender, and I didn't come out of it for a few days. When I woke up one morning sober, with a splitting headache, my first thought was paranoia— *What if he saw me? What if Greg knew what I was doing?* And then I realized how fucked up it was to even worry about that. My drinking wasn't about being seen or not. It had nothing to do with Greg. It had to do with me and my future. I didn't know why it happened, but I was incapable of just having a drink to relax. Once I started with one, I often didn't stop until I was damn near unconscious. What happened to me? I didn't understand it at all. I'd felt near powerless plenty of times. But only alcohol made me feel like I had no control and no choices.

When I was sober, I obsessed over Greg, but not in the same way he obsessed over me—instead, it was pure fear. I was determined to escape his pull by any means I had. But instead of getting professional help, I thought only of protecting myself from Greg, both physically and emotionally. I thought of finding another man to have in my life. Someone strong, someone who could protect me and help me get my life back on track. Despite his threats, I started dating again. Or trying to, anyway.

One of my first "boyfriends" after my divorce was a Dallas Cowboy. He was a reserve player, a special teamer who only lasted in the pros for a couple of years. Not exactly a star, but I was impressed. He came to the club one night, and he was so handsome—not tall, but powerfully built under his suit with sharp features and natural confidence. He found me at the bar after my shift and asked if I'd like to go out the next night. I got asked out on dates nearly every night, but I never said yes. It was just part of the job. But there was something about this guy—he was so strong, so confident, so kind, I thought he'd be the perfect antidote to Greg's hate. Dating him would be like an exorcism, and he wouldn't be intimidated by Greg at all.

He took me out to a nice restaurant, and we had a pretty good time. He also came over to my house one day and played football in the backyard with some neighborhood kids. It was a vision of a life I'd wanted. Dallas "high society," good fortune, laughs. And he hadn't even made a pass at me yet—I thought maybe he was a little shy, or a little old fashioned. After all I'd been through, that was fine with me. I was happy to take it slow. He went away the next weekend to Pittsburgh for a game, and he told me he'd be back to see me that Monday. When he came over, I made him a drink, and I had one myself. Of course, I couldn't have just one, and pretty soon we were both half in the bag. We got to fooling around a little, and when I went to kiss him he winced. He pulled my hand from his chest. "Listen, babe, I just played yesterday. I'm still a little banged up." I told him I'd be careful, and he gave me a look like I still didn't understand. He stood back and unbuttoned his Oxford shirt, and then moved under the light of a lamp. My jaw dropped. He was a powerfully built man, but his body looked absolutely ruined—a jagged black bruise ran from his hip all the way to his shoulder, and his chest was spotted with bruises like an overripe banana.

He must have seen the look of horror on my face, and it seemed to irritate him. "Listen, I don't really feel like being touched. How about you just let me fuck you the way I want, and I'll give you 500 bucks. That's better than what you normally get, right?"

My jaw dropped from half open to gaping. I thought this guy was an old-fashioned gentleman. Turns out, he was just waiting for me to name my price.

"Get out of my fucking house!" I screamed. I couldn't believe it. I felt I'd been insulted in a way I could never forgive. I was a dancer, not a prostitute. I was tired of men not seeing a difference. I still had my boundaries. I never saw that particular Cowboy again, though there'd be others.

Later that year, I met a car insurance salesman who was about my age. I met him at his place of work instead of my own when I needed a new policy, so this time I thought there'd be no confusion about the nature of our relationship. Seth was a nice boy from Nebraska, but he had enough of a tough streak to stand up to Greg's shit. But like me, Seth had his head turned by Dallas nightlife. During daytime Seth was a man responsible beyond his twenty-two years, working long hours toward one day achieving a dream of owning his own insurance agency. During the nighttime, he snorted, smoked, and drank his way to a different place. I went on the ride with him, and it often ended somewhere ugly. I was just happy to have someone my own age, with my own wild independence and lust for life. But that wasn't nearly enough to build a relationship on.

When Seth yelled, I wasn't surprised. I was coming to think that was what being in a relationship with a man was all about. When he hit me, I was simply disappointed, and again not surprised. I was beginning to think this was also par for the course, even if I knew I could—and must—do better.

Then I missed my period. I finally worked up the nerve to tell Seth, and he exploded, demanding I get an abortion. We fought, and he ended up punching me hard in the stomach, again and again.

Finally, he'd shown me a horror I hadn't known before. Unlike with my first child, I'd been drinking heavily and snorting coke before I realized I was pregnant. I ended up getting an abortion, which was one of the most painful episodes of my life. It was twins. The episode pushed me off the edge. I could no longer face my life head on—I needed a drink and a bump every day to keep myself from feeling the horror of what my life was becoming.

After that, I lost myself. I lost weight—I was under a 100 pounds. A toothpick with boobs. I worked almost every night to keep up with attorney bills and mortgage payments, but too much of my money was going to drugs. I just don't even remember much of that time in my life, other than the feeling of being lost—out to sea with no harbor in sight.

The first half of 1992 is a blur in my mind. I only remember a few scenes, mostly the times I was high. I lost my house. I couldn't keep up with payments, and I had nothing in it anyway. I went back to renting, though I stayed close to my son, with the hope that one day things would be better, for me, for him, for all of us, and he and I would be a family again.

And I partied. I think it shows how fast I fell in such a short time that only half a year after I was propositioned by the Dallas Cowboy, I accepted my first money for sex. This time it wasn't an athlete, it was a comedian. A local boy who'd made it that last year onto the cast of a national show and had been cast in a movie to boot. He was flush with cash and ego, and he had returned to Dallas to show off a little. Still, he was a blast to be around, and not a bad guy. We hung out at the club, and a group of us went out afterward to party. Before long I found myself alone with him in his big Dallas-style Ford truck in the parking lot of a bar.

"Listen, I think you're real pretty," he said. "I'd love it if you would give me a blow job. I'll give you 100 bucks for it, and a ride home if you want. I'll take you home if you want either way." I was a little less surprised this time. I was also high. *Well, at least he wasn't sending any mixed signals,* I thought. I went down on him in his truck. I did it for the money, and I did it because, in a weird way, he was respecting me. He wasn't leading me on or trying to manipulate me. He was letting me choose for myself what was going to happen. I believed if I had said no, he still would have driven me home, and that would be that. So I agreed. I found afterward I didn't feel bad about what I'd done, either. He never asked me to be a girlfriend or anything—he made it clear what he wanted, and I could give it to him. Hey, it was the best relationship with a man I'd had in years. Still, I told myself it was a one-time thing, a fun adventure that I'd never have reason to repeat.

I spent the hundred dollars on a couple cases of diapers. I took them over to Chuck and Ellen's at my appointed Wednesday visitation time, and rang the bell. Of course, nobody was home. They never were. I left the diapers on the porch with a note that I would appreciate seeing my son. I'd done that before, but usually with more f-bombs. This time, it was a note of surrender. Then I went home and slept for days.

I was lonely and depressed. I couldn't even think about how lonely and depressed I was, since my thirst for drink and coke always got in the way first. But at some point I became so exhausted, malnourished, and defeated that I didn't even have the strength to leave the house anymore. I rationed a bottle of vodka over a few days and just wept. I had nobody to talk to about my problems.

And that's why I decided to reach out. I decided that day to go to an AA meeting.

I'd been to Alcoholics Anonymous before. In fact, I went to plenty of meetings back in Ohio. Then it seemed like something I had to do.

There was a meeting house ten minutes from my new place. I confirmed the meeting times and showed up, hangover and all. I walked in to a small, cramped room with coffee-stained carpet and folding chairs and looked into a dozen or more faces. There were all sorts of people that day—grandmas and grandpas, kids that looked even younger than me. It might as well have been people I was riding with on a bus. They didn't mean anything to me, but I sat down and listened as a middle-aged cowboy was telling a story, about his own temptations, the things he had to hold onto, all that he could lose if he slipped again.

I had no idea many of this group would become some of my dearest friends. Some would become some of my saddest warnings. They, and others that would enter that room, would come to make up a special corner of my heart. But right then, they were nobodies to me. I stayed and listened, only because I was so desperate.

The cowboy's name seemed to be Doc. At least, that's what everyone was calling him. When he noticed me, he began to tell his story while looking me right in the eye. I could tell he was a little sweet on me. Not really what I wanted, but he at least seemed like a nice guy.

When he was finished, everyone greeted me. They were welcoming enough, but I left not knowing if I would ever return.

Lucky for me, I decided to go back the very next day. It was the second day that I told the story of my ex, my son, my battle in the court. By the time I got to the part about taking my first drink during my custody battle, I broke. I cried and cried, and a woman named Ella took me in her arms. She didn't say anything, but that one hug was enough to make a regular out of me.

I had another court date set with Greg. I almost didn't show. I'd missed one or two before. I'd even done a bump of coke before one. I knew I'd lost that game, and I had no clue how to get my son back. But after a few days attending meetings, talking to people that had suffered my kind of heartache, I tried again. After all, Greg was still defying a court order to allow me to see my son.

This time, he made the same ultimatum he always had: that I submit to private drug and alcohol testing, and if I passed, he would drop his petition against me. He was certain I wouldn't be able to pass, but I knew now I could. I agreed.

For the next couple of months, I would get phone calls at all hours of the day a couple of times a week. I'd have to drop everything and go to a private testing center to pee in a cup. Every test cost me about fifty bucks. I didn't mind. I was going to play the game, and I was going to see Jeremy again. Then I'd work to get him back in my life full-time.

Finally, we arranged to meet at a McDonald's around Jeremy's second birthday. I'd been clean and sober for over two months, though I'd lost so much. The confidence I had when I fought for my independence was shattered. Greg had won—I wasn't independent; I was merely alone. But in another sense, I had won—over time, he'd given up his obsessive hold on me, and was now merely nasty rather than a constant threat to my life and sanity. I hadn't thrived, but I'd survived, and now I had the opportunity to fill my empty heart once again with the first true love of my life.

Jeremy showed up with Ellen. I was there half an hour ahead of time, and the blue plastic booth where I sat was spilling over with presents. My eyes welled with tears. *What if they don't show*, I'd thought. *I don't know if I could go on.* But there he was, his chubby pink hand in Ellen's cold white one. The first thing I noticed was that he looked happy. It made me start to cry to see him excited and smiling, even if I couldn't know if he'd even recognize me. And then I noticed that he looked just like a mini-Greg. The same hair, the same walk, the same broad face. But there was a look in his eyes that was like looking in a mirror. It was that wild streak, that openness to everything in the world, that curiosity that came across in just a glance. This was my boy.

I scooped him up and tried to control my tears. I wasn't going to fight Ellen, even if she provoked me. I'd play any game I had to so that I never had to let go again before I was ready. In that moment, I was certain that I had finally won back all I'd ever need.

We spent the afternoon together, and I let him leave again with Ellen, despite all my instincts. I knew a single fight at this point could set back my cause. Slowly, we settled into a routine, and Jeremy would come visit me on the weekends, and I'd take him out on Wednesday afternoons. The schedule made it nearly impossible for me to keep dancing on big-money nights, but I didn't care. I was ready to find something else anyway. I didn't want the moon and stars. I just wanted to live, and I didn't think I could without my son.

The Energizer Bunny

Philadelphia, PA

Into experimentation / talking / high stamina / pace yourself

"No, I've been married twice, actually. My first marriage ended because I walked in on my wife jerking off our dog. She said it was because of his prostate diagnosis, and that he'd have to ejaculate three times a week. By doing it at home, she was saving us forty bucks a go. What do you think, was that enough to leave her? What would you have done?"

One of the great lessons I've learned about the lives of the affluent is that the relationships of the rich are often made or broken over the family dog. I'd been with a client that stayed with his wife for the sake of the German Shepherds, and here was a client who got a divorce because his wife got too close to Fido, and he was jealous.

"My second wife was into swinging with me. We both messed around. I thought she understood me on that level. But we fell out of love and fought over money. She just wanted to spend whatever I made, and she was spending it on other men! Almost every woman I've been with has cheated on me in one way or another. I guess I have trust issues."

Energizer Bunny talks a mile a minute. We've just met, and I imagine he's spent the morning getting ready with numerous quad shots of espresso. Bunny is a family practice physician, and who knows what else. Clearly he's the sort of client that's trying to fit as many lives as he can into the time he has on earth. Our get-to-know you chat is supposed to lead to talk about what he wants to do, but I'm used to therapy being part of a client session. I'm just not used to hearing a client's entire life story and romantic history told to me at a mile a

163

minute. I'm expecting to have him ask me my opinion on his crush on his 4th grade teacher when we finally start to move things forward. "To tell you the truth," he starts, "I'm more into pleasing you than just getting off myself. What is it that you like?"

Oh god, not this again.

Whenever a client asks the question, I know I'm going to have to work extra hard. It turns out Bunny screws like he talks. He has me model every possible position for him, tickle his ass, stroke his balls, "orgasm" three times, and that's just to get him warmed up. After that, he turns into a machine. The actual Energizer Bunny, only gray and bald.

"It's actually really hard for me to get off," he explains. "I've been to a sex therapist who has me masturbating on a regular schedule, but that's only helping a little."

I've got my limits, and I know I have to find a way to end this, er, gracefully. Besides, if I can get him off, I'll get a great review online, I'm sure. Better reviews mean higher rates. I grit my teeth, rehearse my plan, and go to work. I talk him into stroking himself while I suck and lick his balls. He watches me intensely as I masturbate. I can tell he is getting close.

"Wow, Victoria. That was the best orgasm I've had in a long time. It's been almost a month since I had one at all. We'll definitely have to meet again." He's still paying me, so we talk some more. "Tell me more about yourself," he asks. Bad idea, I think. "For instance, do you have kids? I don't and I think that's one of the reasons I always had trust issues. My new wife and I are trying to conceive right now, and I think it's really bringing us together. Of course, you've seen what I've been struggling with. If my wife knew how to do what you know how

to do, oh man . . ." What do you want. *It always means "figure me out." Tell me about yourself. It always means "Listen to me." I'm paid well to understand that.*

Chapter 12

RUNAWAY TRAIN

"Hi, Doc? This is Jenn."

"Hi Darlin', how are ya?"

"Sorry to call this late. I didn't wake you, did I?"

"No, I was just settlin' in with a book. What's the worry, hon'?"

"Doc, I'm at the club, and I really want to have a drink."

"Alright, babe, I'll be right there."

I wasn't alone anymore. I had people in my life that could understand me, or part of my life, anyway. Doc was one of them. When I felt like I was in trouble, that I was at a low point and the only answer seemed like another drink, I'd call him up and he'd come talk to me. Or, rather, he'd listen to me talk.

Doc had a crush on me, but he was a good guy and didn't push it. He knew I was in a bad spot, and he wasn't about to take advantage of that. Still, he'd take me out, try and cheer me up. He'd take Jeremy out as well. We'd go to the rodeo together, and he'd teach Jeremy how to keep from being mistaken for a city boy. He bought him his first boots. Jeremy loved them, and he'd wear them all weekend during our visits. He'd even insist on wearing those things to bed, right over his pajamas.

Doc wasn't the only one. There was also Grace, or "Birdy," as she was called because she chirped away just like a sparrow. Grace was about my age, but she beat me to the habit by a few years—she was in and out of treatment by fifteen, and had seen a few years of sobriety already. I listened wide-eyed to the stories of the old-timers, but it was Grace who made me feel most like I belonged. Like me, she had a whole life to look forward to, as well as a past she'd always be running from.

I went to AA twice a day, most days. Once at noon and once at 6 pm. I needed that reinforcement. And I needed real friends. Sure, there were girls at the clubs I talked to, but many of them were girls still at the top of the ride. Some of them had been there for years and years, and might never come down. But I knew the more I hung out with the other dancers, the more I was at risk of taking another plunge. Sometimes it felt that I couldn't get any lower than I was, but instinctively I knew there was a lot more ground to lose.

So by 1993, I was maintaining sobriety and seeing my son regularly. The problem with sobriety, though, was the sobriety. By that, I mean I no longer had any easy tools to cloud my mind and memory when the bad feelings started. It could be regret. It could be fear. It could be pure sorrow that kept me crying for days. There was so much I'd lived through already, and episodes from my past would form a line at night and march through my mind like an army, and I had no weapons anymore to fight them off. So I'd cry and cry, and the next day, I'd go to AA, hoping I'd see the same familiar faces there. And I usually did.

And when I was out, during lonely moments in the city or working at one of the clubs, I could make a phone call. Doc would come any time, any hour. Sometimes I'd be dancing and hear some unkind word from a man at the club, and I'd have a flashback to a fight with Greg. Or I'd see a man that looked like my father, or one of the violent men I'd lived near as a child. Or I'd simply feel a moment of overwhelming exhaustion, like I was carrying a load too heavy to bear, and the only way to put it down was to have a drink. That's when I'd take a break and make a call.

Doc would come, and he'd order me a soda. Then he'd ask the bartender to sell him an empty beer can that he would carry around to fit in with the crowd. He got a few funny looks, but the bartenders soon got to know him. They'd fold a napkin around the can and hand it over to him with a wink, and we'd go to the corner and sit together. He'd hold his empty beer can, I'd let my soda sit there, and I'd just talk. Not that I'd be able to talk straight about my loneliness or sadness, or my fears, or the trouble I had when I was a kid. I'd talk about an argument I had with a cashier, getting stuck in a traffic jam, any stupid little thing that bothered me that day. And he'd listen, he'd nod. He'd tell me how proud he was of me that I wasn't going to let these things get me down. That tomorrow was another new start. Mostly, he'd let me talk, and that was all I really needed. I'd feel better, and if I still wasn't right, I'd end my shift early and he'd drive me home.

Other days, I'd have that feeling first thing when I woke up. Getting out of bed seemed impossible, the prospect of facing another day without chemical enhancement seemed unwise. That's when I'd call up Grace. We'd go shopping, maybe for new clothes for Jeremy. And we'd gossip and tell each other embarrassing secrets and crack each other up. I don't know if we ever talked to each other about the worst of the worst from our past. It wasn't about that. It was just about having a human connection, someone to offer a little warmth and safety. We both knew enough about each other's pasts. There never seemed like a reason to go into it.

That darkness never went away. The only way to fight it was to learn to live with it. I wouldn't always beat it, though.

"Doc, thank God you're home."

"You don't sound so good, hon. You need me to pick you up?"

"Doc, I fucked up. I fucked up real bad. Can I come over? I'm worried about what I might do next."

"Oh, God. Jenn, where are you?"

"I'm just around the corner. I can drive over."

"Aw, hell. No, Jennifer, don't drive, just let me know where you are."

But I'd hung up. I was already on my way. I don't remember much about that morning, other than that I'd let the darkness get to me the night before. It always seemed to happen the same way. I convinced myself I was better, that I'd dried out long enough that now I could have a single drink just like all the people around me seemed able to do. It'd take the edge off and help me make it through one more night, and then I'd start over again the next day. Of course, that's not how it works with alcoholism. One drink was never enough. It took me too long to learn that. I'd come to that morning with the sun high in the sky. Apparently I'd passed out behind the wheel of my car without ever leaving the parking lot. Thank God. Who knows what would have happened if I'd driven in that shape.

But a few hours snooze hadn't brought me close to sober. I'm lucky I made it to Doc's house with no trouble. I'd been there before—Doc had a huge, beautiful house. He was a millionaire, having inherited a fortune from land his family had sold off. He owned a successful construction company, too. He was the classic Dallas success story—buy and build, make it big, don't be afraid to spend. But like so many success stories in that city, there was real pain just under the surface. Like me, he was always a drink away from losing everything.

When Doc opened the door, the first thing I noticed was the smell of whiskey. He'd been drinking, too. Why? I was still too far gone to ask, but it's not hard to guess—the pressure of his business, his past, his family, his own personal darkness. He sighed and invited me in. "Well, if we're both going to slip, we might as well slip together."

"Give me a drink," I said.

He did. "I'm glad you're here, Jenn. This has been a tough couple of days for me, and looks like you've had a couple of hard ones yourself." He looked unfocused, and he sounded sad in a way I'd never heard before. "Listen, I'm going to throw this out. I never did like this whiskey much anyway. You know what I really missed was just a cold beer. I'm going to go to the corner store and buy a six-pack, and we'll split it, and then we'll go the hell to sleep, and when we wake up, we'll go get a couple of steaks. Whaddya say?"

I agreed, and I had him pour me one more shot first. He obliged.

I don't remember anything after he left. The next thing I knew, I was in a hospital bed.

I noticed the gown first, and the cool light on my arms. My mouth was dry, and I had a splitting headache. And something else, too—the top of my head felt numb. I was disoriented and had trouble bringing my hand to my head. I realized the crown of my head was heavily bandaged. *Oh my God*, I thought. *I have no idea what's happening.*

The truth is, it wasn't the first time I'd woken up in the hospital, unsure how I'd got there. It wouldn't be the last, either. But what caused it, I soon learned, was the clearest possible sign to me just how fast it could all slip away.

After Doc had left, I'd apparently gone straight to his desk. I knew he kept a .38 there. He'd shown it to me before—part and parcel of his cowboy gear, I suppose. In fact, he had a whole arsenal in the house, one room over from where we were drinking. I must have known he'd be coming back soon, and had to do it fast. I put the gun to my head and pulled the trigger. Lucky for me, I missed my temple and skimmed the top of my head.

Later, Doc visited me in the hospital and told me what he found. "As soon as I walked back in the door, I smelled the gun smoke." He ran to the room where we'd been drinking, and there he found me, bleeding from my head with his .38 in my hand. "I almost had a heart attack. That sobered me up quicker than anything," he said. When he leaned down to check on me, I'd groaned. There was some blood, but clearly I hadn't succeeded. I'd just grazed myself. The bullet had passed right into his gun room, nearly hitting some ammunition. "You nearly blew up the whole damn house," he told me.

"Why, Doc? Why'd I do it? I just don't remember."

And I can't remember my thoughts—only some of my feelings. I remember the feeling that everything was lost. That I'd made a mistake I couldn't take back, that I'd never be sober, I'd never be happy or make anyone else happy, that I'd lose my son, that I'd never be loved or be allowed to love. I just felt completely empty.

Doc and I talked and talked. We both knew something had to change in my life. I could never allow myself to get to that point of despair again. I never thought myself capable of trying to hurt myself in that way, but I'd drunk enough to reach a place I'd never been before. I couldn't drink like that again. But every night I was at the club I was around temptation. "I want to get out, Doc. I really do. I know I'm not going to be dancing forever, I just don't know what else to do."

"Well, I think we can figure out something."

So within a few weeks, I was starting a new job. A day job. It was with a company called Intrepid Publishing, which was run by someone in our AA group. Intrepid did a lot of business publishing, including neighborhood guides supplied by Real Estate companies. I was going to work sales and advertising with my friend Grace, who'd been with the company for some time (we kept a lot of things in the family in our AA group). Gracie and I would sell advertisement space in our neighborhood guides to local businesses, and I'd sketch out the ads—I was finally using my art skills to make money. In other words, I was suddenly a square, and I was damn happy to be one.

I worked hard at that job. I'd have to cold call businesses all over the county, visit their offices, make a deal. I bought new suits and toned down my look. Still, the work I was doing with Intrepid wasn't *all* that different than what I was doing at the club. The ads might have been the product, but I was still selling myself. I think I knew that from the start, and that's why I did well. Those owners of car washes and copy shops didn't care all that much about a $4,000 ad in a local insert. They cared that a pretty woman was asking them for their time and making them feel important. Yes, there was much more to the job than just turning on the charm, but I was damn good at that as well. Sure, the suit was uncomfortable—I never got used to wearing that—but I put long hours into that job, knowing it might be a shot at survival.

I made about $2,500 dollars a month. Not bad, but not good. It was enough to pay rent on the townhouse where I was living, support Jeremy (my child support payments had been lowered significantly) and pay the bills, but not much else. So I was still dancing a few times a month for a little extra cash. I was doing well with it—since I was no longer dependent on the clubs just to live, I didn't feel near as much anxiety when I was there, and far less temptation to go sit at the bar afterward.

Then one night I was working at Satyricon. This was the club with all the old Roman columns and white silk, the place that looked like a coliseum with naked ladies instead of gladiators. For whatever reason, many of the other girls at the club had experience as porn stars or pin-ups, and it was a well known venue for what might be called talent scouts. I'd been approached by men asking to take my photo before, but I'd learned enough already to ignore anyone that didn't come with references.

One night, one of the girls introduced me to a man named Michael. He seemed all right, and I let him chat me up a little. Then he told me who he was. The editor of a magazine called *Hustler*. Had I ever heard of it? He handed me his card. I couldn't believe it.

I'd spent the last few months trying to break away from this world, and here was the devil himself, inviting me back in. Well, I've gotta confess, I've always had a soft spot in my heart for Larry Flynt. Like me, he grew up in a rough family in the brutally repressed small towns around Ohio. He did whatever he could to break free from all that, and he knew his freedom could make him a dime, too. His Hustler clubs started in Ohio towns like Akron and Columbus, and even though they'd mostly been driven out of business by state government by the time I started dancing, they were legendary among the club owners and older dancers. Most of all, Larry had been a survivor, and he didn't let anyone tell him what to do or how to do it.

His editor, Michael, told me he was impressed. He invited me out for a shoot in LA. He said I might even make the cover, that Larry would love me. I debated whether or not to say yes for about three seconds. Of course I'd go. I'd make a load of money, scratch that itch for fame I'd had since I was a kid, and, speaking of childhood dreams, I'd get to go to Hollywood.

Well, the day came, and I'm not going to lie. I had a blast. I met Larry Flynt first in the elevator of the huge building on Wilshire Boulevard. He was in a gold-plated wheelchair, decked out in a loud, lime-green suit. He introduced himself by complimenting my tits, then he shook my hand. I laughed. Of course, if it was some guy on the street saying the same thing, I would have ignored him, or even feared for my safety. But there was no malice in what he was saying. It was his shtick—he refused to pretend that he wasn't thinking about sex most of the time, and he wasn't going to apologize for it. He was just cheeky.

We did the shoot, and while I didn't end up making cover, I had, shall we say, a prominent role cued up for an issue due out the next spring. I made a few grand too, and went home smiling. I had to admit, that wasn't how I saw myself conquering Hollywood when I was a little girl, but hey, even my idol Marilyn got her start taking it all off in front of a camera. For the first time in a long time, I felt like I'd won.

I carried that back home with me. I still worked for Intrepid, and when I got back, we were in the thick of a serious sales competition. Highest total ad sales would win a trip to Mexico. I had a little burst of confidence from my recent shoot, and I dominated that competition. I was the hustler, dammit. And I won.

Unfortunately, Greg caught wind of my photo shoot. He needed to punish me somehow. Through Chuck and Ellen, he also knew about my coming trip to Mexico. I had to tell them that I'd be unavailable for my regular weekend with Jeremy. Two weeks before I was supposed to leave, I got a call from my lawyer. Greg had filed a petition claiming that I was a risk to flee the country with Jeremy and asking that I be barred from leaving the state of Texas. The petition was ridiculous—I wasn't taking Jeremy with me on my award business trip. Still, after talking to my attorneys about places the petition could lead, they decided it was best that I stay around to address questions from the court. So, I canceled my trip. Of course there were no charges and Greg's petition was thrown out, but he didn't mind. He'd got what he wanted, which was finding another way to make me miserable.

Still, I had more important things to look forward to. My issue of *Hustler* came out that spring, and I was giddy. I'd lie awake and laugh, thinking of the scandal it'd cause back home. I wished I had my old high school friends near, since I knew they'd find the whole thing to be hilarious. The issue came out, and Michael sent me over a dozen copies. I didn't know who to celebrate with—I wasn't about to pass naked pictures of myself around AA (talk about giving up on the "anonymous" part), and I didn't want to party with the girls from the club, either.

I ended up finding a bar after a long day at work and decided to have a drink. It'd been nearly a year since the episode at Doc's house. I told myself I was different now—then I was drinking out of pain, but now I was actually happy. It was just a little reward. I had confidence now, so I'd be able to handle it.

Well, after that one shot I left the bar. Then I happened to drive past another one that I remembered I liked even more. So I stopped there and had another drink. Then from there, I found an old Irish bar, the kind of place I used to go to train my liver way back in Ohio. There, I got totally shitfaced. I didn't even make it out of the bar's parking lot. As soon as I started my car and swerved back out of my spot, I heard the sirens. The cops busted me right there, feet from the scene of the crime. I spent the night in Dallas County jail, and my car went to the impound lot. My first DUI.

I had work the next day. I retrieved my car and showed up late to work with the same suit on from the day before. As soon as I walked in, everyone looked up. I could see in the eyes of my boss and the other people I worked with that there was no point making up some dumb excuse. They knew what had happened and they could probably still smell the alcohol from the night before. They could see it written on my face. Some of them had been there before. My boss called me into his office and I cried, begging to keep my job. He said he wasn't about to give up on me, and that I shouldn't give up on myself, either.

I promised I wouldn't, and could only hope that was true.

Orin

Boston

Danger / not respectful / Never see again / do not recommend

Ouch! Oh my god, is he biting? Yes, he's biting.

We all have our baggage we bring to the bedroom. My job is to understand my client's issues while concealing my own. It usually works, more or less. Most of the clients I work with know the boundaries as well as I do. They've been vetted. And some of them are nearly as experienced with the business as I am, only on the paying side. But sometimes something dangerous slips out, even among the vets.

My nipple is aching, my skin is crawling. I can do sadism, but that's something where you've gotta discuss the rules ahead of time.

I gently push Orin up off of me. I want to look him in the eye and distract him in some way so he leaves my bleeding areola alone. But the look in his eye is practically primeval. He's not there behind the eyes, and he goes in for the other nipple like a Rottweiler after a steak bone.

I cringe and cover myself. "Okay, now you're hurting me." I know when to cut off the pretense to protect myself.

The light comes back in Orin's eyes and he looks like a little boy who's skinned his knee and doesn't know whether crying will help or not.

"I'm sorry, I didn't realize it was hurting. Lets try something else."

I agree. I flip around and he starts in from behind, and soon I feel a hand tightly gripping my shoulder, and then his mouth on my other shoulder. Ouch! Holy shit, he's biting again. I leap up. "You're hurting me again." Again, he apologizes. Jesus, isn't this guy a dentist? Does he have some kind of dental fixation? This is worse than the gynecologist

177

who wanted to spend hours with his face buried in a muff. Don't these pros get enough of this at work? I think of Little Shop of Horrors. The guy with the choppers even looks kind of like a twisted, nervous Steve Martin. I wonder if he shot puppies and poisoned kittens as a kid. Maybe he just had a knack for inflicting pain.

I find a way to end the session as quickly as possible. Usually I like to figure out how to give men what they want, but this time I have to bring business to a close and exit gracefully.

After our session is over, I go to the bathroom to clean up and take a look at the damage. I still have visible bite marks as well as welts all over my body from where he grabbed me. I don't waste any time writing a post of warning on the ladies' board of our popular underground website. What else can I do? Part of the career of a call girl and this is just an occupational hazard. Sometimes behavior like that can be a red flag for greater danger, and the website is designed to protect the escort as well as the john.

I take a walk and think about my client. What was there in his past that made him act so anxiously, that made him get off by causing pain? I couldn't figure him out, and that troubled me, since figuring out my clients was how I felt most safe. I'd be fine, but it was one more bad experience to carry with me. Next time I went in for a routine cleaning, I'm sure I'd flinch as soon as my dentist came into the room. And I'd probably avoid the gas if he recommended it.

Chapter 13

FINISH WHAT YOU STARTED

"Mommy, what did they mean you're an umbrella?"

"They were just teasing me, Jeremy. They were being mean. You forget about them."

I was with my son inside Chicago O'Hare Airport, and I was trying my hardest to keep from crying.

"But how can you be an umbrella? That's something silly, right mommy?"

It was 1994. There'd been a group of four men drinking in the back of a bar I stopped in to smoke a cigarette during the layover due to the weather. They'd noticed me.

I had a layover there from Dallas with Jeremy. We had a flight back to Ohio, for my grandfather's funeral. I was already a mess of feelings—for my lost grandpa, one of the few family members who had always been kind. For the anxiety that always crept up when I was set to see my parents. For the return to Canal Bottom, a town I'd left to make something of myself. Well, this is what I'd made of myself—I was a woman who danced on stage for money. I was an advertising associate. I was a young woman struggling still with addiction to alcohol and drugs. I was a divorcée. And I was the mother of a bright, curious boy. One who couldn't ignore something he overheard.

"Oh, look at those puppies," one had said as they approached me.

"Those aren't puppies, man! Those are full-grown St. Bernards."

They laughed, staring at my chest. They blocked my way in.

"Why the hurry, you late for your flight?"

One man leaned in real close to Jeremy. "Excuse me, little guy. Would you mind if we borrowed your mother for a moment? It's raining real hard and she'd make a great umbrella."

They all cracked up. "Yeah, give us shelter! Me first!" another laughed.

I covered myself with my jacket and pushed through the wall of thick bodies and knock-off Cowboys jerseys as the men laughed more. I was upset, and so was Jeremy, and he wouldn't let the moment go, even on the flight up north.

And how was I going to explain? How was I going to tell Jeremy who his mother was, the choices she made and why she made them, the troubles she struggled with? He was old enough now to ask questions. I didn't know if I was old enough yet to answer them.

By the age of twenty-four, I was already living a double life. Victoria McCormick owned the night in Dallas. After my photo shoot in *Hustler* was published, Victoria had become a local celebrity. I was in demand. At the clubs like the Royale, Red Room, and Satyircon, I was available for dances only by special request, and nearly all the gentlemen who I danced for were high rollers. There were the oilmen and the software guys, the sports stars, the glam rockers and country stars, the game show hosts and newscasters, comedians and politicians. I was so popular that I'd also get invites to other clubs around Texas. I was on the marquee! Okay, it wasn't exactly my childhood dream to see my stage name in lights at Ecstasy Ranch outside Lubbock, but the important thing was that I

180

was *wanted.*

I got used to being wined and dined in the best restaurants in Dallas, and showered with gifts like jewelry and clothes. This was Dallas, and in Dallas, after dark, being the city's tastiest arm candy was pretty high status. I had a long relationship with a leader on the Cowboys football team, and I really felt like I'd made it to the top of the crop in Dallas.

There were days I thought I had it all. I was still working part time in advertising. I loved feeling like I could do a good job there. I was seeing Jeremy on weekends, and he'd stay with me for weeks over the summer. And I had the nightlife, too, moving my way up toward what seemed like fame and fortune. Everything seemed possible. There was nothing I couldn't handle. A few drinks out on the town—why not? I had the money to take a cab, or even driven home by my date's driver. I had a few bad nights, but then I'd get sober again, and I wasn't running into any real trouble. I even kept going to AA, though I wasn't being open about the big nights I'd sometimes have.

I'd been through enough to know the dangers, and I was still young enough to look for more. I could be a nice Dallas mom on the edge of the burbs during the day, and at night I could pursue and live the big life I always knew was meant for me. But there were those moments, like the moment at the airport, where my two lives weren't going to fit together. These were two pieces from very different puzzles I was trying to force into place. How was I going to explain to my four-year-old son why those men were teasing his mom? And there I was on my way home to celebrate my grandfather's life, and I could already imagine my second cousins and great aunts pointing and whispering—*What happened to little Jenny's body? She didn't look like that the last time I saw her. I heard she was in a pornographic magazine . . . Oh, and she was always such a good girl.* I could never explain my life to them, and I didn't want to nor did I have to. Where were they when I needed a family?

I spent the trip saying as little as possible and wearing unseasonable, baggy clothes. I let my spitfire son do most of the talking while I cried for my grandfather, who I hadn't seen in years.

When we returned to Dallas, I went to my plastic surgeon and made an appointment to have em taken out. I was grateful to the ol' silicone bags for all they'd done for me. But they only really made sense for one part of my life. I owned the night, but I wasn't respected enough during the day—by family, by coworkers, by attorneys. Like that time at court when my lawyer had me wear a wig, I couldn't really hide the fact that I'd become more Victoria McCormick than not. I didn't want to bury Victoria with the silicone sacks, I just wanted to have a little more balance.

My surgeon was disappointed. "Ah," he said. "Look at this work. Perfect contour. No wrinkling around the skin envelope. No contracture. These could go another decade and still look perfect." He sighed. "I'll do it, but you know this is like asking Leonardo da Vinci to tear up the Mona Lisa. These are a masterpiece."

I thanked him and signed the paperwork to go through with it anyway. It set me back 10 grand and a few weeks recovery time, but I wasn't too sad. I wasn't going to lose too much work (other than as a human umbrella), and I was happy to live life more as Jennifer instead of Victoria.

When I got back to the club, I was working the VIP room less.

Newer, younger girls were coming in. Some with augmentation that rivaled my own previous Da Vinci work, and suddenly I was the grizzled vet at twenty-four. I was a year or two away from being a house mother, dabbing on pasty glue and breaking up cat fights. I was shocked how fast all that was happening, and I knew I had to find something else fast that would build on my success. I was talking to another girl around my age, and she was going through the same thing. How long could she keep up with this work before her career went over the cliff? How long could she face all the temptations of this world and survive? But she had ideas, and she had connections. "Listen, have you ever been in a music video? I used to know this guy from dancing back in Houston, and he wants me to come out to shoot a Van Halen video for a concert tour. Wanna come along?" I was floored. Van Halen? I thought of my old friend who was buried in his Van Halen tour shirt, and I knew I had to go. It would be like another life goal checked off my bucket list.

In the meantime, I met a man while dancing named Paulie, and he let me check another item of the list—to live in real Dallas-style luxury. Paulie ran a software security company, and he'd made it big in the mid-90s computer boom. He had a sprawling new house, a fleet of cars, and a wallet full of Platinum cards. I think he saw me as one of his prize trophies, and he'd usually introduce me to his friends by my stage name instead of my real name. He wasn't a bad guy, though, and was real sweet to Jeremy, even if he spoiled him just as rotten as he spoiled me. Paulie convinced me to give up my day job, and after a few weeks of living in his place, he wanted me to give up my night job as well. In his mind, he was purchasing exclusive access with all his gifts and free rent.

That set off some alarms.

I was enjoying living with a man that didn't threaten me, that treated me like a goddess. But a goddess locked up at home is still a slave. We got along fine unless I went out without telling him where I was going, what I was up to. Then he'd get jealous, and we'd fight. But what was I going to do? I wasn't born the sort of person that could stay home and eat bonbons and watch *Days of Our Lives* while the maid vacuumed upstairs. I'd always worked. I'd always had to take care of myself, and I wasn't going to give that up. So I still took some shifts out at the club. That made Paulie crazy.

"I give you everything! I'd understand it if you had to do it for money, but you don't. So what, you like showing off your tits to hundreds of strangers? Sometimes I don't know about you."

"It's not about that. You knew when you asked me out that I wasn't going to be a housewife."

We worked out a truce and I kept my dancing to a night or two a week. Hey, I had to get out of the house somehow. And for my own wellbeing, I stuck to dancing at the Royale, which had a pretty strict no drugs policy (back at Red Room, girls would be doing lines off the bar—not a great environment for me anymore). But while Paulie was away, sometimes I would drink, waiting for something to happen in my life. Every time, I'd tell myself it was the last time. Other days I'd be happy, spending time with Jeremy, showing him a life he'd never see with his father. Eventually, I found the kind of balance I was looking for. One night, Paulie came home with a present—an enormous rock, almost too heavy for the thin gold ring that held it in place. I was floored, and despite memories of my first marriage, I took it. He didn't get down on his knee or anything. That wasn't his style. But the message was clear. I was his now.

Soon after, Paulie made a big software sale and wanted to celebrate with a trip to Vegas. It was my first time out there. We flew out first class and stayed in a lavish hotel, and took advantage of all the pleasures Sin City had to offer. Paulie wanted to show me a good time, but he wanted to be the one in charge. If he was gambling, I was supposed to be sitting by his side, blowing on his lucky dice or whatever. When he was ready to go back to the hotel room, I was supposed to hop right up and follow. Pretty soon I got sick of the arrangement and made my way to the VIP bar. After an hour or so, after a couple of drinks and a few laughs with the bartender and the couple sitting next to me, I felt a hand on my shoulder. I looked up, and there was Paulie, face as red as a slot-machine cherry.

"Are you trying to make a fool of me? Let's go," he snarled. He threw a twenty onto the bar, and then pulled me out into the lobby.

"You think I brought you here so you could ignore me and flirt at the bar? Why are you drinking, anyway?"

"I'm your girlfriend, not your daughter, and I don't need a curfew," I said.

Somehow, he got even redder.

"Fine. Have it your way. Do whatever you want. I'm leaving." And with that, he marched off. I muttered under my breath and went back to the bar, where I finished one last drink before deciding to call it a night. I thought I'd go up to the room and patch things up, but when I got there, Paulie was gone. So was his stuff. I ran to the lobby, where the girl at the desk told me Paulie had just checked out and said he had to catch a flight. I couldn't believe it. I had hardly any money on me at all, and I couldn't afford another night by myself. I had to have a friend wire me cash so I could stay down the drive at a cheaper hotel for a night until I could get my own plane ticket switched. The day I got back to Dallas, I moved my stuff out. Paulie and I were finished. I wasn't going to make the same mistake I made with my first husband—even if Paulie wasn't physically abusive, I didn't think he'd ever see me as anything other than a trophy. If he couldn't take me as I was, we had no business together.

We had a few blow-up fights on the phone. He couldn't believe I could just walk away. For me, it was a pleasure just to show him I didn't need his stuff to be happy. I even resolved to re-commit to AA, give up drinking completely, and be the best version of myself I could be.

And I was, for a little while.

One night I was dancing at the Royale, and my friend with the Van Halen connection came up to me after I finished on stage. "Hey, he's here," she said.

"Who?"

"Him. The guy that's Van Halen's manager. He was watching you tonight, and he wants you for the shoot down in Houston. Whatcha doin' this weekend?" She gave me a big, mischievous grin. "You wanna go have some fun?"

I was introduced to the Van Halen rep, a guy with a face aged ahead of its time by too much fun, but with a smile that showed he was ready for even more. God, a part of me was a little jealous of that. The manager invited me to the fanciest hotel in downtown Dallas for lunch the next day, and there we hit it off—joking and flirting, though nothing happened. He asked me if I wanted to meet the band. They were staying at the hotel, and if I came by the next day at 8 a.m., I could say hi. I realized it was a kind of test, and so I showed up on time and tried not to freak out. There was Alex and Eddie and Sammy and Michael, all as pleasant as could be. I *wanted* to freak out, but I kept my cool. Afterward, the manager told me when to show up at the airport the next day for my flight out. I was booked.

The next day was a Saturday, and I had a birthday party at a McDonald's to go to for Jeremy's friend before I lived out my wildest dreams. After making an appearance, I was going to drive Jeremy to Chuck and Ellen's and head to the airport from there. Well, Jeremy was on his own schedule, and I didn't trust that far away look in his eyes. After an hour of romping around in the ball pit and slides, I told Jeremy he could make one last trip through the plastic tubes before we had to go. He was determined to make the trip count, and he scrambled up to a spot well above my head, smiled wide from a big, Lucite bubble, and stuck his tongue out. "Come and get me!"

I couldn't believe it. "Jeremy, you get down here right now, or I'm going to tan your hide!" He knew I'd never do anything of the sort, and he just laughed. I had an hour to drop him off and get to the airport, and time was running out on my dream.

I crawled in after him. I got stuck. I started to cry. There I was, dressed in one of my foxiest dresses, hair done, makeup done, ready to win over a group of rock legends, and I was stuck in a purple plastic tube surrounded by "food, folks, and fun." Once again, I was trying to force together two pieces from different puzzles. By the time I got out with Jeremy in tow, I was already late. I called the manager weeping to tell him I'd miss my flight. He just laughed. He had kids too, and he said he could get my flight switched to one an hour later, but I'd still have to hurry to make the flight. I booked it.

By the time I got into the cabin of the plane, my nerves were shot, and I very much intended to use a free drink voucher I'd been given as part of the flight. I sat down in my seat, closed my eyes, and breathed in and out, slowly.

"Long day already?" It was a familiar voice. I looked up to find one of the vets from my chapter of AA had been assigned the seat next to me. *Well, I guess I better crumple up the drink voucher*, I thought. *God: you have a sick sense of humor.*

I made it in an hour to Houston, where my friend from the Royale picked me up. She cracked up while I desperately tried to fix my makeup. Our assignment was to go shopping for sexy lingerie and then head over to the Astrodome, where the concert and video shoot were taking place. We picked up some things, and we had both packed our T-backs and some skimpy bras. We made it to the Astrodome on time and were taken through a series of corridors where we met the manager, who gave us all access passes. As I was putting the lanyard around my neck, I looked up and realized I was standing in front of Bret Michaels. He made eye contact with me, and he looked like a god. I had to stop myself from squealing like a little girl. Then a man to my left began introducing himself, "Oh, do you know me yet?" he said in a joking Irish brogue. It was the Edge. Eddie and Alex were there, and they nodded to me as well. I was the eye in a storm of hot rock superstars. I almost fainted.

Next, my friend and I went to a small room that was set up with a green screen, and we were asked to dance as we would at the Royale. We did our best, though it was awkward in a cold, concrete room with nothing behind us but a green, glowing curtain. Next we went to the greenroom and hung out with the stars who'd come together for the concert. There was food, top shelf booze, and lots of people having a good time, but I was too nervous to really join in. I ended up talking to Alex van Halen himself, who confided in me that he'd been clean and sober himself for six years, and Eddie had been sober for almost a year. It was a short talk, but it was like meeting an oracle. After that, they wheeled in a TV and everyone watched me and my friend dance. "Nice ass on her," one of the guys said about me. Some of the others nodded. I was on cloud nine.

We watched the concert from the sound booth far from the stage, and I stood near Bret Michaels, trying not to pass out. Here was a guy who grew up down the road from me in the backwoods of Pennsylvania, and he'd transformed himself into a prince. If he could do it, why not me? Then Sammy Hagar started tearing into the song "Finish What You Started," and there on the Jumbotron above the stage my ass and sweep of red hair appeared, swaying with the music. It was me, but big as the Statue of Liberty. The crowd roared, and the guys next to me busted up laughing at the look on my face.

After the concert, we went to the after party, and someone handed me Sammy's sweaty shirt as a memento. I was floating. I had a few drinks, then a few more. My life back home seemed so distant. Here I was Victoria McCormick, and it seemed like all that was important, everything that mattered, was having a good time and having men worship me. I drank so much, my friend from the Royale had to pull me aside. "Don't overdo it, hon. You might blow your chance for something bigger."

That's when I got word that the manager wanted to see me in his suite. Sure. Why not. I was escorted up, and he was waiting for me there with a mirror and the biggest pile of coke I'd ever seen. "You ever done this before, hon?"

"Well, once or twice," I said.

I took a bump. Then we fucked. That went on the whole night. *I've finally made it*, I thought. *I'm who I was always meant to be.*

It's hard to believe, but I really thought I was headed up, not down. But I was on the cliff. I was about to fall, and fall in a way I'd never fallen before.

Mr. Baseball

Dallas, Texas

Absolute discretion a must / public reputation / great to be with in private

I'm in a limo outside the Four Seasons, waiting for my cue to enter the hotel to meet "Neil."

He'd called from one of my ads on the internet and booked with my assistant. He claimed his name was Neil. My assistant said he wouldn't give enough information to run a background check, but wanted to see me for an overnight appointment. Well, "Neil," that's not how this works.

I took it upon myself to contact him personally, and he explained that he was in from out of town and had to be very discreet. He said he was a businessman that was prominent and well recognized in his field. I told him that I dealt with gentlemen such as himself quite often (whoever he was). I then asked him where he was staying since he wanted me to come to him. When he told me he was staying at the Four Seasons in Las Colinas, I knew he wasn't law enforcement, and I knew that he had to be affluent, because you can't just walk in to that hotel. There was a security booth to even get in the parking lot, and unless you had a parking pass, you had to give the name of the guest and their room number and they would call them. With him, I had to have a code word to get to the guest that had made the request. "So, what's your code word?" I asked. "Money Bags," he said. What a pompous jerk!

Here at the gates of the Four Seasons, the security guard makes the call, and I get confirmed. I enter. I take the elevator up to the assigned floor. I haven't been told what room number he's in. I'm supposed to walk up and down the hall until he deems the coast clear, and then he'll open the door and say my name as I pass. Normally I'd NEVER do this for anyone. This isn't normal procedure. But I can tell this is a special client.

As I pass down the hall, my heels practically sticking in the quicksand carpeting, a door to my right opens, my name is spoken, and a large hand reaches out to stop me. "Victoria, in here."

The man is young, muscular. He's wearing jeans and a nice shirt. He has a nice haircut, but he's drinking out of a McDonald's cup through a straw. It smells like it could be a rum and coke in there. "So, do you recognize me?" he asks.

"No," I answer, honestly. "I'm guessing a baseball player, though." It was summer, he was an athlete. I knew something about these guys. He wasn't my first, but he was the most mysterious so far. He just smiles, and tells me his real name. I've . . . never heard of him. I might know half the roster of the Rangers for professional reasons, but out of town ball players are kind of hit and miss. "Oh, of course!" I say. "I'm a big baseball fan, but I didn't recognize you without your gear. You're even better looking than you are on TV!"

It works. He comes over and guides me up against the wall and starts kissing me. He's handsome in a weathered, rough around the edges sort of way. But he's a smooth kisser. I can feel that he's already hard. He wants me. A lot. And that turns me on. I think of all the women he could have chosen from the internet. He chose me. He must have been with hundreds of women, at least. And he chose me. I feel an electric charge through my whole body, and I'm eager to get his cock in my hands, then my mouth, then my pussy. We move to the bed, and begin having some of the most explosive sex I've ever had. We fuck for two hours, and as strong and rough-edged as he is, he knows just where to kiss, stroke, and tease to make me go crazy.

The next day, I Google him. I know the best policy is to know only what I need to know about my clients, and to push them out of mind as soon as our session is over. But every once in a while, there's one I do want to remember. One I never want to forget. I order his jersey online. I've had clients try to steal my underwear or take something from the hotel where we met as a trophy, something to remember the experience. It always makes me roll my eyes. But I've gotta admit, sometimes I want trophies, too.

Chapter 14

HOTEL CALIFORNIA

My arms and legs were burning, my skin was icy, rough, and itchy. My hands shook. My lungs ached. I could barely make out where I was. The room was dim, with peeling paint on the walls and almost no furniture. There was an awful smell, and a filthy gray blanket wrapped around my legs. Light came in through a big, open window right into my eyes. I couldn't see, but I could remember a little. I felt my upper lip with my tongue. It was split and blistered at the corner, sore and stiff. *Oh no,* I thought. *Shit. What have I done?* I 'd been awake for nine days—the longest I'd ever been without sleep. I was hallucinating, and I needed more.

I looked down at my bare forearms, where there were red pricks that sat in the middle of large black welts, the size of a quarter. My skin crawled, and my mouth was dry. I couldn't speak. I steadied myself enough to start to stand and almost passed out. Across from me an enormous man slouched against a wall, snoring. I had no idea who he was. I had to leave, immediately.

I was dizzy and shaking, but I pulled myself through the open door of the room. I was on the second floor of a rotting house, and I could hear voices speak softly to each other in a nearby room. I guided myself down a creaky flight of stairs, holding myself up with a banister covered in peeling gray paint. A feeling of needing to puke came over me, but knew I didn't want to make a sound. *Who else is here? Who is in this house with me?* Paranoia had set in from lack of sleep and I needed more coke. I needed it any way-I would do anything for more of it. Powder or rock; my body ached for it.

I found the front door in near darkness and stepped out into the blinding light. My temples pounded. I squinted, trying to figure out where I was. I could remember so little. *Where's John?* I thought. Across the street, three men with jeans sagging way too low and huge white T-shirts were watching me. What had I done for dope? Had I fucked one of them? My paranoia overwhelmed me. One of them said something and the others started laughing, almost doubling over. I had to keep moving. *Where's John?* I thought. *Where's John, where's John, where's John?*

John was a man in my AA group. I wouldn't exactly call him a sponsor. He was different than so many of the others that showed up to the meetings. He had dark hair, wore dark clothes, was rail thin and quiet. He was no cowboy. He could be hilarious, telling funny stories of his life back east and some of the scrapes he'd gotten into. And if his stories were to be believed, he was a guy that had seen more dark times and gotten into more trouble than all of the rest of us combined. But he had an amazing ability to laugh at all of it. Also, if his stories were to be believed, he had an almost inhuman tolerance for drugs of all sorts, and his stories often revolved around the pursuit of massive amounts of coke, crack, heroin, and other assorted goodies. This guy was basically Robert Downey, Jr. caught in conservative Dallas, trying his best to stay clean and stick to a life that was obviously way too slow for him.

Slow wasn't really a long-term strategy for John.

After I returned from my wild party at the Van Halen concert, I was yearning for more. It's a testament to the power of addiction that I didn't even think what I wanted was drugs or alcohol. I just wanted that incredible feeling of being the center of attention again, in the middle of a kind of excitement that seemed so distant from everything I knew growing up. This yearning has always been with me, and when I was young, I didn't recognize it as anything unusual. *Doesn't everyone want to be rich and famous? Doesn't everyone want to be where the action is?* For me, that feeling has always been closely tied to addiction, so much that for me to dream big is really a sign of risk. Looking up to the stars often means I'm close to a fall, I've learned.

At my first AA meeting after the concert, I noticed John was missing. I asked a friend about him and she said, "Well, he hasn't shown up for a few days. He's not returning calls, either. We're a little worried he's fallen off pretty hard."

"Oh no," I said. "Maybe I'll try giving him a call."

"It's worth a try, dear. I think he might pick up the phone for you."

He did. But I made it clear I wasn't interested in getting him to come back to the meeting rooms. I wanted to go wherever he was going instead. We spoke on the phone. "You're sure you want to meet up, Jenn?" He asked. "I'm not your sponsor and I'm not your daddy, so it's up to you." He warned me that even if I'd been around a little, I was probably going places with him I'd never been before.

And that's what happened. The next few months were lost. John introduced me to a wilder crowd than I'd known—and that included a lot of Dallas drug dealers and junkies. I wanted coke, I wanted booze, but I was using alongside people that were facing oblivion with a laugh, trying to find the prettiest way to kill themselves.

John introduced me to crack. I watched the pipe as the swirl of the smoke made me a slave to the feeling I was going to get. I was as addicted to the preparation of it and the ritual of it as smoking it itself. Crack is a demon of its own. I believe the phrase "once you do crack you never go back'" is true enough. Smoking crack offered all of maybe a two-minute high, but it was as high as I had ever been before. I needed more and more. More was never enough.

John could go anywhere in the city and score, and he was used to sampling local delicacies. He was like the best local tour guide in the city, if you were into hard drugs. I tried crack in a nasty corner of Dallas, but everything seemed beautiful after my first hit. I didn't know where I was for hours, though the next day I was embarrassed to see a blister on my upper lip from the hot pipe. I was working nearly every day now to support my binge, and I knew it was a bad look for the stage.

So I went back to powder for a week or two before John introduced me to mainlining. "Listen darling, this is the way I prefer it when I can afford it. Just make sure to use a clean needle, and there's nothing else that compares. You'll feel the best high you have ever felt in your life."

I'd never put a needle in my arm before, but I was on such an extended high, nothing was slowing me down. The thing about coke is, it made me feel invincible. It made me feel fearless. All those hounds nipping at my heels—fear, depression, shame, regret, anger, nightmares—they all fell away when I was using. And when I'd start to come down, all those hounds would catch up again. But when I put a needle in my arm, it was instant. Slamming it for the first time gave me the warmest feeling throughout my body that I had ever felt. It was almost like I had arms around me holding me. I almost felt like I was loved and everything was okay. That warm feeling gave a jolt to my body unlike any I had ever felt. With that first hit, I had an orgasm! Never had anything made me feel that good before. I felt it and I could taste it. What had I been missing? I'd been chasing that high since the first time I put a straw up my nose.

But like other times I'd fallen off the wagon, I convinced myself that what I was doing was gonna end real soon. After the *Hustler* shoot and the Van Halen video, I thought my time had arrived. I just needed this boost to meet people, to stay on top of things, to be my best self and keep self-doubt at bay. I had professional head shots done up and met up with a sleazy agent that built a phony acting resumé for me, claiming I was an extra or had a small role in movies shot in the Dallas area like *Born on the Fourth of July* and *JFK*. I stayed in contact with the manager from Van Halen, hoping to score a role in a real video. And I took calls from *Hustler* too, making sure I was around for a possible photo shoot coming up in the next year. Success was so close; I could taste it. And once I had that, I could have anything else I wanted in life—security, freedom from my past, romance, adventure. I'd be able to do anything. I'd cleaned up when my life had taken a turn for the better before. I told myself I'd do so again, once I'd made it where I wanted to be.

Of course, there was Jeremy. I hid from him at first. I told my ex that I had some work out of town. I did, sometimes. I'd go work at clubs in other parts of Texas. But it wasn't an excuse I could use forever. One day, I cleaned myself up a little, took a quick bump, and went over to Greg's house just to drop in on Jeremy and tell him I missed him, that I'd see him soon, but I had to work really hard and wouldn't be able to call for a couple of weeks. It was a weekend; a time I'd normally pick him up anyway. I pulled up to the vinyl ranch where Greg was living and rang the doorbell. A woman answered. It was Gina, Jeremy's Kindergarten teacher. She let me in like it was the most natural thing in the world. She offered me tea.

"Greg's not here, but I'm sure it's fine if you want to say hi."

Jeremy was in the kitchen, playing with Gina's daughter, who is a chubby little Dallas blonde that Gina entered into five-and-under beauty contests. I played with Jeremy for a few minutes while Gina hovered overhead. Then I turned to leave, using all my power of restraint to keep myself from choking this woman who had snuck into the role of my child's new mother.

"Well, Gina," I said. "Hey, you make a nice family. Don't let me stand in your way." I stormed out and slammed the door.

I was furious, but I was in no shape to be a mother myself. I was starting to realize it, too.

Five days later, I found myself in that crack house, in that war zone of a neighborhood. After I found my way out of the house, I wandered around unknown streets, head and body aching. There was something wrong with me, something beyond just coming down after a long bender. I hurt like I never had before. With the summer sun beating down on me I found my way to a major road, and recognized where I was. *I need to get home*, I thought. That's the first step. *Just go home. Go home. Go home.* Already, though, there was another voice in the back of my head telling me to find John again. He'd have something for me. He'd help me feel better.

Lucky for me, on that particular day, my better angels won out. I went home. But the voices didn't stop. A part of me was aching to go out, to find John, to feel good again. But I knew I was sick, in a way coke wouldn't fix. The better angel kept talking, too, and it kept saying the same thing. *Go home. Go home. Go home.*

I did something next that surprised me. I called my parents.

"Hello?"

"Hi, mom? It's me, Jenny…"

"What is it? Is something wrong?" She wasn't used to hearing from me, other than for birthdays or holidays.

"Mom, I think I need to come home for a while."

I didn't know what I was saying. I had no plan. I just knew I had to leave where I was, what I was, who I was. Ohio was the only other home I'd ever known, as broken as it was.

I spent the next few days alone, in a dark room, trying to fight the cravings of coke. I was in agony. It wasn't just the addiction; I could tell something else was wrong. So after I was feeling strong enough, I went to the doctor. He ran some tests and told me he was worried about my liver. I thought hepatitis. All the needles I'd stuck in my arm. All the near-dead I'd been hanging out with the past couple of months. But it wasn't that, exactly. I was in liver failure. My liver was as banged up as the rest of my life, and the doctor told me if I didn't seek help and stop drinking and whatever else I was doing, I wouldn't have long.

For a moment, I gave in to the idea. *Good,* I thought. *I'm ready. There's nothing left for me here.* I had no love in my life. My "agent" had stopped returning my calls. My biggest claim to fame was being in a nudie mag, and my best asset was my body, which was giving up on me. I couldn't even dance for many more years, I knew that. There were already girls younger than me getting the big tips. I was starting to become second tier, even at the clubs where I used to rule, like the Red Room. I'd disappointed all my friends—I couldn't face AA anymore. And now I was facing painful illness, addiction, and the prospect of admitting defeat and heading home. Most painful of all, my baby had slipped out of my life again, and I'd allowed it to happen. *Maybe it would be best for everyone if I just disappeared*, I thought.

But even if that's what I wanted, I didn't want to just self-destruct. I'd be proving everyone right about me if I just went out and OD'd. I could see the look on Greg's face at that moment when he heard about me found dead in a crack house somewhere. He'd probably laugh.

Instead, I called and made plans with my parents. My dad and brother would come to Texas and help me move back to Canal Bottom. I'd find work in Akron, and I'd go to AA again, and I would make myself better. I'd do it for Jeremy. I'd find a way to be the mother for him I wanted to be. *Who am I kidding*, I thought. *I've already wrecked it all.*

I spent my twenty-sixth birthday alone.

The next night, I had a shift at the Red Room. I wasn't sure what was going to happen in my life, but I knew this part of it was ending soon. I just couldn't do it anymore. I couldn't pretend. But I needed money, as always, and I was focused.

That night I spotted a man right away near the stage. He was cute in a geeky kind of way. Balding, with glasses and a pair of Levi's on that were rolled up at the ankles. I made eye contact and he gave me a big, warm smile, maybe even blushing a little. I noticed he had a nice watch. I was a predator.

I left the stage and went over to his table. I had him pegged as a software guy. They were the best. Happy for the attention, loaded, willing to spend big money to feel like a big man.

"Hi, I'm Victoria," I said. "What's your name?"

"Um, hi Victoria. I'm Tim. It's a Breguet, by the way." He must have seen the confused look on my face. "The watch. I noticed you looking at it. And yes, it was expensive, but no, I don't have a lot of money on me right now. But I'd love it if you let me buy you a drink."

Now it was my turn to blush a little.

Tim Gallagher was pretty damn charming, I soon learned. He had a way of taking me by surprise with nearly everything he said. And he noticed things. He saw me right away, who I was, a little of what I was struggling with. I didn't even have to tell him.

"Listen, Victoria. I'd like to take you out. Is that something you hear a lot? Only every night? I know this is your job. So I'll pay for your shift. Just have dinner with me, that's all I'm asking. Tomorrow, maybe?"

Sure, I thought. He was smart and sweet, and those were two qualities that had been absent from the company I'd been keeping lately. He seemed like someone I could talk to.

And talk I did. The next night we went out, and of course he paid for everything, and he let me talk. It was like a therapy session, except one where the doctor was paying the patient. I told him some of the stories from my life, and I loved watching his eyes get wide. He'd never experienced anything like it. He was from a preacher's family in Louisiana, he told me. He'd studied hard, gone to a great school, and moved to Dallas after college, where he started developing software for a military tech company. He'd had the same job for more than ten years, and he did pretty much the same thing every day. He told me he sometimes fantasized about having more drama in his life, a real adventure, but he didn't think he could find it if he tried.

Well, he'd found me, and I had enough drama in my life for both of us.

We saw each other off and on for a couple of weeks, and then my dad and brother were due in from Ohio. Tim knew I was leaving, but he said he wanted to spend as much time with me as possible. "You bring color into my life," he said. "I like you."

I like you. Somehow I'd never heard those simple words from a man before. *I love you*, yes. I heard that all the time, especially at the club when men were trying to get in my g-string. But to be liked meant something more in a way—he was saying he accepted me for who I was. So, we saw each other a lot, but Tim was dating a ghost. I didn't have any hope of love, romance, or even the promise of "like" at this point. I just wanted to be free. I wanted it all to end.

In the day or two before my family arrived, I made a plan. My dad and brother would be driving the U-Haul. I'd be in my car. When I got to Tennessee, I'd break off from them, and drive to the little town where my grandparents were from. Maybe that's what it meant to go home, I told myself. I could put an end to it peacefully with an 8 ball of coke in my veins on the side of a mountain where many of my ancestors lived and died.

I agreed to see Tim one last time before I left. And once again, he surprised me. "You know, I haven't taken any vacation time at all this year, and I've never been to Ohio. Is it as beautiful as they show it in the movies?" he asked with a sarcastic grin. "How about I take two weeks off and help you move up there and get settled?"

I told him he was crazy. Why would he do that for someone who was leaving town? Why would he want to be around my family, after all I'd told him about them?

"I just want to be around you as long as I can. Plus, I've always dreamed of seeing Akron," he laughed. But I could tell he was serious about being with me. And I could see that he knew more than he was letting on. He had a way of getting into my head when he wanted to, and though I hadn't hinted at my plan in any way, I think he knew I needed someone badly.

So the day came, and he showed up. My dad and brother barely acknowledged him, and they didn't have too many words for me either. But he didn't mind, he seemed to be in a great mood. After the U-Haul was packed and my dad and brother were off to fill up the gas tank, I had a moment alone with Tim.

"Listen," I said, almost crying. "I need you to do something for me." I went into one of my bags and pulled out a Ziploc with an 8 ball of coke and a hypodermic needle. "Do something with this, please. I don't care what. Just don't tell me, okay?"

He wasn't phased at all. I went out to my car, shaking and crying, and he came out a few minutes later. "How about I drive the first hundred miles," he said, as casual as can be.

And we drove. And talked. And for the first time in a long time, my life seemed normal. It seemed real. I thought maybe I'd stick around a while for normal.

The Philly Phanatic
Philadelphia, PA
Married / Big spender / Will take as much as you can give

"Listen, I really want to see you Victoria, but I'm going through some family things right now. Any chance we could negotiate the donation?"

Addiction can come in many forms. We all have times we're tempted to just take off and fly with no plan on how we're gonna land. The Philly Phanatic is notorious among escorts of a certain service. He went from a non-entity on the profile site to having one of the deepest list of bookings and reviews in less than six months. There are "hobbyists" out there with long lists, but nobody that built one as fast as the Phanatic. The guy known as the Phanatic is actually a guy from Penn who was married with young kids. It was unusual to have such an active hobbyist that was also a family man. But the Phanatic would send his wife and kids to England to visit family, and then he'd go crazy. He'd book doubles, or even triples, for multiple hours. He really wanted to try it all. Some girls thought he might have a terminal illness and was trying to get it all in before he left. But he sure seemed healthy in the sack. I chatted with some of the other ladies, and we figured out he must have spent more than $50,000 in just a couple of months on our service alone. How was it possible to do that without the wife's permission? There were plenty of open marriages out there, but none of us had run into any set-up where the wife grants complete financial freedom to fuck around. That's unprecedented.

Now his wife has caught him. He calls me in a complete panic. "She found my extra phone. She saw all the calls. I've gotta be a lot more careful now," he tells me. "And I know I've gotta cut back. It's hard

205

though, I think I'm addicted to this. Victoria is there any way we can negotiate your donation for three hours?"

I feel bad for him, but this is a business. I tell him if he can't afford the usual donation, we can't meet. He understands and hangs up quickly. I guess he's on to the next girl.

Chapter 15

SEMI-CHARMED LIFE

My time back in Ohio was short. I was ready to give up the fight, to accept the life of some many women I'd seen come before me in northeast Ohio. But God had other plans for me.

I'd done my time in rehab, been to countless AA meetings, and suffered abuse and heartbreak. I'd suffered a lot for twenty-six, but I'd caused my fair share of pain too. I'd felt on top of the world, and like I was washed out in the gutter. I didn't know what was next, but I knew what was in my past. No more coke. I'd become something so strange, so weak, I could never imagine living that life again. And no more dancing. It was the only way I knew to afford the life I wanted and stay independent, but so many of my slips came backstage. It was time to stay away from any stage. I just knew I couldn't handle it.

For what it was worth, my time back in Ohio was actually happy. And that's because I was in love. And I was sober. It should be no surprise that staying clean during good times is easier, and I was having a good time despite myself.

I can't lie, it wasn't all good: all my childhood dreams were in tatters. I knew I was far off from fame and fortune, and those dreams were fading the older I got. My idol Marilyn had moved on from pin-up girl to movie actress by age twenty. When Marilyn was twenty-six, she was already a star, in movies like *Gentlemen Prefer*

Blondes (not always true, I've found) and *How to Marry A Millionaire* (harder than it looks, based on my experience). Marilyn was the "It Girl" in her twenties. She was in a mansion in Hollywood. She was in all the papers. She was in all the magazines. Where was I? I was somewhere in the back pages of some yellowing copies of *Hustler* at the bottom of middle aged men's dressers. My ass, projected to the size of one of the faces on Mount Rushmore, was sometimes up on a big screen during Van Halen concerts. My stage name, Victoria, was still whispered between men in polo shirts and casual slacks back at the Red Room. And my name was on the back of a head shot and at the top of a faked resume in the files of a sleazy agent, the guy who thought it'd be good for my career to tell everyone I was an extra in *JFK*.

And where was I living? Back in the very room where I'd hidden from my father all those years and dreamed of escape. I was just like the girl from the Johnny Cash song who came back to the candy store, only minus the success and plus a few scars.

But I did have the boy next door, and that made all the difference. Well, Tim might not have been the boy next door exactly, but it sometimes felt like he was. He was just so kind, so familiar, such a good listener. I hadn't had some of the same feelings toward a man since having Tony in my life, the boy who'd I'd lost to a car crash at sixteen. Tim was visiting from Dallas every weekend, and he made me feel like I'd made it. He was such a kind, gentle man that my parents didn't really know what to make of him. On the one hand, it was clear I'd come back to Ohio with nothing. But here was this amazing prize I had to show for my time in Dallas. They were wondering how I did it.

I started working right away as well. I got a job at a local radio station, where I wrote ad copy and sometimes did voiceover work. It was a step forward from the one legit day job I'd had in Dallas, and it was just one more sign that I'd done some growing up. I remember standing in front of my old mirror in my bedroom, the one with the torn and faded purple Van Halen sticker in the corner. When I looked in the mirror now, I didn't see a young Marilyn Monroe. I saw a young business woman. Someone who would find her strength in new ways. Someone who didn't have to fight just to survive.

And, of course, there was my son, Jeremy. I missed him so much right away. The plan was that I'd put my life together, then he would come and live with me for the summer before he went back to school. But I knew as much as I wanted him back, before I could save him, I had to save myself. I couldn't put him through what I'd already put him through—he needed a mother who could protect him, not put him in danger.

But I was feeling strong maternal feelings. As happy as I was when Tim visited, or when I got to work every morning, I'd have long crying spells at night. At first I thought it was all because I missed my son so much. That was part of it, but I soon learned there was another reason as well. My hormones were changing. I was pregnant.

I didn't even need to go to a doctor to know. After I missed my period, I knew just from the way I was feeling. As soon as the doctor confirmed it, though, I called Tim. He could be hard to read, sometimes, but not after I told him he was going to be a father. He was elated. "You know, Jenny, we've only known each other two months, but lets make it official. Doesn't that make the most sense?

Will you marry me?" I agreed without much hesitation. Not that there wasn't some. I loved Tim, but I hated the idea of giving up my independence. My deepest instincts told me that kindness and charm could quickly turn to something much darker when men moved into my life. I'd never let someone else tell me how to live, how to think, how to feel, and that's what every relationship I'd been in had turned toward at some point. But Tim was different. Tim knew me, the real me, and he loved that person. And I loved him, too, for all his smarts and good humor and geeky good looks. I said yes.

Of course, his job was in Texas, and he wasn't about to relocate to Ohio or anything. I worried. Everywhere I went in Dallas, I'd have flashbacks—I'd pass bars where I had big nights or corners where I'd scored coke. The city was a big map of want and regret for me. I wasn't sure I could go back there.

Tim understood. "Look, we don't have to go into the city. I know you want to have more peace in your life. We'll move out to the suburbs, get the white picket fence, and I'll mow the lawn on Sundays. Believe me, there's no temptation to be had in Plano, Texas."

I laughed. And I agreed. I'd never hung out in Plano. The people that lived there built big new houses with new money, had sprinklers watering their lawns 24/7, and the highlight of each weekend was little league games and Friday night football. In my mind it was like a big black hole of contentment, where nobody needed to travel outside their neighborhoods unless they needed to for work. *If I was set up in a place like that,* I thought, *I wouldn't need a wig to convince a judge I was a real Dallas lady. I'd have custody of Jeremy again in no time at all.* On the one hand, it felt like the sort of suburban stupor I'd spent a lifetime trying to avoid. But on the other, I saw a kind of freedom in it, one where I reclaim my health, my sanity, and embark on the novel experiment of building a loving family.

So after only two months, I was heading back to Dallas, where Tim and I married in his empty dining room in his apartment. His father, a fiery Louisiana preacher, married us. Tim rolled his eyes at every mention of holy covenants. For him, the power of our marriage was in the odd-couple balance we had, the ease of our partnership, the prospect of raising a child together, not religious rites. But I paid close attention to the words Tim's dad was saying. Cause even though Tim's IQ was off the charts, I always thought there were some things he just couldn't—or wouldn't—let himself see. He grew up with so much talk of religion that he was hardened to the whole concept. But I knew, and I think Tim's dad knew as well, that we'd have to find something deeper between us than what we already had, which seemed like plenty at the moment.

After we married, we found our big house with a picket fence in Plano, and I was back to having regular visits with Jeremy while we waited for the second to come along. Every day I'd go to my AA group, and every Sunday I'd go to church, and I'd drag Tim along. He treated it as an amusing diversion, but he also knew it was important to me, and that it gave me a better shot of making it through recovery.

Then, in May 1997, Noah was born. He was a little early, and was born weighing a little less than five pounds. I cried while holding his tiny, precious body, knowing what a miracle it was that he was here at all, that I was here at all, that I'd earned a second chance along with this healthy, peaceful child.

I remember bringing him home and just spending days with him alone while Tim worked. It reminded me of the days I'd spent alone with Jeremy when he was first born, and again I cried, this time with longing and regret and the hope that both my boys would be able to spend time together soon.

A week after Noah was born, we had visitors. One was Jeremy, who was meeting his brother for the first time. And the other was Greg. Of course I'd spoken to Greg and seen him at his own house when picking up Jeremy. But we rarely had much to say to each other, and we went through intermediaries (Chuck and Ellen, his god-parents) as much as possible. Honestly, we couldn't stand each other. But now it was different. For me, it was important to show him that I'd survived after all, and less than a year after I'd been on the verge of destroying myself, here I was, back and better than ever, with a gentleman as a husband, a beautiful home, and a literal new life in my arms. I needed him to see for himself that I was a fit mother. And for him, he no doubt wanted to see the opposite. He wanted to look for clues that I was still drinking, still drugging, still running around.

So Greg came to visit, and he took his shoes off in the entryway, and we had him sit down in an overstuffed leather chair in the living room near the fireplace, and we offered him something to drink.

"How about a beer?" he said, staring straight at me with a scornful smile. "Or maybe you've got something harder around the house?"

"Greg, we don't have anything like that." He was testing me. "You want a soda? Maybe a Dr. Pepper?"

We struggled through awkward silences, broken by Greg's "jokes," mostly made at my expense.

"Nice house. You need a dog in that backyard, though. I've got a cop friend that's looking for a home for a retired service dog, if you're interested. Only problem is, he's been trained to smell things you might not want him to smell."

Tim wouldn't take the bait. "We've got cats, that's plenty for me," he said.

At one point, Tim left to start up the grill, and it was just Greg and I in the living room. He looked at me without saying anything and pushed his Dr. Pepper off the table onto my new white carpet.

"Aw, hell. Sorry. I hope that comes out."

I tried my hardest not to scream. He was determined to show me I could have nice things, but I'd never have a nice life. After a few more jokes about coke, about my dancing, about my redneck relatives, I finally had enough and told him it was time to go. Greg went to go get cigarettes from his car for a last smoke before taking Jeremy back, and I followed him. Then the Ohio girl came out a bit.

"Fuck off, Greg, and if you think you're going to sit in my living room and make your idiot limp dick comments ever again, you're out of your tiny fucking mind."

Greg looked up at me and grinned his shitty little grin, then turned to the left and nodded. "Sorry for the language, ma'am. I'm sure this used to be a nice neighborhood."

I looked up to see my neighbor Carlie Boyd standing outside her Mercedes, watching us. Carlie drummed her perfectly manicured nails on the roof of the car and waited a beat. Then she flashed a big smile back at Greg and said, "I wouldn't know, I haven't lived here long. So far I'd say the neighborhood is shit, but some of the neighbors are starting to grow on me." Then she turned to me and winked. *Oh,* I thought. *I like her.*

Greg left with Jeremy, and that was indeed the last time he set foot in my house. And the next day, I got a knock on my door. It was my neighbor, Carlie.

"Hi!" she said. "Sorry I didn't come sooner. I thought you were probably doing baby things." Without me inviting, she pushed her way into my living room and started looking around.

"Um, hey," I said. "Yeah, new baby. He's asleep now though."

I'd met Carlie before, but we hadn't really talked much. She was just this fabulous, well dressed lady that came and went in a big Mercedes and wore suits and big hats. I thought maybe she was a lawyer, or a politician or something. I didn't really think about her much at all. I kind of saw her as just another nice detail in the background of the nice neighborhood I'd just moved into.

"It's a boy, right? Your husband told me. Don't kill me, I got a little something for him." She reached into her designer purse and pulled out a clear, domed box. Inside was a rhinestone pacifier. "Isn't it the most hideous thing you've ever seen? I had to get it." It was a Dior pacifier. This lady I'd never met got me a designer pacifier for my newborn. She looked at me a little nervously, then reached in her purse and pulled out a water bottle and took a swig. "You don't like it? You can take it back, don't mind me. Oh, you do like it? Good, then I can tell we're going to be best friends."

And we were. Carlie was about ten years older than me, but like me she'd squeezed in way more living than most in her years on earth. She was married for over a decade to a Chicago grocery magnate, and she had a couple of kids, too. But she'd divorced, and when she did, she came down to Dallas to start everything over again.

"Look at me. I'm not dead yet," she'd say. "My life in Chicago was crap, and there's nothing for me there. But I'm still alive, and I'm ready to have some fun."

Carlie would come by a few times a week, and we'd crack each other up with stories from our lives. She thought my time on stage was the funniest thing in the world. "Well, Victoria, just how big were your titties, then? Did they look more like melons or beach balls? Could you let a little air in or out depending on your audience?" And she would crack me up talking about her terrible dates with lawyers and doctors. What else did she do? She served on the board of some charities. Sometimes I'd see her jogging in her designer athletic gear, moving slower than most adults walk. "Go for it Carlie!" I'd yell from the porch. "You're gonna be a champ!" The other neighbors would just stare.

More and more, Carlie was becoming my one outlet for fun. I had so much of what I wanted—a kind husband (though to be honest, any man who didn't hit me I thought of as nice), two beautiful boys, a perfect home, and the hope of a future. But I couldn't help who I was. I didn't need booze or drugs anymore. But I needed something. I needed a challenge.

Six months after Noah was born, I went back to work part-time at an advertising job. Tim was supportive, and Carlie was fascinated. "What's that like?" she asked. "I've never had a 9 to 5 before." She'd been rich all her adult life. It was amusing to her that people might need to work—to live, to support their families, to feel purposeful.

And so I worked, I played, I loved, I nurtured. 1997 was a terrific year. Noah grew and thrived. Jeremy visited often, and I'd take him to little league games and movies. There was nothing I lacked. But. But. But. There was still something missing. It wasn't the substances. I didn't think I needed those, and AA helped when alcohol tempted me. It wasn't fame. I still thought I had a special destiny in some way, but wasn't set on being on the screen or anything. I knew that ship had sailed. I had contentment, but there was something big I was missing. Was it happiness? Was it God? I wasn't sure. I knew for now it was enough to hold on, to give my love to my sons and husband, but if I thought about having this life ten, twenty years into the future, could I imagine myself still holding on, kissing my husband when he came home, cooking, vacuuming, washing, crafting, gossiping, chauffeuring, shopping, jogging, and just, well, coping? No. No I couldn't. Not me.

Dr. Sprinkles

Princeton, New Jersey

Kinky / Has money / Would see again

Okay, I can do this. I try to concentrate. The funny thing is, I really do have to pee. I just can't at the moment. Not into this guy's mouth.

"Oh God," I hear him moan as I move closer. "Come on, baby, just let it go." I'm not really one for inhibitions, but this one's tough for me.

Okay, Jenn, think of the time you've most had to pee. That one time at dinner when you drank that whole bottle of Cakebread Chardonnay the client brought and then he started telling a long, important story about his first girlfriend? Or that one time you had to drive non-stop from Cleveland to Connecticut to meet a generous client and couldn't be late? Nope, all these stories involve clients, and I can't help but imagine peeing on them, and how horrified they'd be. Come on, Jenn. You're a professional. You have to do this. I turn around and look down at Dr. Sprinkles in the bathtub. The white rope tying his wrists together is starting to slip, and his blindfold is crooked. I've never been good at knots, I think. They really should offer classes in bondage..

I turn back around to face the tile wall and close my eyes. Okay, on the count of three. One. Two. Suddenly I feel rough lips on my ass. Jesus! He's licking my ass! Startled, I finally let go. I cringe as I hear him gurgle. Threeeeeeeeeeee. I let it all out. I turn around again, and his blindfold and ropes are soaked. His chest is heaving, and he's come all over the tub.

"Oh, God. Oh, God," he says. "What are you going to do with me now?" Gosh, I just don't know. I feel spent. Well, stick to the script, I suppose. "Look at what a dirty boy you are," I say. "You're bad. Get yourself cleaned up. Then come into the other room for your punishment."

I flee to the other room to regroup. I've gotta admit, I'm a little turned on. Dr. Sprinkles is actually one of the most respected cardiologists on the east coast. He spends most of his days saving lives, and the burden of his responsibility is enormous. Once every blue moon he wants to give all that up, he wants to be dominated, he wants to abandon all control. It's fucking exciting to give that to him. Even if that means pissing on a man that could save the life of a loved one someday.

Chapter 16

SCAR TISSUE

"So, girlie, tell me how it went?"

"Ugh."

"Noooooo. I don't believe that. What went wrong? Tell me all the details, right down to the color of the unmentionables."

I was at the bar of The Mansion, an old fancy Dallas restaurant, with my neighbor Carlie. We were dressed to the nines, having our girls' night out. The second of the week—we had a lot of nights out together. My youngest son was three, and I spent most of my days with him. I was happy then, but I'd been playing the church going housewife for so long, I was starting to crack. I needed fun, and not the kind of fun you have sitting outside the ball pit at McDonalds. For me, that fun was hanging out with my funny, whip-smart friend, Carlie.

"Black. Does that help? It was just a basic black T-back."

"Honey, I'm a square. You'll have to speak slowly and explain everything. What the hell is a T-back?"

"You know, a thong that goes up your ass and straight across, like a T."

"Oh, sounds romantic."

"It was! It was pretty much what I was wearing when we first met. It was like our first date all over again."

"Ha! Okay, so back up a little. What were you wearing over the dental floss?"

"Nothing! I'm telling you, it was just like our first date."

"Um, okay. And what was he doing?"

"You wanna know? I'm too embarrassed to say."

"Please darling, no secrets between us."

"He was doing . . . World of Warcraft."

"Dearie, you're going too fast again. Is that something for his work?"

"No, it's a fucking computer game. You go online and control a little guy that battles orcs and shit, you know, with a big sword, and you play with a lot of other people online. It's just this dorky thing."

"What the hell is an orc? Some kind of creature? Okay, so he's on the computer playing with his sword when he could have been playing with you instead?"

"Exactly. So, I thought I'd at least be able to get him to take a break."

"Honey, you deserve more than a 'break.' So then?"

"So I go down to his office and stand in his door, hair done, makeup on, looking just like I did during my best stage days. I stood there for a minute in the doorway and he didn't look up. I couldn't think of what to say. So I cleared my throat a little, and he barely moved his head in my direction. He looked at me for exactly one second. I'd spent over an hour getting myself ready, spent the last couple of weeks working out, getting into shape, and it's all for this one second look. He says, 'Um, not tonight, Jenny. I'm just ordering a pizza.' Click. He hits a button on his computer and the Dominos guy is on the way."

"No!"

"Yes! You can do it all online now. You can hit a button on your computer and get fed. What good am I anymore? Once computers can drive our kid to daycare, I'm doomed. Carlie, it's been sooooo long. And I'm not just talking about sex. Tim is such a great dad, and when we're all together, we're happy. But ever since Noah was born, it's like I'm not even a person to him anymore. I'm the 'mom.' Once Noah's asleep, we might as well not even be in the same house."

"Well, what else can you do online these days? Maybe he's made his computer his wife. Or he's got a thing for orcs."

"No shit. That's exactly what it's like. I don't think he even checks out porn, but I have this fantasy of making one of those videos and getting it on the internet. I'd love to see the look on his face when he clicks his mouse button and there I am. 'Yoo hoo! Tim! Remember me? Your fucking life partner? Click your mouse on these, asshole!' Why not? You know, it's been almost four years since I danced, but sometimes I think I could have a nice little side business making videos of myself dancing and get him up then. Bring Victoria back. I could make a fortune!"

"Don't you dare! Jenn, you have way too many other talents for that. You know what I think, time to toss out the T-back for good. How's real estate school going, anyway?"

"Fine, but let's not change the subject. Seriously, what am I supposed to do? I'm not that old. I'm in great shape. I'm the same person I was when he was all over me years ago. Now, nothing."

"Did you ever think that maybe that's the problem? That you're the same person?"

"Well, no. I spice things up. My hair's a new color, I change my look sometimes."

"Well, that's not what I mean. It's just . . . Jenn, I know you actually got paid to turn men on, but you can be pretty dense about what men want sometimes."

"What? Screw you, Carlie. I'm the best in the biz."

"Jenn, I'm sure you're very gifted. And I'm sure all the men at the establishments where you used to work would pay lots of attention to you. But, you're too pretty. You've got the body. You just never learned how to play the game."

"Carlie, you were a freaking model. You're the most beautiful woman I've ever met. What are you talking about?"

"You get a prize for saying that, but for my work it was different. To succeed in that job, 99 percent of the men I had to turn on didn't even like girls. It didn't matter—same tactics apply. You can't just tell them what you like, who you are. You have to make them think they're figuring you out. You can't just show yourself. You have to let them feel like they've discovered you. Like they're the only one who can solve the mystery. 'Oh, you think I'm pretty? I don't know, I never thought so. Tee-hee.' It's not hard, obviously. We all learned around the time of our first kiss. But there's more sophisticated versions of it. If you're trying to attract a guy, you can't just tell them you like them. Jenn, emotionally, you're like a puppy. That's you, Jenny. 'I like you, lets have sex!' The more you like them, the more you need to act like you could care less. Like you're disgusted. It's not about teasing, it's about making them feel like they have a chance to change your mind, to find you out, to feel like they're calling the shots."

"No offense, Carlie, but that sounds like some seventh grade bullshit. I'm not interested in playing Clue or Mystery Date or whatever. I just want to get laid by my own husband."

"You think so, don't you! But it's true. And I think you know it's true. I mean, a g-string and nothing up top? That won't work. You're a breast-bearing professional, you should know. It wouldn't be a show if you just walked out on stage naked and scratching your belly. It's about the show. Even if the guys are just sitting on their fat asses, you're creating the illusion that they're the ones convincing you to take it all off. You know, with their dollar bills and the force of their libidos. I mean, let's get philosophical here."

"Shut up, Carlie," I said, cracking up.

"No really, what is a boob? Did you ever ask yourself that when showing em off? I ask you now. It's just a sack of skin. They're made for babies to suckle from. You remember what they looked like after you had your boys, right? We're both mothers here. Not very sexy, but that's what they're really for! The reason men are attracted to them is because they're hidden. Imagine it: you're a baby sucking away all warm and safe and snug, and then one day the boob is yanked from you, tucked in a brassiere, and you never see breasts again until you're fifteen and have to convince Melanie after the Sadie Hawkins dance to unbutton her blouse. It's all about that moment. Having that power to access the forbidden."

"Wow, Carlie, deep."

"What I'm saying is, there's no mystery. It's that simple. You've got to convince him that you've got some secrets. Something he doesn't know about that he'll have to work to discover."

"Yeah, but I worry it's not me, it's him. I don't know what's going through his head."

"Listen, Jenn. If there's something going on with him, I can get the truth out of him without him even knowing it. You know I can. I can talk to him any time."

"Hell no, Carlie! For one, you know the guy's a genius, and he'll see through your sleuthing, no offense. Second, honestly, he doesn't like you very much."

"What!"

"It's true."

"That's impossible. I make him soup when he's sick. I'm perfectly nice to him. He has no reason to dislike me."

"Maybe that's the wrong word for it. Let's just say he doesn't trust you. He loves your chicken soup, how could he not? He just hates our nights out. He says so. He always tries to stop me from coming out at the last minute. He wants my life to be as tame as his, and he kinda blames you for springing getting out." I looked down at my little glass of wine.

"Oh, that's ridiculous. I'm a good influence on you. We hardly ever drink more than a glass when we go out. I would never let anyone see me drunk, and I wouldn't let that happen to you either. See, it's all about being in control. Never let anyone see you compromised, Jenn. Remember that. Besides, he'd change his mind about me if he knew all the good I was doing for you. Right? I mean, don't take this the wrong way, but if it wasn't for me, you'd hardly get out, and you're the sort of person that can't just stay in. And look at us! I'm a perfect chaperone. You never get into trouble when we're out."

"I know, but damn Carlie, sometimes I want what you have.

Look—you've got money."

"Let's not talk about that."

"Okay, just saying, you have money so you're independent, you've got no responsibilities, and when you feel like having fun, you can go do whatever you want, fuck around with whoever. I've seen you pick up guys. And good men, too—like guys out of movies. I'm not going to lie, you're a freaking inspiration."

"Well thanks, I think. It's not hard if you do what I was saying earlier." She takes a dainty sip from her glass and looks around. "Here, just watch and learn."

With that Carlie got up from her stool and moved down the bar to an open spot near a silver fox who looked like a Fortune 500 CEO who flies his own private jet to the Antilles on the weekends. I'd noticed him. But I hadn't thought twice about him there—he didn't have the eyes, the posture of someone looking to flirt at the bar. He was too relaxed, too assured, drinking a scotch and making notes in a book. I'd been hit on so many times at bars, I just had a radar for that kind of thing, and I wouldn't have thought he was looking. Carlie and the man were far enough down the bar that I couldn't hear what she said to him, but he immediately invited her to sit down. And within a moment he was completely fixated on her. He was asking questions, maybe talking about himself. And as far as I could tell, Carlie wasn't saying anything, just nodding, making soft little noises in response to whatever he was saying—"hmmmm," "hmmm?" "ohhhh…" I swear, she said nothing the whole time, and the guy was looking at her like he was going to propose.

After ten minutes, she got up, again hardly saying anything. He gently grabbed her arm, handed her a card, and looked about ready to sign over his private jet if only she'd call him. She looked at the card without much interest, gave him a polite smile, and walked back over to me. I was trying hard not to crack up.

"Let's go, sister. Listen, when you learn how to do what I just did, you'll be able to wrap any man around your finger, whether he's your husband or not."

"What the hell, you just sat there like you were just nodding and smiling at the most boring teacher's lecture just because you wanted a good grade. It was so phony! How'd you do it?"

"Because it didn't matter that I said nothing. The less the better. It was all in the eyes. That he understood, and the less I talked, the more he could project whatever he wanted or whoever was the one that got away. It was the look. I just had to make him feel like if only he used the right words, I'd have something amazing to share with him. A secret only he could really discover. That's all it takes."

"If you say so, Carlie. Lets get home anyway before I order another glass. Once I get home I'll practice my mysterious lady eyes in the mirror. Or maybe I'll just dress like an orc."

Another night, another lesson learned. I became who I became partly because of Carlie, who was a mentor in more ways than one. She taught me how to cook, and she taught me how to dress. What shoes to wear, what watch to wear, how to do my hair. She taught me what to look for in other people, too. She taught me how to figure out what they wanted. She was like Sherlock Holmes, and could deduct a man's motives, marital status, and money in the bank by the slightest clues. She taught me not to wear my heart on my sleeve (a lesson I'd often forget), if I wanted to stay in control. She taught me to not get drunk in public, to keep my voice down, that power in any situation could come from subtlety first.

Later, when I started sleeping with men for money, it was the lessons Carlie taught me that allowed me to create Victoria McCormick, the escort. Because of her, I could read men like a detective on a crime show, and I could give them what they wanted before they knew themselves. And I'm not talking about just sleeping with them. Carlie taught me it wasn't just about that with men (though of course sometimes it really is). It didn't surprise me the first time a client paid just to talk to me all night, and it didn't surprise me that very wealthy men might pay me well to dress in the right dress, go with them to the right party, cling to them in the right way, and look at them just so when they wanted it, and then send me home when the party ended without so much as a kiss and a hand job.

Carlie was right about a lot of things, but that didn't mean she was right about everything, or that she was always in control. I knew like me, Carlie had run into problems in her past from drinking too much. And we would occasionally have our glass of wine at the bar. But I never saw her even a little slurred. She never drank like that in public. What I didn't know, and what I didn't find out until too late, was that the water bottle Carlie would take out with her on her snail-pace jogs around the neighborhood was filled with vodka. I didn't know that when she was alone at night, she'd drink herself into oblivion more often than not. I didn't know any of that for the longest time, until Carlie started to deteriorate ten years later from the acute damage she'd done to her organs. What I didn't know, and what I didn't understand, was that Carlie wasn't living her life to the fullest—in fact she'd given up on life before I met her, abandoning all hope and everything else except the appearance of happiness and prosperity, and a devotion to small amusements (as I must have been). In that way, Dallas was perfect for her.

She wasn't in control, and neither was I, but Carlie convinced me I could be. That I could be someone on my own, living life on my own terms. And so, when nothing improved between Tim and I, I filed for divorce in 1999. It was an amicable break, as far as these things go. Carlie always told me that I needed mystery to keep Tim interested. Hell, maybe that was the problem, since in some ways he knew me better than I knew myself. He wasn't surprised when I began to separate from him. He only wanted to make sure we did what was best for Noah.

As for me, I moved out of my perfect house with the white picket fence for something a little less separate from it all, a little more connected to other lives. I moved into a beautiful apartment and got a job with an apartment management company as a leasing agent. I was studying to get my real estate license, and everything seemed to make sense—I'd be a powerful woman on my own terms, with the kind of career that I'd seen others in the city pursue to incredible fortune and influence. I'd raise my kids and provide for them, too. I saw myself becoming someone like Carlie, someone who could impress anyone she met. I'd go to bars, have a glass of wine sitting in front of me, and make CEOs with private jets fall in love with me just by giving them the right look. As in the past, though, as soon as my dreams started to look like reality to me, I found myself humbled pretty quickly. I was still filling my place up with furniture when my life fell apart once again in the fall of 1999.

Chris
Highland Park, Texas
Gentleman / Great tipper / Loyal client

"And what do you think should go around the pool? My gardener is thinking hosta, but I don't know, it seems a little boring to me. It's like a grandma thing to plant. What do you think? He says it has to be something that won't shed leaves into the pool. Hon, you've always been good with this kind of thing, what would you want by the pool?"

I almost start to cry. What would I want? I look around me, at the walls of the whitewashed brick mansion. At the new grotto pool being installed. At the pitcher of sweet tea perspiring on the veranda, looking like a detail in the background of an Architecture Digest photo. I have to remind myself, this is not my real life. This is not my real home. It doesn't matter to me what gets planted on the slope above the pool. I've been doing this too long to fall all over again, but sometimes, some gestures, some questions, still get to me. "Well, I think mountain laurel has always looked pretty by water. Maybe that. Not sure it thrives down here in the heat, though." I clear my throat. "So, Chris. You were gonna show me this year's Ferrari?"

The light goes on in his eyes. We're back to sharing a fantasy, not a reality. "Oh, you're gonna love this year's. When you see the color, you're going to lose your mind." Every time I come back to Dallas and see Chris, he shows me his toys. For instance, every year, he trades in his old Ferrari for a new one. He had to buy a certain number in the first place before he was allowed into the "exclusive club" that made it possible to buy new directly from the factory.

We go for a ride through Highland Park in his new mint green

Ferrari and we leave the top down. I'm glad not to have to talk for a few minutes. I close my eyes and let the wind blow my hair back. Not that I hate talking to Chris. He's charming, he's handsome. He's gentle and even considerate in bed, he treats me like a lady, and he always gives me more than a little extra. He's a dream of a man, and one of my best, most faithful clients since I started the work ten years before. But he's not mine.

We pull back into his carport, and he shows me more of the toys he's acquired since we last met up. We always meet at his house. He always wants to show off his toys. Like many of my well-off clients from the area, Chris didn't grow up well off. He worked hard, he made his money, then he wanted to play.

Chris takes me to a locked cabinet in a small room just off his garage. "This," he says, "is my latest acquisition." Chris types in a code that releases a lock on the cabinet, reaches in, and with both hands carefully pulls out a large, black assault weapon that looks something like a movie prop. "Don't worry, it's not loaded," he says. Check this out. He flips on a few lights and lasers, has me look through the scope, and takes my picture toting the thing like I'm some kind of post-apocalyptic mercenary.

He shows me the photo, and it's ridiculous. For some reason, I get angry. I'm tired of posing. I'm tired of artifice. I'm tired of playing. And I'm tired of being teased by all these trappings of success. Chris puts his newest toy carefully back in his toy chest, and I wait. When he turns around, I jump him.

I never do this. But right now, today, I'm doing this.

I push Chris down to the floor and unbuckle his belt. I'm hovering over him, my face inches from his. He's startled, but I can tell he's

230

already hard. I pull him out of his pants and tease him.

"Oh, shit," he says. "Can you do what you did last time?" No. This time I'm going to do what I want. I'm going to take what I want from the moment. I've been with Chris many times, we're comfortable together. But I have no idea how he's going to handle this. And I don't care. I will him to give me what I want, on my terms, and afterwards, I'm completely satisfied.

"Good lord," he says. He looks bewildered. "Good lord," he says again. "I guess you must like big guns." I don't dignify his joke with a response. Instead, I get up and swagger around his house. I know this isn't going to happen again. I know I'd never try to get away with this with any other clients. But once, just once, I had to show a client what I really wanted.

Chapter 17

PRETTY GOOD

I thought I was at peace, but I was never meant to have peace for long. I was enjoying my new life on my own. Yes, in some ways I was lonely, and in some ways I was scared, but I was free, and I had love. My friends, my sons, even my ex were all important people in my life. Maybe because we were such an odd couple to begin with, the divorce didn't hit either of us as hard as it could, and we still felt a lot for each other. We just both recognized we'd become good partners as parents, and little more. Even if there was some pain, some awkwardness, we both realized we'd be in each other's lives as we raised our child together. Noah was still so young, it was all hard for him to understand, but he never really saw his parents fight, and I think it helped that he could see that we still cared for each other.

That wasn't the case with my other son. Jeremy was such a special boy, with an IQ off the charts, real talent at sports, and a big, wide open personality. But unlike Noah, Jeremy watched his parents fight all the time, and he had to live with the obvious truth that his mom and dad despised each other. By the time he was ten years old, his father and I had come to avoid each other whenever we could, and that was good enough. I thought it was working, but my first husband had other ideas. One day at work I got a call from my lawyer that Greg had filed to move out of state with Jeremy.

He was going back to Ohio.

By our original legal agreement, neither of us could move out of state with Jeremy. It was one reason I couldn't send for him after I'd moved briefly back to Ohio myself. But Greg was going to try it anyway, and he filed a motion in family court before he told me one word about it.

My lawyer didn't sound too concerned—"If he's going to Ohio, he's going without your son. That's just the nature of the agreement." My lawyer was wrong, though, and the judge granted Greg the right to take Jeremy away. I couldn't believe it. Just when I'd reached a point in my life where I was fully in power of myself, when I wasn't drinking (other than that occasional glass of red with Carlie), when I was working, back to school, standing up for myself and my sons, it was all blown up by an hour-long court date. It's like Greg knew just when to strike to cause me the most pain. In court they brought up all of my past—my work, and my addictions. It didn't matter that I was practically a child then myself and was now a perfectly competent adult. Once that record's in place, it's there forever.

And my problems were about to get worse. I was about to have a pity party, and all my demons were invited.

November 4, 1999, was the day I learned I was going to lose Jeremy. That night, I went to a Mexican restaurant not far from the court and sat at the bar. I was by myself. I had a little food, but mostly tequila. It wasn't a lot, not by the standards of my party days. But I was out of practice, and it hit me particularly hard. I was feeling those same feelings I'd had before I met Tim. Completely alone. Hopeless. Yep, it was crazy to think that, but that day wasn't about living in the present. It was about being stuck in the past. I was fixated on the worst times in my life, and soon enough I started remembering the ways I used to make myself feel better. Get drunk. Get high.

I'll never know if I would have really gone through with it. But I suddenly had the idea to drive out to where I used to score coke in downtown Dallas. Just to see who was down there, I told myself. Well, I didn't make it far.

Not far away from the restaurant, still in Collin County, north of Dallas, I ran a red light in my brand new silver Infiniti and just missed a blue sedan crossing an intersection. The moment I thanked my lucky star for the close miss, I saw the cruiser lights reflected in my rear view mirror.

I didn't try to argue or bargain. I just told the officer I'd been drinking and put my hands out for the cuffs. It was my second DUI.

The first thing I did at Collin County jail was call Tim, who posted bail and came to pick me up.

"I'm sorry, I'm sorry, I'm so sorry."

"Don't apologize, Jenny. What happened, happened. What you've got to do now is take care of yourself."

I suddenly wasn't sure how I would. I just had an overwhelming feeling that everything could be taken away from me, and there was nothing I could do about it. Losing everything I loved, like Jeremy, felt inevitable.

Though my court date and sentence wouldn't be for a few months at least, the fallout began sooner than that. Though I tried to be discreet, my employers at the apartment management company found out about my DUI and terminated me. Because my apartment was deeply discounted because of my employment with the company, suddenly I could no longer afford it.

So shortly before Christmas, I found a new townhouse just in time to set up a room for Jeremy and Noah, who would be staying with me for Christmas. In all the chaos, I managed to have plenty of presents to put under the Christmas tree, but no time to pick up the Christmas tree itself. In fact, when my boys came to stay, the new townhouse was about as festive as a half-abandoned warehouse, with moving boxes stacked everywhere and nothing on the walls, let alone Christmas decorations. The boys and I picked up a tree late on Christmas Eve, but they were both too sleepy to help decorate it, so they went to bed that night with the Christmas tree leaning up against the door.

I felt horrible. I was determined to give my sons the Christmas they deserved, even if I had to stay up all night. I started decorating, but nothing was looking right. The tree leaned to one side, I broke a glass ornament all over the floor. Soon enough I remembered a few bottles of wine a neighbor (someone who didn't know my history) had dropped off as a housewarming present. I decided I'd have a glass and calm down.

I wasn't ready to have just one glass, though.

The next thing I knew, I was waking up out front of my townhouse at dawn, my arms wrapped around the Christmas tree and my cheeks streaked with wet mascara. I wasn't sure what happened, but I knew I'd got drunk, got mad, got into a fight with a Christmas tree, and lost. *Oh my God! How in the hell did I end up outside on top of the Christmas tree and how many of my new neighbors saw me like this?* I managed to pull myself back into the house, tree included, and finish decorating it before the boys woke up. They were as excited as any children are Christmas day. They never knew the difference, but I did. I'd lost control again.

In 2000, I pulled myself back on my feet and finalized my divorce, but also had to pay some consequences. On my thirtieth birthday, August 31, 2000, I was sentenced to 90 days in jail for the DUI I'd been charged with the year before. I thought I was going to die. For all the problems I'd run into, for all the trouble I'd brought on myself, I'd never spent time behind bars. The sentence was harsh, but that's Collin County for you, what they call a "hangin'" county in the Texas legal system. I never stood a chance.

Because I'd found more work back in leasing apartments, I was able to spend the days of most of my sentence on work release. I'd work from home and Tim brought Noah over to stay with me most days before he'd go to work. At night, I'd go back to Collin County jail, which seemed like pure hell at the time. Ironically, later I'd come to think of it as the Hilton of the Texas correction system. The facilities weren't bad—there was even carpeting! But the experience was soul crushing, partly from the company I kept. There were truly terrible women in with me, and some whose lives were just tragedies. One young girl I was with was from a wealthy family but had got involved with drugs, and a car that she and her boyfriend stole was later linked to a murder. I remember traveling with her in the back of the police van, both of us in chains. We just talked and tried to comfort one another. Both of us were equally bewildered to find ourselves where we were in life, and both of us knew we'd made the decisions to put us there.

So every morning of the week I'd change into a business suit at the jail and drive to my townhouse where Tim would drop off Noah. We'd play together, and I'd work some, and it wasn't all that bad. But come 7:30, I was back in my jumpsuit in the dorms with all the other women, some looking at much worse fates than my own. Then, just before Halloween, I was out front with Noah carving pumpkins, got distracted, and severed an artery in my thumb with the carving knife. I passed out almost immediately, and Noah, at only three, found a neighbor who called 911. It was the first time Noah saved my life, but it wouldn't be the last.

I spent the rest of my ninety days in the prison infirmary, work release unceremoniously over. It was in the infirmary that I met some of the worst of the worst, the mothers who had lost their minds and murdered their own children, the violent psychopaths in lockdown when they weren't being medicated into vegetables. I promised myself once free, I'd find a way to never see this side of the world again. I'd seen enough real evil to last a lifetime already.

By March 2001, my divorce was finalized, I had finished real estate school and become a licensed agent, and had begun work as an apartment locator. I loved it. I was entering maybe the best, most productive time of my life. I made good money, I had my son Noah half of every week, and my son Jeremy would come home every summer and for holidays. Jeremy was growing like a weed, and his mind was developing as fast as his body. I was determined to make enough money to help send him to a fancy private school near Cleveland, since otherwise he'd end up in the same sort of ramshackle education system I'd been put through. I wasn't going to let that happen. Only the best for my boys. I was making money, but I was spending it, too. I still couldn't get past the idea that I had to prove to everyone that I wasn't just independent, I wasn't just a good mom, I wasn't just a successful business woman. I had to be the best, and I had to make sure everyone knew it, even the strangers on the street as I drove past in my Infiniti, my manicured nails strumming the steering wheel. Hey, it was a Dallas thing.

That year I was doing so well, I started my own business. I joined up with my old friend Lee, a real estate tycoon who had been a friend since way back in my dancing days after I first moved to Dallas. Lee had always treated me with respect, and even if the first time he saw me he saw me half naked on stage, he always seemed to be more impressed with my brains than my beauty. Of all the men in my life, it was Lee who saw the person I could become if I only kept my head above water. I was thrilled he was taking a chance on me, and along with his son Dave, he invested in an apartment locating company that I'd run.

We started off well. He had the Rolodex, and I had the determination. But we just happened to pick a crappy year to start a new business. That September, terrorists flew two airplanes into twin towers in NYC, and one airplane into the Pentagon in DC, and the shockwaves spread all around the world. Beyond the tragedy of the moment, there was a recession, and many of the wealthy business people from outside the area that we catered to were in no mood to move in a new apartment and relocate at that time.

Still, we got by on sheer determination and grit. We kept the business going. But I wasn't making enough to keep myself going. All those lavish expenses, rent, car payments, private school tuition wasn't going to take a rest while I pulled my new business through hard times. Some months we'd do well enough that I could pay everything off. Others, I had to put everything on credit. It wasn't sustainable for me.

I ended up taking a trip back to the Red Room, where I used to be queen. I was still friends with the owner there. I was in my thirties now, and I'd added a little around the middle. I wasn't about to get up on stage again, but he gave me shifts as a waitress. I'd work the nights that Noah was with Tim, and it was enough to provide a steady income stream during those down months, but it was also embarrassing for me. I felt like it was a huge step back. What if one of my real estate clients saw me there? I'd be mortified. But I didn't know what else to do to make money. Lee knew. He didn't care. It's where we'd met, after all. He just wanted to make sure I wasn't giving up on my dreams. I wasn't. In fact, they meant more than they'd ever had in some ways. I knew what I had to lose. I knew how bad things could get if I didn't bury the past and keep looking forward.

But the past never stays buried forever.

The Red Room was the best option I had, financially. But it wasn't a great option emotionally. So much had passed for me between those walls—friendships made and lost, bad fights, long boozy nights, coke in the bathroom stalls, dates with Dallas big shots. Now I was just one of those ladies—the kind I'd always pitied a little when I was younger. A mom working late in the smoky barroom, just trying to keep out of the way of the grabby hands of horndogs and get home in time to get four hours of sleep before driving the kids to elementary school the next day. I can't say I even remembered many of their names.

One night I had a long, hard shift, with bad tips, busy hands, and a crowd of shitfaced donkeys who didn't know how to behave themselves. I was especially stressed out because the very next day, Lee and I had an important meeting scheduled. We were set to talk with students at a prominent real estate school in the city where we could pitch our company and try to recruit students as real estate agents. It would mean more income, less running around the city for me, and more management experience. I sure didn't feel like a boss that night, though. In fact, I felt as low as I ever had.

Once the crowd died down a little and my shift ended, I sat down at the bar to catch my breath before heading home.

"Hey gorgeous, can I buy you a drink?"

It was a line I'd heard, oh, at least ten times that night alone. Without looking up I said, "No thanks. About to head home."

"Really? You look like you could stand to have someone to talk to. I'm nice! I promise."

I looked up. Here was a silver haired, well-built guy with a confident grin. He didn't seem like a creep. He seemed to be someone who was comfortable with himself. And from the way he was dressed, didn't seem like the type who had a second job just to make ends meet. I wanted to know what the hell his secret was. What any of these people's secret was. How were there all these men and women that seemed to make it in this city and never have to look back? Of course, it took me the longest time to realize very few of them had lives as polished as their shiny watches or as stable as their piled-high hair dos.

I let him buy me a little glass of red wine. I remembered my friend Carlie's absolute control over this kind of guy. I thought I'd try my hand at it. Only, I never had Carlie's control.

I woke up the next morning at a hotel not far from the Red Room. I was alone, and there was $200 on the nightstand. I looked at the clock—it was five minutes until I was supposed to have my meeting at the real estate school. I leapt out of bed and began looking for my clothes, which were strewn all over the room. *Shit! I've got to be across town!*

My head was pounding, and all I could think about was the meeting. It took me a moment to realize the clothes strewn all over the floor included sequined, butt-hugging shorts. Then I remembered that I didn't even have my car—it had a breathalyzer in it, and I couldn't have driven it even if I'd wanted to. I guess that explained the money on the nightstand, a little. Money for a cab. And, I suppose, a little extra for . . . I pushed the thought out of my mind. I had to call Lee.

"Alright honey, I understand. Please, don't worry about it. I'll come get you."

Lee was there in moments, dressed in his pressed suit, with perfect hair, as always. And there I was in my sequined shorts and dripping mascara.

"First things first, Jenn. Lets get you home."

"But the meeting!" I stammered.

"That's off, honey. I called it off. Not a problem. Lets focus on you right now. Wanna donut?" he asked with a crooked smile. He had a big box of Krispy Kremes in the backseat that were supposed to be for the meeting. "They're all ours now."

"Lee, I wrecked everything! This was our big chance to grow the company. I just fucked up everything, like always."

"Now Jenn, just relax."

"No, Lee, I don't want to relax. I'm terrible. I don't know why I keep fucking up my life. I'm just terrible."

"No, Jenn. You're not. You're not terrible. You're pretty good."

"Pretty good?! What the hell does that mean? Pretty good."

"Jenn, you're pretty and you're good; which means you are pretty good. You're a good person. Just remember that."

I was quiet after that. He drove me home, and I showered, had a coffee and a cigarette. Then I got back to work.

Arnold

Myrtle Beach, SC

Gorgeous / stylish / No longer looking for companionship

"I'm sorry, Victoria, you've always been good to me. But please, I'd appreciate it if you took my number out of your phone. I've made some changes in my life. I've found a new church. I have a new girlfriend. She's a yoga instructor, and she's brought me peace. She's helped me live a healthier life. Victoria, I'm finally at peace with myself."

I wish him the best, and I hang up. But I'm skeptical that he's finally at peace. It's small consolation that I'm not the only one who can't figure out exactly what she wants. Some of my clients have taught me that. Arnold is one of them.

Arnold is a regular client I'd look up whenever I was in South Carolina. Or he was, anyway. Arnold was in some ways another dream client. His body was smooth, and his muscles were as strong and defined as a body builder. In fact, he was a body builder. He was tanned, groomed, and handsome. I've had clients that owned many fine things, but Arnold was a fine thing—his body was like a precious luxury item. I'd practically dream about it.

Sex with Arnold was another matter entirely, though. He'd invite me to his beach house, which was so carefully and tastefully put together, I thought maybe he was an interior decorator. He'd answer the door, always a little nervous and distracted. "Shush, Pearl!" His toy poodle would always be there, yapping by his side. We'd sit, and he'd need some time to get comfortable. We'd chat on the couch while he smoked a joint or two. "Sorry," he'd say. "Work's been crazy. Just trying to relax a little."

Eventually, he'd pinch his joint, sigh, and invite me to go down on him. Sometimes he'd ask for a strip tease first. I learned after the first time or two not to be alarmed or offended when, after putting on a show, we'd get started and his dick would still be half limp. I've been with clients old and young where I had to do a little extra work. No problem.

He'd close his eyes, I'd get to work, and he'd start trying to talk dirty. "Oh, yeah, I love getting my cock sucked by a beautiful chick! Damn, I'll never get enough of a gorgeous red head . . . uh, woman . . . riding me!" I tried my hardest not to laugh. It didn't take long into our first session for me to realize what was going on. I wasn't going to break the illusion, either. Sometimes I might have to play therapist, but I know it's not my job to help my clients discover themselves. I'm not getting paid to help Arnold realize he's gay. I'm there to tell the story Arnold wants to hear about himself, that he's a man who likes women, and that he's a man that women like.

I never know whether or not Arnold's new yoga instructor is real, or if she's really a woman. I hope she's not. I hope he's figured out what he really wants, and I hope he's found it.

Chapter 18

LONELY NO MORE

I started as a high-paid escort in the Dallas metropolitan area in 2005. At the time I started that line of work, I was in my mid-thirties, was the mother of two children, and had been a successful real estate agent for years.

What started as a small, secret part of my life changed everything over the following decade. The whole time I was a working girl, there were only a few people in my life who knew how I was making a living. But I've never been very good at keeping secrets for long.

My path I took to meeting my first client began in 2002.

After starting up my own apartment locating company and making it work for a little over a year, I had decided to give it up. Though I'd been successful early, real estate in Dallas was in a huge slump after 9/11, and I'd also fallen off the wagon once or twice, which had affected my relationships with clients and business partners. I was determined to learn from my mistakes, and also to keep my career moving forward, and soon after letting go of the business I joined the largest real estate company in Texas.

Ellie Holiday was a giant, and it was run by a proper Texas Lady. Ellie had been selling property in Dallas for over sixty years, and in a city where business was dominated by shit talking, hard-drinking men, she stood out as a real role model for a young businesswoman like me. That she could command a room without swearing made her an anomaly in the Dallas business world.

With my experience, I was able to sign on with Ellie as an apartment locator and realtor and brought a herd of corporate clients along. The money was great, and I felt like I was finally on the right path. But what a hell of a lot of work it was. I'd be on call all the time, and I had to be ready to drop everything to show an apartment or house, whether it be eight in the morning or ten at night. One of the reasons I'd let go of my own business was to have more regular hours, but this new job was making my hours less predictable, not more.

I could have managed if I was on my own, but I had two boys that needed my attention. Jeremy was eleven and Noah was seven, and they had needs too, needs that I couldn't just spend money to satisfy.

At eleven, Jeremy was still living with his father in Ohio. During the school year my only contact with him was by phone, but he'd fly down for some holidays as well as summers. He was already becoming a tall, handsome, strong man, with a stubborn streak. He'd been forced to look after himself in a lot of ways, but I wasn't going to leave him alone more than I had to. I knew better than anyone that there was a lot of trouble to get into in Dallas.

Noah was my real sweetheart. He was always ready to pick me up when I was down, and even at seven years old, he never seemed bothered when I had to leave him with my babysitter an extra hour or two. Still, the guilt I felt in leaving him at home was huge. My heart was sick with every missed milestone.

For a while, I did try to make it up to the boys with money. I'd go all out for birthdays and Christmases now that I had a good income, showering the boys with new bikes and baseball gloves, video games, and huge parties for all the kids in their classes and camps. I knew that wasn't the sort of mother I wanted to be, and that something had to change.

Across the office from me at work were some of the home sales crew. What they did was something I envied. Rather than a small commission on every new rental, they made as much as 6 percent on every home sold, so a single deal for them could be the same income as dozens of deals for me. Sure, they had to hustle, but it always seemed like they could take breaks, go on vacations, block off hours with kids and still be in business. It's exactly what I wanted. So that's what I did.

After a few months of training and apprenticeship, I started selling houses. With connections all over the city I started hot. I closed on over $1 million in houses my first month, and I felt like I was just warming up. And what's more, I did well enough that I could take a few extra days that first month. I remember closing a deal early one Saturday morning and swinging by my ex-husband's place to pick up Noah. I took him to the park, kicked off my pumps, and lay in the grass practically giggling while Noah skittered across the monkey bars. *Now this,* I thought, *is the life I've been waiting for.*

I should have known by then not to take the good times for granted.

After that first month, business slowed. I'd make deals, but sometimes closings wouldn't happen for months after initial agreements. I was going weeks, sometimes months without income, other than a few apartment lease deals I could cobble together when desperate.

And though there were some days when it felt I'd left all my demons (and ex-husbands) in the dust, I should have known that they never really went away forever (that goes for both demons and exes). Part of my daily routine was still trips to my AA group. I still had friends there I'd known for almost fifteen years, and they helped me hold on when darkness arrived on my doorstep. After all, I was doing much better in some ways, but I was a single mother with no family around and little time for a social life or dating. I also had an ugly past I'd never fully faced and anxiety that I didn't know how to deal with in healthy ways.

All that's to say, even though I was doing much better, I still fell off the wagon every once-in-a-while. I'd have nights alone in my townhouse when both kids were with their dads. Or I'd have a long work week with little to show for it. Or a night out with my friend Carlie, where one little glass of wine would lead to a trip to the liquor store for one little bottle of scotch. Or my regular trigger—my first husband saying something terrible to me over the phone or in a letter. Maybe there would be no real trigger or cause, just a decision that a drink or two was something I could handle. It wasn't. I was an alcoholic, and "a drink or two" wasn't really on my menu of choices.

When I slipped, I'd be lost for a day, or maybe a week, depending on what else was going on in my life. But I'd always go back to AA, and even this cycle started to feel like just the way my life was going to be. I thought back to my friend and business partner Lee and what he told me in the car after I blew an important meeting by oversleeping with a hangover—"Jenn, you're pretty good. You're pretty, and you're good." That carried me forward, and it helped me keep trying even after I slipped.

But I wasn't always good. In 2003, I got my third DUI. There wasn't much to it, really. I'd slipped, had an extra glass of wine or two and been pulled over for running a stop sign. As soon as the officer asked me to exit the car, I knew both how silly a mistake I'd made and how deadly serious a mistake it was at the same time. DUIs don't drop off your record in Texas, and this was the third I'd received since moving to Dallas. So much had changed for me for the better in seven years. But this. There was still this, and now I knew my mistake would be with me forever. A third DUI was an automatic felony.

I hired a big name attorney in Collin County and I was given ten years' probation with no jail time. I felt like I dodged a bullet, and remembered some of the horrors I'd seen in Collin County jail during my last arrest.

And so the cycle all began again. I got myself back to my AA meetings, doubled down on my commitment to raise my kids right, and get back to work. I had one more plate to spin now, though—regular check ins with my probation officer, both scheduled and unscheduled. Lucky for me my probation officer was a decent guy—he wasn't a bullshitter, and he'd tell me exactly what I had to do and where I had to be to stay out of prison. And I did it. I managed for another two years before I ran into another wall.

In 2005, I was keeping up on house sales, but my expenses had long-since outstripped my income. I had child support and private school payments for my first son, some similar expenses for my second son, rent, Realtor fees, and fees related to my probation. I was slowly sinking. Some months I'd be able to make up a little of my debt, but other months' closings would be put off, the sales wouldn't be there, and I'd slip a little further into debt. By early 2005, I'd even started making ends meet by getting cash advances from shady payday loan places, sometimes giving up 20 percent of my closing commission just to keep up with the bills. I was willing to give up a lot to keep my life going. I'd sacrifice my time, pleasure, friends, nearly anything. But I wasn't going to give up on my kids. And I wasn't going to give up on my independence.

One afternoon after pulling a few hundred bucks from a payday loan place, I decided I needed to get a grip. I needed a way to make more money. I didn't have any more time to sacrifice, since all my waking hours were already divided between work and kids. I'd have to find a way to make a few extra bucks without adding another regular job. In the good old days, I would have taken a few shifts at the Red Room or another club. But I couldn't go back there—I'd resolved to put those days behind me, and besides, I was a thirty-something mother of two. It's not like I'd lost my looks, but I was realist enough to know that the only thirty-five-year olds hired to strip were working the decrepit bars next to the gas stations out by Route 175.

Still, just thinking about the old days awakened something in me. I didn't miss the clubs. The drunk business men and gangsters, the dressing rooms caked with grime and coke residue, the cat fights, the constant feeling of danger. But there was still that part of me, a part I'd long tucked away, that was ready to be noticed. The young woman who dreamed of being a star one day, and who savored the power she had when she first got on stage and commanded the attention of every man in the room. I remembered the feeling of being really *good* at dancing, of flirting, of being an object of desire.

Sure, I got a lot of satisfaction from selling houses. But it wasn't quite the same. It was gratifying, but there wasn't the same physical *rush*.

After I used the loan to pay a bill or two, I sat down with a stack of newspapers and a legal pad. I was going to figure out how to make money, and I was going to do it my way. I made a list of jobs I'd done in the past, including illustration, advertising sales, radio voiceover, and, of course, shaking my ass in nothing but a g-string. Then I started to flip through the classifieds. Of course, by 2005, the papers weren't where you'd go to find a regular ole day job. But that wasn't what I was looking for. I was looking for something special. Something a little out there that might fit me a little better than some extra temp work.

I found it, right in the back of the *Observer*. WANTED, the ad said, BEAUTIFUL RED HEAD TO TAKE PART IN AN EROTIC PHOTO SHOOT. SAFE AND PROFESSIONAL ENVIRONMENT. MAKE GOOD MONEY, NO EXPERIENCE REQUIRED. *Good lord*, I thought. My heart leapt into my throat. I felt just like I felt when I was seventeen, standing at the counter of the pizza shop with my friend giggling over the ads in the back of the paper. That was how I wound up getting my first gig on stage. Back then I'd known the moment I saw the ad that I was going to go for it, despite my fears (or maybe because of them). My skin tingled. *I can't let anyone know what I'm doing*, I thought. *But this could help make ends meet, and, shit, it could be fun.*

I called the number and a young woman answered. I was a little relieved. "Hi," I said, "This is, um, Victoria. I'm calling about the ad in the *Observer*." The voice on the other end was indeed professional. She sounded like she was booking an appointment for me at the dentist's office, not scheduling an erotic photo shoot. She asked me some questions, and I asked her some as well. I told her I used to dance in clubs, and after that, she scheduled a time for me to come by.

I knew from the address alone that the shoot wasn't going to be in some scummy dive. But I wasn't prepared for a sprawling, suburban mansion at the end of the long driveway winding up a hill. In front of the garage sat a sparkling white Escalade with tinted windows. What the hell was this place, and who were these people? I checked the address again. I had it right.

Before I could ring the doorbell, a young woman opened the door. She smiled, wide. "Hey, the red head. You must be Victoria. Come on in. We're just getting set up." The woman was dressed in a silk robe. She was in her mid-twenties, with ash blonde hair, full lips, and a full body. A porn star body. That much was clear to me, despite my lack of pro experience. "I'm Cass, by the way. I'll be doing the shoot with you. And please, get comfortable, this should be a fun one today."

She led me to a living room where two other beautiful women sat chatting. They looked more comfortable than I felt.

"You want anything to drink?"

"Um…"

"Sparkling water?"

Phew. I'm glad she didn't say vodka, because I would have jumped at the chance just then. "No thanks, I'm fine."

"Okay, well let me introduce you to Betty and Veronica, we're all going to be working together today." Betty and Veronica were also much younger than me, but I was sure I could hold my own with, well, whatever the hell we were about to do.

I could see through an archway off to the side that a photographer was setting up lights and equipment in a large, empty room. Another assistant seemed to be there to move furniture and props around, including a stack of white sheets, white towels, and what looked like a tall rack of sex toys. Oh boy.

I tried to make small talk with Betty and Veronica, but they were deep in conversation about hip downtown bars and secret clubs I'd never heard of before. I guess I was out of the loop. The only club I'd been involved with in years was my seven-year-old's chess club.

Cass came back in a moment and sat next to me, close. I instantly felt more comfortable. She explained what was going to happen. "Today we're just doing a photo shoot, no filming. No script. The four of us will just be messing around with the goodies we have over there, okay? Feel free to have fun, but take cues from the photographer when he gives them, and if all goes well this won't take more than an hour."

I took to this new job like a fish to water. It didn't hurt that I was rolling around with three other beautiful ladies. I remembered some of the women I'd messed around with, and it occurred to me that some of the hottest moments I've ever experienced were with other women. I never fell in love with another woman, so I wasn't ready to switch teams, but I had to admit, other beautiful women turned me on. It was only a few moments of setup before we were in the middle of a session of tangled legs, contraptions I never knew existed, and even a little creative finger painting. If I started a little shy, I wasn't by the end, and at one point caught myself practically trying to run things: "Betty, why don't you get under me like this, right, and Veronica, you take that double-ended purple thing—no, the twelve-inch, and you sit behind me like . . . right." Then I turned to the photographer, who had gone quiet. "Is that okay? Can you get that shot?"

"Uh, yeah. Nice."

Afterwards, I almost felt like apologizing, but Cass was tickled. "You rocked. You've really never done this before? Well, you've got work here whenever you want."

"You mean it?" I felt like I'd just gotten an A+ on my Algebra test.

"Yeah, of course! Do you have to go right away? I could tell you about some other opportunities. How about some coffee?"

Soon we were in the kitchen, where Cassie set in front of me two crisp c-bills for my work and a hot mug of black coffee. I had nothing else going on that day, and we talked all afternoon.

"This house is amazing," I started. "So this is yours?"

"Nah. This is the photographer's place, but if you hadn't guessed by now, you can make some real money in this business."

I had trouble believing it. I'd known girls from the clubs who'd gotten into porn, and it never seemed to pay as much as straight dancing, and the occupational hazards seemed higher. I asked Cass about it, and soon she was telling me her story.

Like me, Cass had left home as a teenager, booted out by parents who had no patience for their own daughter's problem with drugs or drinking She ended up at age eighteen at the Kitty Ranch in Nevada. According to Cassie, it was awful. The women would be lined up like cattle at an auction, and johns would walk up and down the row, grabbing here and petting there until they settled on the right girl. They were mostly drunk tourists, were never respectful, and then the house took most of the money. It was a terrible life, she said, but it wasn't because of the job itself. She didn't mind fucking for money, she said. It was just the way things were run that bugged her. Clients were practically encouraged to disrespect the women. If a client did something gross or out of bounds, and the woman resisted, the house seemed to almost always side with the client. She didn't think what she was doing was wrong, she just thought she was being vastly undervalued and under-protected for what she offered.

Then one day a client made her a new offer. He was a producer with a porn company, and he offered her far more money for just taking her clothes off in front of a camera than she was getting for doing much more work than that.

She took her client up on his offer, did a couple of films, gained some notoriety, and started to travel.

"So that's when you started to make real money?"

"Um, not quite. I was doing okay. But I didn't start to really get paid until I started fucking guys for money off set."

What?

It turns out, Cassie's job in a bordello led to a career in porn, which led back to sex for money. Only this next time around, she was in control of the circumstances. She only had sex with guys she knew who could be vouched for. Soon, those clients began vouching for her, and she found she had slipped into a network of men and women who traded sex for money who had gone through extensive background checks and shared information with each other.

"The men are called hobbyists. Well, they aren't all called that. But the really serious ones are. The hobbyists are the guys that take being a john to the next level. These are the guys that have life lists. You know, if you have a bird watcher, he might search all over the woods until he spots a ruby throated woodpecker or whatever and can check it off his life list. A hobbyist might search all over for a blonde Japanese giantess who will lick his ass, and then he'll check that off his life list. Or, you know, a hobbyist might just be a guy who really likes to have a lot of sex with a lot of different women and is smart enough to be careful about it by going through the network and paying for discreet, professional women."

"So like, do the women all have the same pimp or something? Is that even the right word anymore?"

"Ha! No, that's not how this system works. Most of it is done online, or by phone in some cases. I'm known as being an 'independent.' The 'assistant' is basically a roomful of women in an office park somewhere in Ontario, Canada. They keep all these records current, and it's kind of like part restaurant review service, part private investigation service. See, they'll check out guys based on recommendations from working women, and they'll find out if maybe he's not who he says he is, or if he could be a cop, and if he checks out, he'll go in the system. Then every girl who works with him can write up a review that he can't see—basically, what he's in to, if he's safe, all the basics. Then when you're starting up with a new client, you can call the office and confirm the details. You can even talk to the other women around the country who have been with the guy. It's a great system."

"Damn. Well, if you don't mind me asking, how much can you make?"

"Well, it depends on a lot of things, including how many reviews you've got in the system yourself. But starting out, you could probably make at least $250 an hour. And that's a conservative estimate. I don't want to be presumptuous, but if you're interested, I could help you out."

"Oh, me? I don't know. I'm a mom. I've got two boys."

"Well, I have a son, too. It's possible. No pressure of course, but if it seems like something you want to ever try, even just once, here's my card."

For a moment, I hesitated. I wanted to laugh, and once again I felt like the teenager peeking at the ad in the back of the paper for the nudie bar. Though I didn't say anything as I took the card, a part of me already knew I was going to try it.

I was busy, I was avoiding it, I was a little unsure, so I didn't contact Ashley for two weeks. It was never out of my mind for long, though. Finally, one night I held that simple white business card (it just read CASSIE OF DALLAS with a phone number), and thought about my options. I could do this once or twice. I'd make a little money, have a life experience, and no one ever needed to know. Or, I could really *do* this. Cass was younger than me, but she seemed perfectly at peace with herself. She'd worked as an escort for five years, saved up a ton of money, and was just about secure enough that she was looking to get married and start her own limousine company. I figured if I could add work as an escort to my day job selling houses, after a couple of years I'd be secure enough to make whatever schedule I wanted, maybe even start my own business again without having to worry about making big deals every single month.

I called Cass. After a quick conversation, she hung up to contact some of her clients. I chewed my nails while waiting for her to call back.

"Okay," she said. "You're booked for tomorrow at 1 p.m. His name is Rick. He'll be perfect for your first time. He's easy to get along with, and a total teddy bear. Oh, and he likes red heads." She gave me the address and explained it was a space she held just for this purpose. Rick would pay $250 an hour, and $50 would go to Cassie for arranging things. Any time I wanted a client through her recommendation, it'd be the same deal. I couldn't believe it. I was really going to do this, and I was going to do this with a guy named Rick. More than that, it was happening the next day, somewhere between a scheduled house showing and taking my son to swim practice.

The next morning, I put on some lacy lingerie I hadn't worn since my second divorce. On top of that, I wore a wool suit with a skirt and a white blouse. I felt utterly ridiculous while cutting up banana slices into Noah's Wheaties. But soon enough he was on the school bus and I was about ready to start my very, very long day.

First, I had to figure out what to bring with me. I got out my gym bag and threw in a change of clothes. But what else? It wasn't a question I'd thought to ask Cass. Condoms? She said Rick was "safe," but that could mean a lot of different things. I decided to stop by the pharmacy, just to be sure. What else? Makeup? Perfume? Pepper spray? Would he be the sort that wanted to be handcuffed to the bed posts? Would he be the sort that wanted to chain me instead? Would he want anything inserted somewhere I was uncomfortable having something inserted, either on his body or my own? Would I be responsible for bringing things that the client might want to insert or have inserted? It was all too much to think about. I decided that for now, I'd stick with jeans, a T-shirt, and normal underwear to change into after.

I spent the morning showing an old Victorian house out near Highland Park, and then skipped lunch and just sat in my car blocks from Cassie's working apartment. I hadn't eaten all day. I was starving, but figured I didn't want to go into this thing with bloating or coffee breath. I was getting by on Tic-Tacs.

Finally, at 15 before, I rang the bell and Cass was waiting for me, and she gave me a tour of the place. The bedroom wasn't some S&M dungeon. It just looked like a nice, sunny bedroom. The kitchen looked like a kitchen. The living room looked like a living room. In fact, it was set up a lot like a model home I might show my other clients—cozy and tasteful, if not quite lived in looking. The bathroom also looked like a bathroom in most ways, other than it was lined with drawers around a large sink. "Upper left is where you'll find the basics," Cass said. She opened it up to reveal condoms neatly arranged in rows by type and unopened tubes of Astroglide. She didn't show me what was in the other drawers. Maybe she didn't want to intimidate me my first time out. "Take your time afterwards," she said. "Towels are in closet just outside the bathroom. And, oh, please no sex in the shower. It's not really set up for it."

With that, she left, and I was alone, thinking about what the hell came next. Should I use a different voice? Should I pretend to be someone completely different? I was Victoria again, after all, not Jenny. I watched the clock. When Rick was five minutes late, I thought maybe the whole thing would be off, and I could go home to my sane, suburban life and forget all this ever happened.

But then the buzzer rang.

"Hi," said a friendly voice. "This is Rick. Sorry I'm late."

"Um, no worries," I said. "Your reservation's still good. We saved your table." I cringed at my own bad joke, and buzzed him in. *Oh Jenny*, I thought. *Just calm down.*

Rick knocked on the door a minute later, and I peeked through the peephole. The man outside was tall, with black glasses and a shy, geeky smile. He looked kind of like a hyperactive Clark Kent.

I counted to ten, held my breath and opened the door. "Hello, Rick," I said in my smokiest voice.

Rick walked right in and hung his jacket on a hook by the door. Clearly, he had been here before.

"Hi, Victoria, it's good to meet you," he said, a little red flushing his cheeks. "Listen, no need to be nervous. Cass already told me it's your first time. Well, not your *first time*, like your first time ever with a man. Ha. That would be a little weird. Your first time with a client. It's cool, I'm into it."

Who was this guy? There was something a little familiar about him, but I didn't think I'd met him before. Then it dawned on me. He was a type I knew. So many men like him used to stuff money in my g-string back when I danced. Lonely, single men who relocated to Dallas to work as engineers, as software developers, as finance guys. They were always attracted to a girl like me, someone that didn't try to hide anything, that made sexuality seem so simple and straightforward.

Rick and I hit it off right away. He made a drink from supplies in the kitchen and made one for me, too. I accepted it. Then we sat down on the couch and chatted. *Am I getting paid for this?* It turns out he was a banker, and had been in Dallas for a little over a year. He'd been visiting Cass and some other women that used the

260

apartment for six months. "Cassie's great. A real professional. By the way, she told me you used to be an exotic dancer or something. Is that true?"

"Ha. Well, sort of." I recognized the cue. "You want a little dance?" From there, I was more in my comfort zone. I danced for him, and really muscle memory took over. I could tell right away he was into it. From there, we went to the bedroom, where we fooled around like we'd been dating and this was just a lazy Saturday. Pretty standard stuff. We even cuddled after. I'd later learn that this is what clients might call the GFE—the girlfriend experience, which usually involves a little chitchat, usually some pretty vanilla face to face sex, and then some soft whispers after. I liked Rick. I was almost sorry to see him go. "Can I see you again?" he asked. "Um, Yes. I think so, yes." Why not? This hadn't been so bad. Kind of a thrill, really.

I showered, changed, and waited for Cassie to return to divide up the money. I left that day with $400 and a whistle on my lips. *Hell*, I thought, *I could get used to this.* And soon enough I was used to it.

Duncan

Denton, TX

Safe / Would see again / DO NOT DATE

"*Thanks, hon. I love it. And I had a wonderful time with you. But listen, I've thought about it, and I don't know if our plans for today are such a good idea. I've been thinking...*"

Duncan and I are sitting on the floor of his living room beneath a big ole Christmas tree that I helped set up. My cat is by my side, warm and purring. A fire crackles in the fireplace. But suddenly I feel a chill.

Duncan was a client I met a year before. Sure, he was a hobbyist. But he seemed to hone in on me, and we got together often. He's a urologist, single, safe, and kind. Sure he's a little older, a little staid, but I like seeing him.

When he wanted to "take things to the next level," I thought, Why not? Sure, I'd been burned by falling for clients before. But this relationship was so easy, and I'd been single so long, it seemed right. Besides, I was thinking maybe it was time to get out of the business. There was too much danger, too much indignity, too much uncertainty. And I knew as I got older, it would only get harder. Sure, Duncan was a doctor (I sure saw a lot of those in this business), and could certainly provide, but that wasn't what it was about. It was about settling down and putting some of my recent dark years behind me. It made sense with my life, and Duncan wasn't so bad either. He was a gentleman, funny, engaged with life. I could maybe even fall in love.

This morning, Christmas morning, we're supposed to drive to West Texas where he's going to introduce me to his parents. It feels like a big step. Turns out, a step he's not willing to take.

"... So you see, Jenn, that's why I think we should go back to our old setup. I think it might be better for me—for both of us—if we're professional again."

I read between the lines. I knew he'd been having money trouble, between his ex-wife and debt towards his practice. Turns out, "the next level" had meant him getting it for free until his financial situation was better. I can't fucking believe it. I'd practically moved in. I'd even moved my cat over.

"Fine," I say. "Then you won't be needing this." I snatch back the Sharper Image doodad I'd just given him as a present. "If that's the way you prefer it, that's fine by me." And in a way, it was. Sure, he'll be a client again. His money spends just like everyone else's.

But that's it. I am so fucking done with Dallas, with its $30,000 millionaires and its fake manners. I make a resolution to get the hell out, finally, the first chance I get. Victoria of Dallas will soon be Victoria of Fucking-Anywhere-But Dallas. And I remind myself, once again, for the hundredth time: A client is a client. A boyfriend is a boyfriend. They can never be the same person.

Chapter 19

NOT AFRAID

It's February 2010, and I'm driving through a snowstorm. *Where am I?* It's hard to say anymore. All the states are starting to blur in my mind into one vast open road with mountains in the distance. *Montana? Minnesota? Nah, just passed through Kansas City a while ago. That's right, I'm in Missouri.* The radio is warning me of the snowpocalypse just east of me and coming in fast, but I'm nowhere near a turnoff yet. I could stop, maybe I should stop, but the storm is following me, and I don't want to get buried, alone, on the side of the road. I could turn back and try to make it to Kansas City. But I won't. There's something ahead in the road. I have faith that there is. And I'm not turning back to where I was, even if that means risking my life.

The snow is coming in such long squalls that I almost feel like I've lost my peripheral vision. Everything is white but the narrow ribbon of road ahead of me. Behind me all I can see is all my stuff jammed in every corner of the car. I'm awake. I'll make it to an exit ramp. I'll find a place to sleep for another night. I just need to concentrate on the road.

The snow narrows my field of vision even further, and against the backdrop of solid white, my mind begins to jump. Memories flood my mind with such vivid clarity, I feel like I'm hallucinating. Visions of what I'd left behind. Visions of what was yet to come. *What am I still doing on the road? When will I make myself stop? When did I even start?*

My mind jumps back to 2005, when I first started sleeping with men for money. What was scary when I first started was just how smoothly it all fit into my life. The hobbyist services I used made everything safe, convenient, and *extremely* lucrative. I could fit a client meeting between showing a house and picking my kids up from baseball practice. If the kids were on vacation with their dads, I could book clients all week and make a fortune. On top of my day job, I could easily make $1,000 a day. And the men weren't the sort of johns you might meet by advertising in the back pages of the local paper. They were doctors, lawyers, successful businessmen. Many of them were a couple of decades older than me, but still handsome, still fit, and quite refined. When I started, I thought the hardest part would be faking interest. That was sometimes part of the job, for sure, but the hardest part turned out to be not losing my heart.

I moved past my mentor (with her help) and paid for advertising on a number of sites that catered to wealthy men. They could review me, and I could review them. It was like Yelp or AirBnB reviews, except about sex. As my reputation grew, so did my requests.

I was independent, I had everything I wanted, and I was happy. Well, almost happy. Other than my clients, I was still single. After divorcing my second husband, I had no idea what I wanted in a man. I'd married an abusive asshole. And I'd married a supportive friend. Neither marriage had worked out, and frankly, I was afraid to go through it all again. Men, I liked. Picking up the pieces of a broken heart—that I was getting a little tired of. *But I was happy. Almost happy. What went wrong?*

My mind flashes to a moment I hadn't thought about in years, when I had awoken to the sound of rushing water and the feeling of my head being partly submerged. The whole left side of my face was pressed against the glass mosaic tiles that made up the bathroom floor of my Plano townhouse. The floor was flooded with half an inch of water, and my hair, heavy and wet, was splayed in front of my face. I'd left the sink faucet on and then just passed out, and the water was cascading over the edge of the bowl like a falls. I realized my cat was inches from my face, sniffing me and lapping up the water. My head pounded. I'm not sure what time of day it was, or what I'd been doing before I passed out, but I knew it was drinking again that brought me where I was.

The pattern with drinking had been set. I was sober and attending AA religiously, but there were those days . . . there were always those days. It could be a bad trigger from the past that set me off. Or a client that convinced me to split a bottle of wine—I often drank half a glass on dinner dates, but some of my clients were drinkers, and sometimes I didn't say no. Maybe it was nothing more than a night when I was alone and felt alone, with nothing between me and the darkest moments of my past except the mind-numbing power of a bottle of vodka.

I wasn't drinking and driving. I couldn't, even if I slipped. My car had a breathalyzer, for one. But I knew drinking was always dangerous for me, and that with three DUIs in my past, the complications of a secret identity, and young children to care for, every time I lost control to alcohol risked making a mess of everything I'd built.

I'm shaken from my memories by a wind that almost drives me off the road. The guy on the radio is saying that there's a ban on all non-emergency vehicles on all roadways in the region—even if I survive, I might very well get pulled over by a cop if I can't make it to safety. The heater has gone out again in my car, and I'm starting to feel like the winter is creeping in. *I wish I'd stayed in California.*

After I left Texas at the end of 2010 at the age of forty, I'd first driven straight north to Oklahoma. My goal was California or bust, but there was no way I was going to drive through west Texas. No matter what else happened to me the rest of my life, I just wanted out of the whole fucking state. I stayed in Oklahoma long enough to sell off 25 grand worth of furniture (for about 2 grand at auction), open up a PO box, and apply for Oklahoma plates. I wanted to wipe Texas out of my life completely. After all that, I'd headed west to the promised land, a place I thought I might want to start over. After I crossed from Arizona to Cali, I'd got out and kissed the ground. It was almost like a religious ritual. All the bad spirits from Texas seemed to float away. But it didn't take long to realize California wasn't my home either. I was still searching for peace. I was still searching for a home. Hell, I was still trying to figure out who I was. I wasn't going to pick a home until I knew what I wanted next.

My mind flashes back again, this time to spring of 2006. A phone call from Tim. He wanted to know what I was up to. "Why do you have to jump up and leave in the middle of Jeremy's baseball games sometimes? Why are you being so secretive? Is something wrong?" I knew it was useless trying to hide anything from Tim. The guy can see through me like I'm a clear bottle. I'd always used the excuse that I had a house showing. The schedule of a real estate agent and the schedule of an escort line up pretty well, actually, and for most people my day job was an easy excuse for my moonlighting. But Tim wasn't most people. Maybe he noticed the gym bag I was always carrying around, or the way I'd head out to "show a house" and come back with my hair different, my makeup different. He knew my drinking history. He had reason to be concerned.

So I told him. I told him everything. And he didn't hate me for it. "I know I don't need to say this, Jennifer, but please just make sure you're not ever putting Noah in danger. I couldn't live with that, and I know you couldn't either."

Tim wasn't the only ex to know. By fall of 2006, Greg knew what I was up to. He'd found my profile on one of the sites. Maybe it was a bad idea to stick with the old alter ego. He'd known me as Victoria when he first met me. He'd watched Victoria dance in the Red Room from his sullen perch against the wall. And he no doubt Googled "Victoria" and "Dallas" as part of his lifelong campaign to stalk me and make me feel uncomfortable. Greg called me to let me know about it. "Well, Victoria. Seems like you've been busy again." My heart sank down to my shoes. He threatened to tell our son Jeremy about it. I had to beg him not to. Finally, he proposed a terrible bargain. "Well, you say you care so much about your son, but this is what you do to show it. What are you doing with the money, huh *Victoria*? You're not spending it on Jeremy, and you're not reporting it. If you love him like you say you do, prove it." He knew I was headed to Vegas on a trip in a week or two. He proposed I make it a "working" trip and earn enough money to buy Jeremy a car for his sixteenth birthday. "You go to Vegas and work your whore ass off, or he's gonna know everything."

Jeremy looked like a man, but in most ways he was still a kid. He'd be devastated to find out what I was doing. Not that I was ashamed—I knew the clients I worked with, and I knew the skills I had and what they were worth. But no young boy wants to find that out about his mother. Never!

I took the deal. I went to Vegas, and for the first time I worked on the road. It was the beginning of a pattern that would last years. I bought Jeremy an old Trans Am for his birthday that fall. And Greg printed out my profile, put it all in a Manila envelope, and left the envelope out on the kitchen table at their home in Ohio for Jeremy to discover. My double life had lasted about a year before the walls separating my two worlds began to crumble.

The snow is blowing horizontally, but it's still accumulating in little igloos all over the side of the road. I've never see anything like it. Finally, I spot signs for the next exit, which is to Thimblefuck, Missouri. I've never heard of it, but I'm willing to spend the night there even if the whole town is nothing but a gas station and a stop sign. I shiver, grit my teeth, and keep pushing forward. I've been in worse trouble before. I'd always survived.

My mind flashes again, this time to a hotel just outside Dallas. It was April 1, 2007, and I'd had a rough year already so far. Other than my first son discovering what I did to help pay for his private school and his new ride, I'd also lost some of my best friends from AA. When you live life with addiction, it doesn't take much of a slip to fall hard. One good friend had fallen recently after a foot injury required pain meds. Being laid up and being on meds led to drinking, which led to drinking and meds, which led to him overdosing and dying alone. His body wasn't discovered for days.

I had my own problems then with medications. I was on anti-depressants, and my psychiatrist was trying all sorts of new pills on me at the same time, including near psychosis-inducing 3 mg time-release Xanax. Three times a day. I also took Ambien occasionally to sleep when the nights of worry grew too long. The combination was bad, and I'd sometimes have blackouts and not be able to remember what happened to me the night before. When I finally slipped again with alcohol one night, I ended up getting myself arrested for public intoxication. I didn't remember what happened when I woke up in the drunk tank the next day, other than that I knew I needed to contact my probation officer right away.

It was bad news, and a technical violation of my probation. But after talking to Lisa, my new bitch of a probation officer, it sounded like I was going to be fine. I was wrong. I remember it started with me actually calling the police. There'd been a break-in at a storage facility I rented and some of my stuff had been taken. I called in to report it, and the police asked me where they could find me so they could come take a report. I was at a hotel after meeting a client, and I was planning on spending the day by the pool. Other than the break-in, I was actually in a good mood that day. I even ordered a round of pizzas to be delivered to a group of boys that played soccer and their parents who were hanging out by the pool.

My mood got worse, quick, though. I wasn't surprised when a police car pulled up outside my hotel room. It did seem strange that the lights and sirens were on, but I was expecting the police, after all. Then four more squad cars pulled up. *They're not here to talk about my missing duvet*, I thought. When the police barged in and threw me on the ground like I was some drug kingpin, I remember thinking that this must be some really well planned April Fool's joke. What a fool I was.

I was taken to Collin County Jail, once again. Before long I learned what I was facing. When I'd been booked for public intoxication and thrown in a drunk tank, I'd apparently spit at a corrections officer. I don't remember it. But whatever I'd done I was charged with "Harassment of a public servant."A felony. When the write-up reached my probation officer, she'd put out a blue warrant for my arrest. Then when I called to report that some of my stuff had been stolen from my storage unit, the warrant popped up and the police were happy to personally come to take my report. I should have known when they were so eager to come to me personally to take the report.

I knew there was no hope of bail. I knew I wasn't going home. My lawyer couldn't do anything for me. I'd violated parole on a felony DUI charge, and now was facing a second felony. I was going away for a while. I ended up taking a two-year plea deal, with the chance of parole after one.

Before I was transferred to state prison, I had papers served to me from Tim. He was suing me for full custody of Noah unless I agreed to a set of conditions, including spending a year at a substance abuse facility after my release from prison. I wouldn't budge. Tim came to jail with a weasely-ass little lawyer to get me to sign the agreement, and I cursed them out. *If you motherfuckers think I'm going to just sign over the right to be a mother to my son, you've got another thing coming. If you wanna play ball Tim, let's play ball!* Tim and I had always been friends and worked well as partners in raising my son, even after I'd told him how I was finally making money. But this was a declaration of war.

We went to court and had our case heard by the same judge that adjudicated our divorce. I remember Tim tried to use my own probation officer as a witness against me, and the judge wouldn't allow it. Ultimately, he took my side. I remember him saying, "Jennifer, you're about to go away to a bad place. You're are probably going to have a tough time in there. But when you come out, I expect you to be the great mother that I know you are. We'll examine custody then." I promised I would be.

I remember going back to jail to a heroes welcome from the other prisoners. How many mothers had lost their children after being sent away? How many had no fight to put up after their lives were shattered by convictions? I wasn't going to let that happen to me. But early the next morning after I won in court, I was awoken by officers and put in a paddy wagon for Gatesville, Texas and off to prison. Now that my civil matter was over, I was off to serve my time.

What is there to say about my time at Gatesville? It was indescribable. The place was once a mental institution, and it still felt like a dungeon years later. I fought. I fought other inmates to save my life, and sometimes I was beat up. I ate food that I wouldn't serve to an animal. I cried night after night for my lost children, and I spent the few hours I could sleep dreaming of the time when I'd see them again.

They worked us at that prison—I did hard labor. And when I had a moment to "myself" (in a giant dorm filled with hundreds of bunks), I read novels. I remember spending July 4, 2007 alone in my bunk, thinking of the past years when I'd spent the holiday with my boys. Of all the hard nights I've had, I think that night alone, thinking of better times, was the hardest.

It was there that one night, alone and afraid, that I heard the words of God call to me. "Be still, and know that I am God." I looked it up later, and it was a verse from the book of Isaiah. Whatever caused me to hear that voice, I don't know, but it was all I had when I was in prison: the promise of a more peaceful time in the future.

I was granted parole February 8, 2008. The prison gave me a set of donated clothes that smelled like mothballs and despair, a $100 check, and a phone call. Because I was close to Houston, I called an old friend who lived in the city named Christopher to come get me. Christopher was a cop, and we'd dated years before. Christopher was a guy that could help. And he was a guy—he wasn't going to help for nothing. The first thing we did is drive to get a Pepsi and a pack of cigarettes. It's amazing the sort of thing you miss most when you're in prison. Then we went to Target and I got a pair of jeans and a new shirt, and then on to get a real sandwich. It was like heaven, but also overwhelming to have so much to see and experience again. I remember almost breaking out in tears looking at the rows of toothpaste available at the store. In prison, we'd only had something that looked like moldy green baking powder—they called it "tooth powder."

I couldn't believe how fast the outside world was. Technology had changed. I didn't even know what a text was on a cell phone, let alone how to send or type one. Nothing was slow in the real world and I had to learn fast how to adjust back in to society. I trusted no one and was scared of everyone at the same time.

Christopher helped me get on my feet the first couple of days, but when I told him I wasn't interested in having sex with him, he got upset. He ended up giving me a couple hundred in cash, pre-paid for a motel room for a few nights, and wished me good luck.

I was eager to get back to Dallas to see my son, but I wasn't sure I wanted to live there again. I thought perhaps my best hope of picking myself back up was through a fresh start, close enough to see my son regularly but far enough away to be clear of all the old demons that lived in Dallas.

So after I visited my son, I came back to Houston. I got a job at Denny's serving pancakes. I got an apartment. I found new work at an art store, managing the paper department. It was there that I began meeting new friends—some of Houston's artists, who would invite me out to gallery openings and shows. Then I began to meet wealthy art patrons and fall into their circles. Wasn't it just like my life: within a few months I went from recent ex-con refilling coffees for 50 cent tips to hanging out on a yacht in the Gulf with the mayor of Houston's colleagues? Once again, I was living a beautiful dream, but my dreams have never been reality for very long.

Finally, I pull off the interstate, just as it feels like the storm is going to swallow me whole. Not far off the exit ramp is a divey family motel. *I'll take it*, I think. I've stayed in worse. I've stayed in much better, too, but I can't think about that right now. I have to think about getting into a warm room, settling in, and making it through another day. I've learned by now that every time I get hung up on making it big, I end up struggling to make it at all.

As I pull into the motel parking lot, navigating the quickly forming icebergs that used to be parked cars, I breathe a sigh of relief and close my eyes.

Suddenly in my mind I'm back again in Houston, heading to a party where I'd meet up with some of my new friends.

It was July 4, 2008. Exactly one year from my lowest moment in prison, the night I spent longing to be with my sons. Once again, I was alone without them. I was working to repair my relationship with them after going away, but it was going to take time. I'd missed so much. Alone without them again, another summer flying by, I committed to making the most of the life I had. I called a cab to the party, and by the time the cab showed up, I was already half in the bag. Okay, all the way. The cabbie knew what kind of shape I was in and charged me double what he should have. We got into an argument, and he called the cops. Though I talked my way out of it, I wasn't out of trouble for long. Once I got to the party, my friends had already left. I was drunk. I ended up getting into an argument with some young women who smirked at me and whispered insults. Someone called the police, and soon enough I was talking to the cops all over again. This time, they arrested me. Another public intoxication charge, and once again I was in violation of parole. I was headed back to prison to face the rest of my sentence.

I spent the next three months in Harris County Jail. It was hell on earth. I regularly watched prisoners get pulverized by the out of control prison guards and other prisoners. The only way I survived was by acting crazy the whole time. After that, I was transferred to prison, and finally released for good in March 2009.

I'd been away from my life for two years. Jenny was a distant memory for me, and so was Victoria of Dallas. I didn't have a double identity—I had none at all. This time, I decided to face my past and live in Dallas again. I'd find a way to make it work. And I couldn't bear having that distance from my son again. But restarting after time served as a felon isn't easy. They definitely don't make it easy. I had to have my ex-husband Tim rent an apartment for me in his name, since few landlords would rent to me with a felony on my record. I had no hope of starting back up as a Realtor after my license expired with the record I now had. And other employers were just as unconvinced by my resume. I finally found a job at a mom and pop operation that hooked up businesses around the city with janitorial services. I was back to selling, going from office to office to convince them to use our services. It was definitely a new world for me and it didn't last long. I was laid off in October of that year. 2009 wasn't exactly the best year for the economy and money was tight.

So once again, I was back in Dallas seeing old clients. Some had moved, some had moved on, but there was enough business there to keep me on my feet. I also started traveling for work—some of my best clients were now in New York, Boston, Philadelphia, and Las Vegas. I'd make working trips and make big money, all while seeing a little of the world. Back in Dallas, I worked on improving my life, on steering clear of alcohol, and fixing my broken relationships. I can't say I was doing too poorly. I even enrolled in college again. I think I had a shot then of making it in Dallas, despite having come to hate the city.

Then I made a mistake. This time, it had nothing to do with drinking. I got lazy, or desperate, or both, and I put an ad up on a site that I should never have trusted. The johns weren't vetted. It was the equivalent of advertising in the paper, or writing my phone number on the bathroom wall. I got a call from a man with a nice voice, and we made an appointment to meet at a local motel. As soon as he showed up, I knew there was gonna be trouble. He was nervous. He was asking strange questions.

And then when the door was closed, he pulled out a 9 mm and put it straight to my head.

"You fucking whore, where's the money?" I felt surprisingly calm. A part of me had expected this with almost every client. It was finally happening. *If I had any money, why would I be here with you?* I remember thinking. He went through my purse and dug out fourteen bucks. It was all I had. He started looking at my phone. I kept calm. "What else you got?" I had nothing. Nothing at all. I wasn't worried about being killed. I was worried about being raped. I decided if he tried to force me, I'd go for his gun. I'd rather be shot. I talked to him. I made up a story about daughters I don't have, my family. I asked questions about his life. I could tell he was angry when he wasn't really interested in money. He wanted someone to hate. I stayed calm. Whatever he did, I promised myself I'd stay calm. Eventually, he got frustrated in trying to scare me. He put on a ski mask, stared at me for a full minute, and then left with the few dollars he found on me.

I called the police. I knew I had to. I'd heard about guys like this that prey on women like me. They rely on us being too afraid and too ashamed to talk to the cops. The police ended up catching the guy, and I testified against him. Because it was my word against his, he ended up not getting convicted. The physical evidence they had was thrown out by the judge. Why? I don't know. The whole time he was in jail, I was getting phone calls trying to intimidate me, I suppose from one of his friends. But I testified anyway. And he got out of it anyway. Months later, he slashed another working girl with a knife. This time, he finally got put away.

I was determined to push it all down, live with the experience like I'd lived with so much else. Then in fall of that year, I got a call that someone had broken into my old home in Plano when I was married to Tim. It was the middle of the day, and my son was supposed to be coming home soon after school. I freaked out when I saw the police cars surrounding my old house. I'd dealt with enough that year already. The police wouldn't let me in the house, saying it was an active crime scene investigation. It turns out one of the burglars was still in the house, hiding under my son's bed.

Both men who broke into my old home were arrested. But I realized I wasn't safe, and either was my son. If it had just been an hour or so later . . .

The incident also set off my ex. He revealed that he'd obtained a secret judgment against me while I was in prison, and despite sharing custody since my return, he was actually entitled to full custody. He'd told the courts about my double life and made the case that I was putting my son at risk. In his mind, the break in confirmed his fears. He was going to take full custody of Noah.

I was so angry; I was worried I might do something I'd regret. I was going to take Tim to court again.

Then I realized what our fighting was doing to our son. He was suffering. I wasn't helping him. I'd always be his mother, and I'd always be there for him, but dragging him into court wasn't going to help him thrive. And it wasn't going to help me, either. I needed to survive. I needed to leave.

That's when I packed all my furniture into a POD and took off. It was at the end of 2010. I'd been living in Dallas (with a few planned and unplanned breaks) for over twenty years. I'd thought it was the city for me. But it had only brought me heartbreak. Where was I going next? Anywhere but Texas. What would I do when I got there? That was a worry for another day. All I knew was that I couldn't survive any longer where I was.

After pulling into the motel in Thimblefuck, Missouri, I'm greeted outside by the nice Indian-American couple that owns the place. They bring me a blanket and a hot cup of tea and ask me what I was doing out on the road. I don't even have a story to tell them, and just thank them for their kindness. That night, we're snowed in by the worst storm in decades. The whole plains region is snowed under. I spend three days in my motel room, wracked with fever.

I'm tired, I'm sick, but I'm not afraid. I feel like I'm as lost as I've ever been, but I'm not afraid. I've survived. I know I'm going to survive. Whether I have someone to take care of me or not, I'll survive. During this road trip, my nights have been full of regrets for the past, but no fears for the future. I'll survive. No matter what life throws at me, I'll survive. I think of the voice I heard while I was in prison. "Be still." I feel it now. No matter what happens to me, I am still. I have only myself, but I'm finally at peace. I've proven I can survive.

Now it's time to prove that I can thrive.

Daniel

Cherry Hill, NJ

--- (All mine, will not share)

I pull my Ohio State baseball cap down over my forehead, sling my gym bag over my shoulder, and hurry up the stairs to my apartment. I'm almost late for my hour with Daniel. It's a time of the week I don't want to miss.

Then, from the top of the steps leading to my door, I look down into the parking lot and see his car pulling in. Shit. Too late to get ready now, he's already here. Daniel parks and gets out of the car and his eyes move instinctively up to my balcony. We lock eyes. We both begin laughing. He's got his Ohio State cap pulled down over his eyes as well, with the same gym bag slung over the shoulder.

"Well," I say. "You caught me, I'm late and you're early. Might as well come on up!" With Daniel, it doesn't really matter that I haven't got all dolled up. I don't need to do dress up with him. I don't need to pretend to be some long lost ex for him. I don't need masks. Daniel is the first client I've had, maybe ever, who wants to be with me—the real me. It's thrilling, and unnerving. He won't mind that I'm not wearing makeup and got stuck running errands. He's made love to me in my diamonds, cashmere, and furs in a hotel room overlooking the city. And we've fooled around casually on the couch. When he asks, "What do you want?" he actually means it. It practically leaves me tongue tied, and I'm still learning how to answer honestly.

He comes in, and I hand him a Diet Mountain Dew, his favorite drink. We sit on the couch and talk about our week. Half the time I'm getting paid, it's for the therapy portion of my meeting with men, but

280

that's not what this is. I don't charge for the talk time with Daniel.

Then we start tearing off each other's clothes. Daniel is in his fifties, but he has the body of a thirty-five- year old. He's handsome, he's mannered, and he gives me the most explosive, full-bodied orgasms I've ever had in my life.

Daniel isn't my fantasy man. He's not a cowboy hat wearing billionaire who promises to give me everything I want. He's not a movie star. He's better than those things. He's the finest reality I've ever experienced.

As we make love on my couch, I know it's too late—I've slipped again. Not into drinking. Into love. My other vice. I know Daniel and I will start seeing each other outside of our professional relationship. And I know there will be heartbreak. There always is. Because as much as he knows how to push my buttons, he has his life. He's a married man, with a teenage daughter. And I have my life. I have my own kids, my own past to deal with.

As Daniel and I hold each other on the couch, panting, I make a decision. I'm going to go for it anyway. I'm not looking for perfect anymore. I'm holding onto pretty good. And this right here is pretty damn good.

SOMEWHERE OVER THE RAINBOW

My road trip in 2011 lasted about six months. I kissed the ground in California, and in doing so, I shed that childhood dream of a purple mansion in Hollywood. I visited old friends. I met new ones. I even stayed a few days with my parents and worked on setting those relationships straight. I stayed clean, I stayed sober. And I thought about my future, and made some decisions.

The love and the needs of my sons would still be the foundation of my life. But I knew for right then, I wouldn't be able to live under the same roof as them. Not until I could build the home they deserved to live in, or the home they could crash whenever they wanted as they got older. I'd always sacrifice whatever I could to support them financially, and to make amends emotionally for any hurt I'd caused them. And I could still watch them grow.

I settled in late 2011 in the suburbs of New Jersey to be closer to Jeremy in New York City. I already had clients all up and down the eastern seaboard, and Jersey was the perfect mid-point home base for me. I signed the lease on a furnished apartment and set up my business. I started making money quickly, but I wasn't spending it on things anymore. I was buying myself a life instead.

And I watched my children grow. After high school, Jeremy was accepted at Columbia University in New York. I worked hard to help pay for his school, and to make sure he wasn't starving while he got his degree. He's grown into a strong, brilliant young man. Okay, so he can also be hardheaded like his mom and temperamental like his dad. Jeremy had to go through a lot growing up, with drama on both sides of the family. He's found his own way, and I've watched him become a confident, ambitious young man, even if there's still much work to do to repair our relationship. I know I've left him with some baggage to unpack, and I know that one day we'll work out our differences together.

Noah is still my angel. Around the time I left Dallas, he moved with a "host family" to another city in Texas and began training to become a world-class swimmer. Despite the distance between us, we've remained close, and I've always been there with him as he travels the world to compete. I'd do anything to make him happy, and as he now leaves home and starts college, I find myself crying sometimes out of pure pride and happiness that he remains a bright light in my life.

And it wasn't just my sons I watched grow. I watched myself grow as well. I have to confess, traveling the country to meet clients has been one of the greatest sustained adventures of my life. I've met people and seen places I wouldn't have imagined existed when I was a little girl living in Canal Bottom. I've been on the back of a Harley in the Rockies out west, I've been on the floor of the New York Stock exchange when the bell was rung. I've met people from Congress in DC, men that work for the government, and famous movie stars. Professors, college coaches, school teachers, sports stars, physicians, dentists, attorneys of all kinds. They're living a double life as well, I suppose, and it's possible we're all addicted to excitement of the adventure, of new beginnings.

Even when I'm not working, I travel. One thing I've learned about myself is that I'm a rambler. I'm not good tied down, as any of my exes would attest (though I'm always willing to be tied *up* for the right price). When I've had the time and the change, I've traveled the world. I've visited the ruins and sapphire-tinted waters of Greece. I've toured Italy, France, Switzerland, and Spain. I've seen the Northern Lights and been pulled in a dogsled in Lapland near the North Pole. I've been to the top of Mont Blanc and I've gazed at the frescoes in the Sistine Chapel. And I've cheered on my son Noah on three continents. I've learned to get by speaking Spanish, Italian, and French. I know I've had one hell of a life, and I've lost a lot along the way. I've had a lot of lonely nights, and a lot of days where I didn't know where I was going next. One thing I've gained, though, is the knowledge that wherever I am, I'm home. I've moved beyond the fear of being alone. I can be happy—and happy with myself— anywhere on earth.

Okay, anywhere on earth except Dallas.

The last time I returned to the city was in February 2016. I went to see my son Noah compete. Noah's the only thing worth showing up in this city to see anymore. In 2016, though, I wasn't showing up to the city alone. I was with my boyfriend Daniel. Daniel was a former client, and the first man I'd given my heart to in years. I thought it was time I showed him something of my past.

Seeing the city again, so much had changed. Or maybe it hadn't. I laughed at the thought of the rose colored glasses I used to wear around town when I was young. But I was also wistful to see the city had continued to grow without me—more young men and women with dreams, more new families with the hopes of making it work.

Daniel and I went back to my old house. The one that I used to share with Tim. What once was my sacred place had turned in to a bachelor pad beyond recognition. My flowers and landscaping were gone. The perfect white picket fence I'd put in was crumbling. The place looked trashed. I was sad to see what time (and a lack of maintenance) had done, but it was cathartic. Another old dream evaporated. Another burden of the past was lifted.

More than anything, the city that once seemed to be my Hollywood and New York City rolled into one now seemed a small city, like many others, full of strivers (as I once was). My ex Tim was there for the competition as well. We'd mended our differences over time. We'd never be best friends again, but we understood each other and were both committed to seeing our son flourish. We all had dinner together, and it was nice, but I felt something I hadn't in a long time—the need to go home.

I see my parents sometimes. We even vacation together down in the Carolinas. Things may never be great between us, but I'm hoping to get to pretty good. My other ex-husband lives alone in the woods in Ohio. We don't talk. And that's another blessing I count.

And back in Jersey, I joined another AA group. I've learned to take my sobriety one day at a time, knowing a single slip can have big consequences. At the same time, I've learned not to beat myself up either if I have a bad day. I'm hopeful for the future, because I know who I am.

I still have dreams. I'm in my mid-forties now. It may be time to get out of the business. I know that. I'm only getting older and I know I will never find a true companion staying in this business. But these days I don't dream of meeting the billionaire, of having the mansion, of being the big screen star. I dream of having fulfilling, creative work. Of taking care of myself. Of having friends, and having companionship. Work can be as much of an adventure as travel. Other than the journey of this book, I've been a production assistant on the set of a show. I write and illustrate greeting cards. I dream up businesses and other ideas to keep me busy and content. I've also tried to not just be good, but to do good. One of my childhood friends died of ALS, leaving children behind. I led the effort to establish a fund in his name to make sure his kids could go to Ohio State. I know that helping others in difficult times is maybe the best way of getting through my own.

A place that I love to go and that is very spiritual to me in the US is just outside of Denver, Colorado in the Rockies to a place called Red Rocks. I remember one day heading up there after finding myself on my own and contemplating the next chapter in my life. After hiking mostly uphill for a few miles I sit in what's called the "Amphitheater" in between the two massive slabs of Red stone which kind of reminds me of Epidaurus, Greece. But these natural formations are unlike anything I've ever seen before. I see Denver from a distance. I'm blanketed by blue skies and white clouds.

This whole hike I prayed to God with the sun shining on my face. I asked Him what he wants for my life, and what His plan is for me. It's funny how God answers all prayers if we would just be quiet, still and listen.

I love my life; it may not be the one everyone wants but it works for me. While sitting there praying in Red Rocks, I prayed about a future opportunity for me. I had an opportunity to go back to Italy and finish this book and have three months of solitude.

After Daniel and I started a relationship, I found myself in couples therapy. During the final visit (which I didn't know would be the final one) I had told him I would walk away from my double life and go back to selling houses so that we could develop a stronger relationship and start a life together. Turns out once I said I was finished and would settle down, he walked away and ended things with me! Hindsight is always 20/20 and today I realize he wasn't the one for me and never accepted me for who I am. It didn't take him long to find a new girlfriend, and he's still married! The tangled web we weave. Nonetheless, it absolutely tore my heart out and I knew at that point I had to heal and be true to myself. I don't need to change for anyone. From ashes I realized I was reborn. So I sold everything I owned in my apartment and rid myself of everything that reminded me of him and the toxic relationship we had. I packed a few suitcases and my cat. After a few months of preparation, I flew to Sardegna, Italy. I rented a beautiful villa bigger than the state of Texas surrounded by the sparkling waters of the Mediterranean Sea. It's sprawling, gated and terraces off every bedroom. I have a marble staircase and floors. It's what I have always dreamed of, but far too big for just me. Close to me is Poetto Beach where there are bright pink flamingos in the bay. It is so wonderful to see such amazing birds in their own habitat. When they fly they are so large and astounding to see their bright pink and black markings under their wings. Their contrast to the aqua and azure sea is a sight I will never forget.

While here I decided to go to London for a week. I had an opportunity to do a podcast interview with a famous gentleman that wanted an American courtesan's view of the differences between America and London where prostitution is legalized. In addition, he wanted to know about this book and if I would recommend this life for anyone. My answer was no! I met some new friends along the way there that I am meeting in Amsterdam this week and attending the tulip festival. Recently I took off to the mainland and went to Milan where I was able to see Duemo and have Easter mass there. The view of the magnificent structure outside that has over 3,400 different statues, 135 gargoyles, and 700 figures adorning it has more than any other cathedral in this world. Inside the cathedral I stared at the grandeur of statues of prophets and saints that go back to Biblical times. I was able to see Michelangelo's final piece before his death in 1564 at Sforza Castle. From there I visited Florence to see Leonardo da Vinci's exhibit and of course stare at my favorite statue; the Statue of David. Then on to Pompeii; the most interesting place of ruins on earth. Then from Salerno to the Amalfi Coast on the southern coast of the Salerno Gulf on the Tyrrhenian Sea where the water glistened like diamonds and I have never seen anything more aesthetically beautiful in my life in this world. This has been the most incredible spiritual journey of my life and what I needed to complete this book. It seems that those of us that wander are never lost and find the rarest gems. My life only ten years ago—I was sitting in a Texas prison cell thinking that it was the end of my life. Well it was an absolute beginning to a new one where I have come so far with so little and a new chapter of my new life begins here.

I'm not sure exactly what the future holds. But I know that without my faith and perseverance I would not be here today. We're all born in this world without hurt and without hate. We only have the need to be held, fed, touched, and loved. Without those things, we'll always be striving and kicking against life. Beyond that, we have the power of free will. And we all have the power to find peace. Aren't we all just searching for something larger and vaster than us? Vaster than the universe? Aren't we all just looking for peace?

I pray that this book gives ONE person the strength to not make some of the mistakes I have made and gives hope to anyone suffering and to never give up. When we take care of our life our lives will take care of us. We might not all find the lives we dreamed of, but we all have it in us to be pretty good.

www.ingramcontent.com/pod-product-compliance
Lightning Source LLC
Chambersburg PA
CBHW031937090426

42811CB00002B/210

*9 7 8 1 7 3 2 3 0 7 6 0 5 *